Just Another
Crisis?

The **ISEAS – Yusof Ishak Institute** (formerly Institute of Southeast Asian Studies) is an autonomous organization established in 1968. It is a regional centre dedicated to the study of socio-political, security, and economic trends and developments in Southeast Asia and its wider geostrategic and economic environment. The Institute's research programmes are grouped under Regional Economic Studies (RES), Regional Strategic and Political Studies (RSPS), and Regional Social and Cultural Studies (RSCS). The Institute is also home to the ASEAN Studies Centre (ASC), the Singapore APEC Study Centre and the Temasek History Research Centre (THRC).

ISEAS Publishing, an established academic press, has issued more than 2,000 books and journals. It is the largest scholarly publisher of research about Southeast Asia from within the region. ISEAS Publishing works with many other academic and trade publishers and distributors to disseminate important research and analyses from and about Southeast Asia to the rest of the world.

Just Another Crisis?

The Impact of the COVID-19 Pandemic on Southeast Asia's Rice Sector

Edited by
Jamie S. Davidson

First published in Singapore in 2023 by
ISEAS Publishing
30 Heng Mui Keng Terrace
Singapore 119614
E-mail: publish@iseas.edu.sg
Website: http://bookshop.iseas.edu.sg

All rights reserved. No part of this publication may be reproduced, stored in a retrieval system, or transmitted in any form or by any means, electronic, mechanical, photocopying, recording or otherwise, without the prior permission of the ISEAS – Yusof Ishak Institute.

© 2023 ISEAS – Yusof Ishak Institute, Singapore.

The responsibility for facts and opinions in this publication rests exclusively with the authors and their interpretations do not necessarily reflect the views or the policy of the publisher or its supporters.

ISEAS Library Cataloguing-in-Publication Data

Name(s): Davidson, Jamie Seth, 1971–, editor.
Title: Just another crisis? The impact of the COVID-19 pandemic on Southeast Asia's rice sector / edited by Jamie Seth Davidson.
Description: Singapore : ISEAS-Yusof Ishak Institute, 2023. | Includes bibliographical references and index.
Identifiers: ISBN 9789815011661 (soft cover) | ISBN 9789815011920 (ebook PDF)
Subjects: LCSH: Rice trade—Southeast Asia. | Rice—Government policy—Southeast Asia. | COVID-19 Pandemic, 2020—Economic aspects—Southeast Asia.
Classification: LCC HD9066 A92J96

Front cover photo: Varieties of rice for sale, Cipinang Market, Jakarta, Indonesia, 2016. Reproduced with kind permission of Jamie S. Davidson.

Cover design by Lee Meng Hui
Index compiled by Raffaie Nahar
Typeset by Superskill Graphics Pte Ltd
Printed in Singapore by Mainland Press Pte Ltd

To the rice growers of the region

CONTENTS

List of Figures — viii

List of Tables — x

Acknowledgements — xii

The Contributors — xiii

1. Introduction: Just Another Crisis? The Impact of the COVID-19 Pandemic on Southeast Asia's Rice Sector — 1
   Jamie S. Davidson

2. The Role of Path Dependence in Malaysia's Paddy and Rice Policy under the Pandemic — 34
   Fatimah Mohamed Arshad

3. Impact of COVID-19 on the Philippine Rice Sector — 78
   Roehlano M. Briones and Isabel B. Espineli

4. The Indonesian Rice Economy during the COVID-19 Pandemic — 105
   Bustanul Arifin

5. From Controlling to Abandoning: State–Rice Sector Relations in Thailand — 135
   Thanapan Laiprakobsup and Manthana Noksawak

6. Impact of COVID-19 on Singapore's Rice Supplies, and Future Food Security Challenges — 161
   Jose Ma. Luis Montesclaros and Paul S. Teng

Index — 191

LIST OF FIGURES

2.1	Historical Timeline of the Paddy and Rice Industry in Malaysia, January 1961–December 2021	39
2.2	Market Interventions in Malaysia's Paddy and Rice Industry	41
2.3	Deviation of Farm and Retail Prices from the Border Prices, 1995–2016	46
2.4	Share of Paddy Buying by Institutions, 1996–2017	48
2.5	Rice Price, January 2002–August 2021	50
2.6	Policy Response to a Rice Price Crisis in 2008	52
2.7	Input and Output Subsidies for Paddy and Rice and SSL, 1979–2021	56
2.8	Paddy Input and Output Subsidies and Paddy Yield, 1979–2021	57
2.9	World Rice Stock-to-Use Ratio, Production and Utilization	58
2.10	Rice Prices, January 2015–August 2021	59
2.11	Malaysia: Rice Production, Consumption and Import, and SSL	60
2.12	Malaysia's Rice Trade, January 2000–December 2021	64
3.1	Annual GDP Growth, Philippines, Selected Years	81
3.2	Quarterly GDP Growth, Philippines, Selected Years	83
3.3	Monthly Rice Retail Prices, WMR and RMR, Philippines, 2017–18	90
3.4	Quantity of Philippine Rice Imports, June 2018–December 2020	92
3.5	Unit Landed Value of Rice Imports and Wholesale Prices of Regular and Well-Milled Rice, June 2018–December 2020	93
3.6	Shares of Rice Expenditure, by Type of Household, 2015	95
3.7	Paddy Rice Output and Yield, 2010–20	96

List of Figures

4.1	Disparities of Rice Yield in Indonesia by Region	110
4.2	Coefficient Variation of Medium and Premium Rice Prices, 2017–21	113
4.3	Global Price of Rice of Different Quality and Wheat, 2007–22	116
4.4	Price Fluctuation of Staple and Strategic Foods, 2018–22	118
4.5	Coefficient Variation of Strategic Food Prices in the Domestic Market, 2017–21	119
4.6	Retail Rice Prices from BPS, PIHPS, and Food Station, 2017–21	124
4.7	Domestic Procurement of Bulog, 2016–20	126
4.8	Price of Medium Rice (Panel A) and Premium-Quality Rice (Panel B) at Global and Domestic Markets, 2017–22	129
5.1	Operation Procedure for Receiving and Disbursing Funds for the Project "Upgrading the Mega Farm with Modern Agriculture and Connecting the Market"	147
5.2	Number of Mega Farms Participating in the Programme, 2016–21	149
5.3	Summary of the Project's Data Comparing the Government's Goal to the Present Project Advancement on Rice, 2020	150
6.1	Contribution of Singapore's Key Sources of Rice to Total Rice Supplies	169
6.2	Comparative Import Prices by Singapore from Key Sources (Vietnam, India, Thailand) and from Alternative Sources	170
6.3	Singapore's Rice Import Quantities, for Three Major Sources	172
6.4	Singapore's Total Rice Import Quantity and Price	173
6.5	Singapore Rice Import Diversification after Vietnamese Rice Export Restrictions	174
6.6	Singapore's Rice Import Prices from Three Major Sources	176
6.7	Minor Changes in Retail Prices for 5-kg Pack of Premium Thai Rice in Singapore	177
6.8	Number of People Undernourished in ASEAN	183

LIST OF TABLES

1.1	Rice Share as Percentage in Urban and Rural Household Expenditures	12
1.2	Average Annual Economic Growth (Gross Domestic Product) Rates, 1980–89	16
1.3	2020 Gross Domestic Product Rates	19
2.1	Paddy Guaranteed Minimum Price and SSHP, Selected Years	42
2.2	Recommended Retail Price of Rice and Imported Rice Price, Selected Years	45
2.3	Concentration Ratios and HHI for Malaysia's Rice Market, 2018	48
2.4	Market Protection and Comparative Advantage Indices for Paddy and Rice Sector, Selected Years	49
2.5	Food Security Strategies in 2008	54
3.1	Real Cost of Rice to the Consumer, 2017–20	95
3.2	Coefficient of Variation of Regional Monthly Paddy Prices, 2018–21	97
3.3	Cost and Returns per ha for the Average Rice Farmer, 2010–20	98
3.4	Distribution of Respondents' Estimate of Monthly Retail Price Change, January 2019–January 2020	99
3.5	Distribution of Respondents by Agreement/Disagreement with Open Importation Policy	100
4.1	Productivity Performance of the Indonesian Rice Economy, 2018–21	107

4.2	Total Rice Imports during the Jokowi Administration, 2014–21	127
5.1	Difference between Distorted and Undistorted Price in Thailand, 1970–2004	139
5.2	Total Amount of Subsidies Received by Each Department	143
5.3	Summary of the Project's Data Comparing the Government's Goal to the Present Project Advancement on Rice, 2020	148

ACKNOWLEDGEMENTS

A number of people deserve recognition for helping in the publication of this edited volume. Jacob Ricks of Singapore Management University and Colum Graham of the Australian National University participated in the December 2021 online seminar on which these chapters are based and provided useful insights on the presentations. An HSS Seed Grant from the National University of Singapore (A-0003599-00-00) helped to finance the online gathering, and Ngoi Yao Jie Wesley of the NUS Political Science Department aided in disbursing those funds. Saharah Bte Abubakar of the Asia Research Institute displayed superb copyediting skills on the chapters, and Ng Kok Kiong and Rahilah Yusuf of the ISEAS – Yusof Ishak Institute professionally oversaw the volume's publication process.

THE CONTRIBUTORS

Bustanul Arifin is Professor of Agricultural Economics at the University of Lampung, Senior Economist with the Institute for Development of Economics and Finance and Professorial Fellow at the Bogor Agricultural University. He has over thirty-five years of experience researching food and agricultural policy. He has held visiting professorships in the US and Australia, and presently serves as food policy adviser to Indonesia's Coordinating Ministry of Economic Affairs and to the Executive Office of the President.

Roehlano M. Briones, a Senior Research Fellow at the Philippine Institute for Development Studies (PIDS), conducts policy research for the Philippine government on agriculture, rural development, food security and international trade. He is a board member of the consultancy group Brain Trust Inc., past board member of the Philippine Economic Society and a Fellow of the Foundation for Economic Freedom as well as of the Social Weather Stations.

Jamie S. Davidson is Associate Professor of Political Science, National University of Singapore, and head of the Food Politics and Society cluster at the Asia Research Institute of the same university. He has written extensively on Southeast Asian politics, including three sole-authored books on Indonesia. His book on comparing rice politics in Indonesia, the Philippines and Malaysia is currently in progress.

Isabel B. Espineli is a Research Analyst at the Philippine Institute for Development Studies. She graduated with a bachelor's degree in Sociology from the University of the Philippines. She has since worked in areas of community organization, agriculture and environmental management. She has contributed with Dr Roehlano Briones of PIDS in publishing research papers on policy research on a number of topics.

Thanapan Laiprakobsup is Associate Professor of Political Science at the Department of Government, Faculty of Political Science, Chulalongkorn University. His research focuses on rice policy and politics in Thailand and Southeast Asia. He has published in *Asian Politics & Policy, Asian Geographer, International Review of Public Administration* and *Journal of Rural Studies*, among others. He is currently researching farmers' adjustment to urbanization in Bangkok's suburbs.

Fatimah Mohamed Arshad is Fellow at the Laboratory of Agricultural and Food Policy, University Putra Malaysia. Over four decades she has written several dozen publications and reports on the economics of the paddy and rice industry, commodity price analytics, supply chain and food security. She relies on econometrics, multivariate analyses and system dynamics to address growing complexity and interconnectedness of agricultural and food systems.

Jose Ma. Luis Montesclaros is Research Fellow and PhD candidate with the Non-Traditional Security Studies Centre, S. Rajaratnam School of International Studies, Nanyang Technological University, Singapore. His work on food security deploying dynamic models has been used by Singapore's Inter-Ministry Committee on Food Security and the ASEAN Secretariat. He was one of LKYSPP's two "Leaders of Tomorrow" at the 44th Saint Gallen Wings of Excellence Awards in 2014.

Manthana Noksawak is a Public Sector Development Officer at the Office of the Public Sector Development Commission, Thailand. Her research focuses on rice-related agricultural policy analysis. Presently, she is writing an independent study on Geographical Indication in agricultural products and the notion of food sovereignty. She holds a master's degree in Government Studies from Chulalongkorn University.

Paul S. Teng is Adjunct Senior Fellow, S. Rajaratnam School of International Studies, and concurrently Managing Director and Dean, NIE International Pte Ltd, both of Nanyang Technological University, Singapore. He is also

Senior Adviser (AgriFood) to A*STAR Singapore. Paul has held leadership positions in the Worldfish Centre, the International Rice Research Institute, Monsanto Company and US universities. He is a Fellow of the World Academy of Sciences and other professional societies.

1

Introduction: Just Another Crisis?
The Impact of the COVID-19 Pandemic on Southeast Asia's Rice Sector

Jamie S. Davidson

INTRODUCTION

Caustic policy debates have raged over the direction of the rice sector in Southeast Asia. The clashing views of governments, opposition parties, donors, international financial institutions, academics, consumer groups, private traders, rural activists and paddy cultivators have contributed to the rancour, although these actors are of uneven clout. One principal fault line pits the policy prescription of liberalization against protectionism. This is especially acute in countries in the region that are significant rice producers but import regularly due to cultivation totals that fall short of national requirements. Indonesia, Malaysia and the Philippines compose this special group of importers. Annual production figures vary, but even with the occasional bumper harvest that can lift cultivation totals to nearly meet consumer demand, total national requirements typically encompass additional supplies for filling public stockpiles. Governments draw from these reserves amid price surges or in cases of emergency such as drought, pest infestation, storms and floods that occur with regularity in the region. Although these net importers grow the vast majority of their rice requirements domestically—customarily, the closest to reaching self-sufficiency in rice is Indonesia (93–99 per cent), followed by the Philippines (85–95 per cent), and then Malaysia (59–75 per cent) (Otsuka 2021, Figure 4, p. 326)—the combined population of these countries is large. It amounts to about 425 million people. As such, together these governments acquire roughly 4.2 million metric tonnes of foreign rice each year, at a very approximate cost of US$1.68 billion on average.[1]

Pro-market advocates would prefer to see higher volumes of rice imports in these countries (and private traders, not governments, in the main do the purchasing). Why? Chiefly because more imports are thought to be capable of bringing down the high price of rice in these rice-deficit countries. Rather persistently their prices exceed those of their rice export counterparts in mainland Southeast Asia, sometimes as much as a factor of two to three times.[2] The reasons behind high costs for net importers can be summed by two factors. First are policy choices, which include heavy government intervention in the sector exemplified by the political and financial support of food parastatals that monopolize the import business (Rashid, Gulati, and Cummings 2008). And intervention in its many forms—from the farm level to palace politics—leads to price distortions and other inefficiencies (Anderson and Martin 2009). The second are geographical factors. High population-to-arable land ratios lead to elevated production costs compared to those in rice-abundant Thailand and Vietnam. There, wide river deltas and lower people-to-arable-land ratios keep production costs down (Dawe, Moya, and Casiwan 2006).[3]

Why are high rice prices of concern? Supporters of the comparative advantage point out that they worsen poverty. How? Principally the poor spend above national average fractions of income on food. If higher quantities of cheaper imports lower rice prices in the receiving country, this in turn enables the poor to spend more of their scarce resources on other such essential items as children's education and healthcare, leading to positive development outcomes. Price reductions, so the argument goes, have other beneficial effects as well. They would minimize smuggling, for instance, which is pervasive in the net importing countries. The large profit margins that incentivize smugglers would be squeezed as price differentials between exporters and importers narrow. Then there is the saving of public resources. If private traders are permitted to buy the bulk of the imports, and concurrently governments de-emphasize rice production, importing governments can shift expenditures from wasteful production subsidies that amount to hundreds of millions of US dollars per year to more beneficial or efficient pro-poor programmes such as targeted, direct cash transfers. Even if governments were to continue support for smallholders—the majority of whom remain net consumers of rice—material support can be deployed to shift planting toward higher-value crops, like fruits and vegetables. Lastly, if private rice traders were to profit more regularly from imports, it has been suggested that they would be enticed to invest in the industry more broadly, boosting underfunded research and development (for higher-yielding seed varietals, for example) and reversing the deterioration in post-harvest logistics (Alavi et al. 2012).

Despite decades of international pressure of varying degrees, these governments have refused to liberalize their rice sectors for a number of reasons.[4] They argue that rice is their respective country's staple food; it contributes more to daily caloric intake averages than any other food item for the majority of their respective populations: Indonesia—52 per cent; the Philippines—46 per cent; and Malaysia—30 per cent.[5] Rice is thus essential to achieving what these governments conceive of or define as food security, which demands that this foodstuff be managed responsibly. This is regardless of the precipitously declining economic significance of rice cultivation in these national economies over the years. If the rice trade is left entirely to market forces, these governments contend that social conflict and unrest may result—for example, when periodic shortages arise on the international market. Violent conflict may be directed at the governments themselves, or between rural and urban sectors if policy too conspicuously privileges one sector over the other. In short, balancing the demands of urban consumers who prefer cheap rice with those of cultivators who seek higher farmgate prices requires careful public management. Cultivators also must be shielded from the wild price fluctuations characteristic of the international rice market. (Compared to other grain markets, the rice trade is more volatile since only 8 to 11 per cent or so of global production is traded internationally.) Given producer preference for cost certainty, rather than the maximization of returns on investment, reliable price stability has proven to incentivize growers to plant paddy in higher quantities (Timmer 1989). Moreover, these governments warn that the flooding of their respective countries with cheap imports will have dire consequences.

It will further impoverish tens to hundreds of thousands of small-scale producers by depressing their already meagre incomes, which in turn will accelerate the sale of land by farmers. National food security is further imperilled as these lands are converted to non-agricultural uses such as housing estates or golf courses.

These governments would also decry the disappearance of the smallholder for reasons that extend beyond material matters: To different extents, the former is apt to celebrate images of the rice farmer as an exemplar of such societal ideals as the authenticity that are closely associated with these countries' agrarian pasts. The stuff of Indonesian, Malaysian and Philippine nationhood, respectively, is frequently romanticized as rooted in the bucolic simplicity of rural life. As such state support of the rice cultivator aligns nicely with these ideological beliefs, just as the pursuit and attainment of self-sufficiency in rice can fulfil nationalistic aspirations. When such perennial importers as the Philippines (in the early 1970s) and Indonesia (a decade later) reached rice self-sufficiency on account of the widespread adoption of Green Revolution technologies by farmers, these achievements were proudly celebrated as national accomplishments.[6] (Importantly, they were lauded by the international community as well.) These past successes, however fleeting, are one reason why dips in rice production and comparable increases in imports are often discursively framed in these countries as developmental failures or episodes of national embarrassment. Furthermore, these governments bristle at the hypocrisy of western governments that push the prying open of agricultural markets elsewhere while protecting their own farmers with unflinching political support and ample financial inducements and have long done so. Lastly, because labour-intensive manufacturing has slowed in these countries of late, these governments would be hard-pressed to provide opportunities for a majority of their rural citizens to gain adequate formal urban employment (Rigg, Salamanca, and Thompson 2016).

Alongside these public reasons lurk private considerations too. Corruption in these Southeast Asian countries is prevalent and vested interests inside and outside government routinely capture lucrative rents and other (illicit) gains from state intervention in their respective international and domestic rice markets. After all, each country supports a food parastatal—National Rice and Paddy Corporation (BERNAS) in Malaysia, State Logistics Board (Bulog) in Indonesia and National Food Authority (NFA) in the Philippines—that for decades has been a magnet for criticisms of alleged corrupt or unethical business practices. Market economists euphemistically refer to them as price distorters or pockets of inefficiency. Furthermore, the holding of competitive elections in each of these countries facilitates government intervention; it politicizes the distribution of resources among key voting constituencies—for example, free or highly subsidized rice for urban voters, cheap chemical fertilizer, seeds or hand tractors for producers. These allocations (and others) fuel broader, complex and entwined patronage networks that are sustained throughout non-election years too.

Production versus Livelihoods

In addition to the policy and political friction between liberalization and protectionism, a second and corresponding line of contention regarding the rice sector in Southeast Asia sets state production demands against the livelihood of growers. Whereas in the former debate, domestic and external actors are often found on opposing sides, the production versus livelihood argument tends to sow division within countries. At first blush, the relationship between production to livelihood appears complementary—the more farmers produce, the more income they earn. And while this relationship can and does hold, it is less robust than one might surmise: The complementarity does not hold uniformly across space and time, and among different classes of rural producers. Frequently, traders, who ordinarily possess better market knowledge than growers, can gain disproportionately from swings in commodity prices. Moreover, many agriculturalists are either smallholders or landless leaseholders incapable of harvesting sufficient paddy needed to cover household expenses, repay debts (most often to traders) and accumulate savings critical for overcoming health emergencies. Many farmer advocates lament that government fixation on rice production keeps producers poor because public financial help is inadequate, or that whatever aid is available is tied exclusively to paddy cultivation, thus preventing diversification to higher-value crops.[7] There are also proven concerns that whatever material support exists flows disproportionately to larger farmers with political connections among local administration, thereby exacerbating rural inequality. Advocates also gripe about low public investment in rural economies more broadly that fails to generate sufficient non-farm employment, for both permanent and seasonal work. Today, a rapidly dwindling percentage of growers rely solely on income gained from planting; smallholders do not earn enough money from their tiny plots to support household finances (and large-scale farmers tend to invest in non-farming economic activities, again exacerbating rural inequality).[8] Equally troubling is government neglect of smallholders who grow commodities of secondary importance to food security, like copra or tubers, or who cultivate crops of duller ideological or political resonance, such as maize. Materially, these producers on average are worse off than the majority of landowning rice farmers. Farmer advocates prefer governments to link poverty and development policies in ways that encompass the primary commodity sector more holistically (Akram-Lodhi, Borras, and Kay 2007).

Although the production versus livelihood dilemma as sketched above pertains broadly to the three net importing countries, for decades a similar predicament has also entangled Thailand, a traditional major rice exporter. To be sure, if we narrowly focus on rice, Thailand's governments have had far less to fret about food (in)security than their archipelagic neighbours. For more than a century, Thailand's rice surplus has helped to feed the region (Ingram 1971). But this does not mean that balancing production imperatives with Thai farmer welfare has been free from contention—far from it. For decades, especially from the 1950s to the early 1980s, Thailand's authoritarian governments adopted characteristically pro-urban policies, exemplified by taxing rice exports. While these taxes suppressed producers' income, the revenue extracted was redeployed to industry and manufacturing (and the personal use of corrupt high-ranking officials). Even as the Thai economy boomed during this period, including rural livelihood improvement, urban income growth rates far outpaced those of the rural (Siamwalla 1975; Ricks 2018).

As the country gradually shifted to more open politics in the 1980s and elections became more competitive, the political significance of rural voters was provided with a boost. To the exasperation of urban elites, these voters backed local candidates who pledged to improve rural livelihoods. This resulted not only in more development funds expended in the countryside to build roads, markets, hospitals and schools, but also led governments to pledge to pay higher prices for paddy. Over time, a paddy mortgage scheme that softened seasonal fluctuations in farmgate prices was introduced and the export tax was essentially eliminated. (Stable rice prices on the international market also helped Thai governments to adopt these new policies.) Rural development and pro-peasant spending by the state accelerated apace to the extent that, by the turn of the century, the anthropologist Andrew Walker could declare that Thailand had become, generally speaking, a nation of middle-class peasants (Walker 2012). Meanwhile, as elections progressively gained popular acceptance as the appropriate means for transferring political power peacefully—no small feat in a country renowned for the frequency of its coups—arose Thaksin Shinawatra, then the country's richest businessman and his Thai Rak Thai party (TRT, Thais Love Thais). Fuelled by their pro-rural platform, constitutional changes that favoured the building of stronger parties and the rise of money politics, they won elections in 2001 and 2005 by unprecedented margins.

With Thaksin's popularity and his populist policies threatening urban elite interests and especially that of the monarchy, which traditionally had depicted itself as the undisputed patron of the Thai villager, the military overthrew Thaksin's government in 2006. After elections were restored, and with Thaksin in exile because of corruption charges he faced, Thaksin's sister, Yingluck Shinawatra, and her Pheu Thai Party— an offshoot of the TRT—triumphed in the 2011 election. As premier, Yingluck pledged to buy paddy from farmers, a key electoral constituency, at inflated prices. (As noted above, the paddy pledging scheme had been used by Thai governments in different forms since the 1980s.) Yingluck's government intended to pass the high prices onto the international market but prices fell, resulting in catastrophic losses to Thai public coffers estimated at over US$8 billion. The military used the paddy pledging debacle as a pretext to topple her elected government in 2014. Although Thailand produces an annual excess of rice, with heavy state intervention in the sector and with an unresolved production versus livelihood conundrum, it is no stretch to conclude that rice is no less a political commodity in Thailand than it is in the importing countries of Indonesia, the Philippines or Malaysia.

THE COVID-19 PANDEMIC AS A RICE CRISIS?

The outbreak of the 2019 novel coronavirus (COVID-19) pandemic in early 2020 slammed unexpectedly and dramatically into the unfolding of these debates and developments, overwhelming some concerns and amplifying others. This pandemic has constituted the most disruptive global health crisis since the end of World War I and the gravest threat to the world economy since World War II. As of this writing, known COVID-19 cases worldwide have surpassed 600,000 million with over 6.5 million deaths. Figures will continue to rise. Not only are infections and reinfections still occurring worldwide as more contagious (but less lethal) variants of the virus emerge, but pressure, too, will mount on governments that have grossly underreported death tolls to release more realistic numbers. Models estimate that the true number of fatalities is two-to-three times greater than official counts.[9]

When governments around the world began implementing unprecedented lockdowns to control the spread of the coronavirus from early 2020 onward, worries were immediately raised not only about peoples' livelihoods as factories shuttered, mass transportation slowed to a crawl and entire industries teetered on the brink of collapse. Fears also focused on the viability of supply chains, where severe bottlenecks at local, regional, national and international levels had the potential to imperil the access and availability of basic food items for hundreds of millions, if not billions, of already vulnerable people.

Today's COVID-19 pandemic aside, due to the rice sector's high susceptibility to an array of disturbances, from poor weather and pest outbreaks to geopolitical earthquakes, a backlash against ethnic minority middlemen and economic meltdowns, the industry is prone to crisis. Southeast Asia is no exception and no stranger to rice crises, although of varying magnitudes and triggers. Harvests plummeted throughout the region during World War II due to the forced requisition policies of occupying Japanese forces; millions died in ensuing famines, particularly in Indonesia and Vietnam (Huff 2020). After the war, it took years for struggling economies and devastated agricultural systems in occupied Southeast Asia to recover to pre-war rice production totals. By the mid-1960s, as birth rates boomed, poverty worsened and with power-hungry communist parties ascendant, chronic rice shortages convinced Western governments to invest heavily in modernizing rice cultivation in Southeast Asia as a means for ensuring food security and in turn bolstering (non-communist) political stability. Plant breeders, funded by wealthy Western donor organizations and governments, developed new high-yielding, fast-maturing seed varietals that, in conjunction with the application of copious quantities of chemical fertilizer and improved water control, would both boost production yields and allow farmers to harvest paddy twice a year with regularity (Griffin 1974; Cullather 2013). In the early 1970s, however, widespread drought precipitated a regional rice crisis, rolling back the early gains of this Green Revolution. International prices remained elevated for years, as the ensuing oil crisis precipitated by the Organization of the Petroleum Exporting Countries ratcheted up prices for inorganic fertilizers (Timmer 2010, p. 2). The rice crisis also prompted the Philippine, Indonesian and Malaysian governments to redouble efforts in convincing as many cultivators as possible, regardless of landholding size, to adopt the Green Revolution package of technology. Illustratively, unprecedented state funding was made available for growers to purchase pricey inputs (high-yielding varieties, inorganic fertilizers) and for bureaucrats and engineers to expand modern irrigation systems. By this time, the governments' trust in international markets and domestic ethnic Chinese traders who dominated the industry had grown thin; as a result, the import monopoly powers of each of the food parastatals were by now firmly in hand.

Notwithstanding controversies unleashed by the Green Revolution, including its mixed record on poverty alleviation, in the main, the subsequent regionwide rice crisis did not materialize until 2008 thanks to these national production programmes.[10] (Individual countries did in the meantime experience the occasional rice crisis, including the Philippines in the mid-1990s and Indonesia amid the 1997/98 Asian Financial Crisis and its challenging political transition from authoritarianism to democracy.) The 2008 rice scare, unlike the 1970s crisis, was neither weather-induced nor occasioned by a dip in production. Instead, in late 2007 speculation in world grain markets, especially in those of wheat due to poor weather and of maize due to rising demand for ethanol—a prime ingredient in biofuel projects—spilled into the characteristically unstable rice market. A large overpay by the Philippine government of Vietnamese rice and (subsequent) export bans by Indian and Vietnamese governments prompted by shortage fears roiled the rice market more roughly than the wheat and maize markets had experienced. Rumours about Thailand's intent to impose its own ban further drove up prices as more panic buying and hoarding by domestic traders and households took hold. International prices tripled in a span of just six months (December 2007 to May 2008) from slightly over US$300 per metric tonne to slightly over US$1000. Once Japan acquiesced to requests from abroad to sell its reserves in the international market, the crisis abated (Dawe and Slayton 2010). Afterwards, although the price bubble of the crisis had been pierced, for years the world price of rice remained over US$400 per metric tonne, failing to return to pre-crisis levels. Experts rightly asked whether policymakers and the international community had sufficiently learned from these series of events to help break the rather regular cycle of rice crises or at least mitigate the effects of the subsequent one when inevitably it would emerge (Timmer 2010).

Accordingly, when COVID-19 began its contagious spread throughout Southeast Asia and the pandemic's manifold adverse effects gripped the region, it was of little surprise that policymakers and politicians turned their attention to the health of their respective rice sectors. But so too did agricultural economists and other scholars with similar research and public welfare interests. It was in this context that foremost experts on rice policy in Indonesia, Malaysia, Thailand, the Philippines and Singapore gathered in December 2021 for a one-day virtual workshop to consider and analyse the multifarious dimensions that today's pandemic has had on Southeast Asia's rice industry, chiefly at the national level. Workshop participants, who possess ties to past or current policymakers, were tasked with addressing any number of the following questions:

- What lessons were there to be learned from past rice crises? Did policymakers apply any of them prior to today's pandemic? Why or why not?
- In a historical context, how distinctive has this current crisis and its effect on rice policy been?
- How well have policymakers adjusted to the demands and pressures of today's crisis? What main constraints have policymakers faced?
- Have the effects of the pandemic—on poverty, for example—been as damaging as feared or have their impact been less severe than first predicted? What factors account for either outcome?
- To what degree has the pandemic forced changes in government priorities in development planning and/or practice, especially regarding the rice sector?
- Has the state shown the capacity and skill to handle both a public health crisis alongside challenges in the agricultural sector? Or do we see bifurcation, or silos, where one sector operates independently of crises in other sectors? Or do we see a compounding effect wherein, like dominoes, the crises destroy the capacity of the state in other areas?
- Rent-seeking has been notoriously endemic in the rice sector. Has the

current crisis worsened or blunted this behaviour? What accounts for either outcome?
- Given the pandemic's initial threat to the viability of international trade, to what degree has the crisis forced changes to the government's approach to domestic production? Has the government adopted more autarkic policies in response? Why or why not?
- What surprising benefits, if any, has the pandemic brought to the rice sector?
- What future beckons for the rice sector? To what extent will the current crisis affect the future? Will any reforms that have been implemented in response to today's crisis take hold and endure? Or do they merely pay lip service to mollify short-term, growing dissatisfaction with the sector's governance?

The revised papers that comprise this volume constitute attempts by their writers to grapple with some of these overarching questions.

TWO MAIN FINDINGS

Rice Crisis Averted

As of late 2022, the multiyear pandemic has not precipitated a serious rice crisis of either variety—one primarily caused by production shortages, like the early 1970s, or one caused by uncertainty and speculative buying that unfolded in 2008. One prime reason for this favourable outcome is simply luck, namely, good weather. Another is that COVID-19 transmissions, thriving in the expansive density of social interactions, have been more highly concentrated in urban centres than in rural settings, especially throughout 2020 and since then. Comprehensive stay-at-home orders hurt urban economies disproportionately. (As a result, urban poverty worsened, as did urban inequality [Kang et al. 2021].) Therefore cultivation totals in the main producing states have held steady. Milled rice production in four major rice-producing countries in 2020/21 was more or less in line with annual averages from 2016/17 to 2019/20: Indonesia—35.5 million (metric) tonnes; Thailand—19.3; the Philippines—12.0; and Malaysia—1.8.[11]

Moreover, attributable to continued economic growth, the share of rice expenditures in the cost of urban *and* rural consumption baskets in these four countries had declined during the decade or so since the 2008 rice crisis (see Table 1.1). This means that developmentally speaking, these Southeast Asian populations were in a better position to confront a COVID-19-induced rice crisis if it had become acute.

The lack of a severe rice crisis did not trivialize the validity of fears in the first half of 2020 of a repeat of 2008 or worse from occurring. First, concerns over the immobility and compromised health of agricultural labour and the overall stress applied to international and domestic logistic networks were understandable and pervasive; these networks, as it turned out, were more resilient than many had surmised. Second, Vietnam had again imposed an export ban, potentially prompting similar restrictive trade measures among other exporters. By April 2020 when Vietnam announced its ban, the world rice price from earlier in the year did increase by some 27 per cent from US$429 to US$543 per metric tonne. Fortunately, with adequate regional and global supplies and international logistics operating reasonably well, the international (Bangkok) price subsequently began trending downward, from US$459 in November 2020

TABLE 1.1
Rice Share as Percentage in Urban and Rural Household Expenditures

The Philippines	2009 (national)		2018 (national)	
	13.1		10.8	
	9.5 (urban)	16.7 (rural)	8.5 (urban)	13.3 (rural)
Malaysia	2009/10 (national)		2014	
	1.9		1.2	
			1.0 (urban)	2.0 (rural)
Indonesia	2005 (national)		2020 (national)	
	16.5		11.2	
	10.8 (urban)	25.6 (rural)	9.6 (urban)	13.9 (rural)
Thailand	2014 (urban)		2014 (rural)	
	9.2		7.5	

Sources: TDRI (2014), pp. 2-12, 2-13, 2-14, https://tdri.or.th (accessed 15 April 2022); Department of Statistics Malaysia 2019, Table 3.3, p. 129; https://www.dosm.gov.my (accessed 15 April 2022); Economic Planning Unit 2020, Table 3; https://www.epu.gov.my (accessed 15 April 2022); PSA (2009, 2018) (calculations by PIDS researchers, personal communication); https://psa.gov.ph (accessed 15 April 2022); BPS (2021), Fig. 1.3, p. 18; BPS (2006), Tables 2.1 and 2.2 (author's calculations).

to US$415 in July 2021 and US$389 by November 2021, returning to pre-pandemic levels.[12] These trends were in part transmitted to domestic rice prices in the countries under study. In the early phase of the pandemic, international prices began to rise. They then plateaued, and throughout 2021 retreated from US$536 per tonne to US$384.[13] Rice prices began to rise in 2022, slightly re-breaching the US$400 mark, more because of the impact of Russia's invasion of Ukraine on the markets for grain and oil—a critical component of inorganic fertilizers—than the pandemic itself. But throughout 2022, as wheat prices spiked, rice prices held rather steady on account of bumper harvests in major exporting countries.[14]

Refining, Not Reforming, Policy

On account of reliable production and comparably stable prices, the governments under review were less compelled by the dire circumstances caused by the pandemic—mounting death tolls, overwhelmed health sectors, sharp macroeconomic contractions, high unemployment, severe incomes losses and near collapse of tourism and related food and beverage and entertainment sectors—to introduce drastic policy changes in their respective rice sectors. Instead, quite serendipitously, nearly each of the governments under review in this volume enacted rather impactful policies *before* the eruption of the pandemic in early 2020. The source of these significant pre-pandemic policy decisions mostly resided in the domestic political realm, but they had direct effects on the rice industry. In this way, we can conclude that the impact of the pandemic served more to accelerate or amplify recent government policy changes or decisions rather than act as a catalyst of reform per se. We address each country's case study in turn.

MALAYSIA

A major policy decision that demanded attention prior to the 2020 COVID-19 outbreak in Malaysia concerned extending the rice import monopoly licence of BERNAS. BERNAS (and its predecessor) has held the monopoly since the early 1970s; this arrangement is a product of that period's own rice crisis. BERNAS's import permit—periodically renewed ever since—was set to expire in 2021, and there was nothing to indicate that the government was motivated to alter the status quo. Then shockingly, in 2018, the political opposition, known as the Coalition of Hope (Pakatan Harapan, PH) scored a historic electoral upset against the National Front (Barisan Nasional, BN), the incumbent coalition. The BN, led by a political party known as the United Malays National Organization (UMNO), had dominated the country's elections uninterruptedly since the 1950s. Soon after taking over the reins of government, the reform-oriented PH administration announced its intent to revoke BERNAS's licence. Not only was BERNAS earning monopoly rents from its rice imports, but also it was considered an integral part of decades-long UMNO-led patronage networks that the PH had vowed to disassemble (and which had seemingly resonated with the electorate). The new PH agricultural minister announced that study teams were in place evaluating alternative import models.

In an equally stunning turn of events in early 2020, a breakaway PH faction, in collaboration with non-PH political allies, toppled its own government. When the political dust settled, Muhyiddin Yassin, a former UMNO power broker, emerged as head of a new coalition government, called National Alliance (Perikatan Nasional). Subsequently, Muhyiddin's government agreed to a ten-year extension of BERNAS's import permit. To observers the extension failed to elicit surprise; the new prime minister had long been a political patron of Syed Mokhtar Al-Bukhary, Malaysia's richest bumiputera (native son) businessman and principal owner of BERNAS. Under a prior UMNO-dominated government, in 2014, Syed Mokhtar's Tradewinds conglomerate was permitted to purchase and take BERNAS private. Put differently, since 2014 when BERNAS was delisted from Malaysia's stock exchange, about one-third of the national rice supply, approximately equal to its annual average imports, was more or less controlled by one man. When we consider BERNAS's one-third market share of domestic procurement, the magnitude of Syed Mokhtar's control is closer to two-thirds of the total supply. In return for holding the monopoly licence, BERNAS has been mandated to fulfil a range of public service obligations that range from managing the state's rice stockpile and distributing subsidies to farmers and Malay millers to ensuring safety standards in the rice supply system (Davidson 2018a).[15]

When the COVID-19 pandemic hit, the urgency of the Muhyiddin government to introduce wide-ranging measures to the rice and paddy sector was blunted, as Fatimah Mohamed Arshad shows in Chapter 2, since many subsidies and pricing policies were already in place.[16] Having been implemented decades ago under pro-Malay directives or during the 2008 rice crisis, these included considerable production and input subsidies for (mostly Malay) growers, special subsidized rice for low-income consumers and increased emergency stockpiling (about which BERNAS habitually complains adds to its costs). As a result, the government, as elsewhere, focused its energies in 2020 on stymying a complete economic meltdown amid unprecedented movement control orders (MCOs).

The government introduced some seven stimulus packages that through 2021 amounted to over US$91 billion in financial injections. These packages could not prevent the economy from contracting a painful 5.6 per cent in 2020, but they laid the foundation for a modest rebound of 3.1 per cent growth in 2021. According to Fatimah, the lower income groups in Malaysia have suffered disproportionately: As unemployment rose due to the MCOs, incomes and consumption declined; many precarious Malaysians slid further down the country's socio-economic ladder. Malnutrition, a worrisome concern prior to the pandemic, worsened, especially among children of low-income households. The pandemic did, however, prompt the government to produce its first-ever government policy paper on food security; prior exercises had concentrated narrowly on the rice and paddy sectors. The paper, however, failed to address the major impediment to improving the competitiveness and furthering the modernization of the country's rice and paddy sector, namely, BERNAS's stranglehold on the sector, which is dulling competitiveness by denying new market entrants and thus stymying innovation, both in upstream and downstream activities. All told, as Fatimah puts it, "Clearly, crises and changing political landscape are important drivers in the policy matrix of the paddy and rice sector in Malaysia" (p. 36).

THE PHILIPPINES

In the Philippines, the major decision taken prior to the COVID-19 pandemic was President Duterte's surprising move to liberalize the country's rice imports. To be sure, for decades there had been a small group of market economists in the country who decried the debilitating state intervention in the rice trade and who pushed for liberalization to lower the country's artificially high retail rice prices, which in turn, it was hoped, would deliver tangible health benefits to the country's tens of millions of citizens who lived near or below the poverty line (Davidson 2016). Pro-market advocates have had some success in opening up other sectors in this country's notoriously protectionist economy over the years—for example, in retail oil and in telecommunications in the 1990s. This protectionism in the main explains the country's sluggish growth rates of the late twentieth century compared to some of its Southeast Asian "tiger" economy counterparts (see Table 1.2).

Still, even these economists expressed surprise when the irascible Duterte in early 2019 announced he was revoking the NFA's monopoly rice import permit. Aside from the prominent presence of an economic reformer in Duterte's cabinet—Carlos "Sonny" Dominguez served as Finance Minister—the Duterte administration also was spooked by a bout of inflation in early 2019, a significant contributing factor of which were elevated rice prices. A pliant Congress subsequently passed a law on the matter. It established new (variable) import tariff rates—in effect, meaning that liberalization was partial—and set aside special assistance monies (10 billion Philippine pesos annually for six years). Chiefly supplied by rice tariff collections, this fund is designed to help soften the sector's transition to more market conditions, especially for the country's hundreds of thousands of smallholders, by (supposedly) improving the industry's competitiveness.

As a result of liberalization, as Roehlano Briones and Isabel Espineli recount in Chapter 3, the wholesale price of regular milled rice dropped appreciably, by about 18 per cent from mid-2018 to late 2020. Unfortunately, this price decrease was less sharp than the dip in farmgate prices,

TABLE 1.2
Average Annual Economic Growth
(Gross Domestic Product) Rates, 1980–89

Thailand	7.0 per cent
Singapore	6.1 per cent
Indonesia	5.3 per cent
Malaysia	4.9 per cent
The Philippines	0.7 per cent

Source: Wu (1991).

suggesting that traders were benefitting handsomely from rice liberalization (Montemayor 2020). While recognizing that producer incomes have been squeezed, Briones and Espineli note that, first, cheaper rice prices have resulted in a net positive gain for society as a whole, and, second, some income losses of farmers have been offset by the disbursement of the aforementioned Rice Funds. Revealingly, Briones and Espineli highlight figures from a consumer survey that shows conclusively but quizzically that Filipinos believe that retail rice prices have in fact increased since liberalization, despite indisputable evidence to the contrary. Briones and Espineli are rightly puzzled by this outcome, although some of it may stem from the heavy coverage in the media of the steep fall in prices farmers have been receiving for their crops. Misinformation campaigns that prevail on social media surely cannot be discounted here (Ocampo 2020).

Since the matter of rice import liberalization continues to be politicized, especially as populist rhetoric gained steam ahead of the May 2022 presidential elections, Briones and Espineli worry about the fate of this historic policy reform and the possibility of its reversal. Not only is the new president, Ferdinand Marcos Jr., a vocal opponent of rice trade liberalization, but we also know from studies elsewhere that the fight to maintain policy reforms can be more daunting than the struggle to enact them in the first place (Patashnik 2008). Still, Briones and Espineli conclude that liberalization most likely spared Filipinos from the ill effects of another rice crisis during the COVID-19 pandemic. The Duterte government did implement some of the most comprehensive movement restriction measures in the region, which contributed significantly to the steep 9.6 per cent contraction of the country's economy in 2020. Yet signally Briones and Espineli are grateful that the NFA was no longer in a position to mishandle rice imports—as it had done on several past occasions—that would have wreaked further economic havoc, leading to additional developmental harm to tens of millions of Filipinos during the already destructive pandemic.

INDONESIA

Unlike in Malaysia and the Philippines, governments in Indonesia did not move against its parastatal (Bulog) to curb its rice import authority prior to the 2020 pandemic. It was once attempted by the International Monetary Fund (IMF) amid the 1997/98 Asian Financial Crisis (AFC). By lending billions to Indonesia's New Order cash-strapped government, the IMF had sought, in exchange, to reform Indonesia's partially closed economy, including eliminating Bulog's rice import monopoly. With liberalization in this sector, the IMF hoped that not only would domestic prices more closely track cheaper international prices, but also that liberalization would dislodge the deep and expansive invested interests in the trade that had accumulated over decades of policy status quo under President Soeharto. But with few trade barriers remaining and even fewer regulations in place, private traders brought in record amounts of foreign rice, which caused many Indonesians, including top policymakers, to take umbrage (Sawit and Lokollo 2007; Davidson 2018b).

As the AFC waned, so did IMF leverage. Indonesia's now democratic governments, especially under Presidents Megawati Sukarnoputri and Susilo Bambang Yudhoyono, restored Bulog's import authority—principally over medium-quality rice—and expanded the agency's responsibilities to include other commodities as well. Meanwhile, a commodity boom and the country's competitive elections have helped to stoke economic nationalist sentiments, of which particular resource and agrarian variants have been vocal (Graham 2020). Bulog has been able to take advantage by extending its control over the rice import business and other basic commodities, even if politicians persistently continue to squeeze rents from it, making the agency particularly scandal-prone. All told, rice liberalization in Indonesia is equated with not only undue foreign interference in the country's economy, but also that of its sovereignty too. If Indonesia's low-income rural and urban consumers would benefit from sizeable reductions in rice prices brought about by liberalization—as seems to have been the case in the Philippines—they are currently a silent majority (Davidson 2018c).

As Arifin Bustanul describes in Chapter 4, there are striking similarities between the effects of the 1997/98 AFC and the COVID-19 crisis. In both instances, a "ruralization phenomenon" took hold, where suddenly unemployed urban workers returned home to work, especially in Java's micro-sized rice plots. (Average rice plots on this infamously crowded island are below 0.5 hectares.) Also in both instances, most workers returned to the cities once economic conditions improved. Another similarity between the two crises has been an economic recession, although of differing magnitudes. In 1998, Indonesia's economy recorded an astonishing 13 per cent contraction compared to about 2 per cent in 2020. Politics explains much of this difference in outcome: During the AFC Indonesia suffered a twin crisis that included acute political instability and uncertainty surrounding the fall of the country's long-time authoritarian ruler, Soeharto. During the COVID-19 crisis, political conditions have been far more stable. But why did Indonesia's economy in 2020 experience the least acute slowdown among this volume's cases? (see Table 1.3). One reason lies in the lax approach the government adopted in locking down the country, as second-term President Joko "Jokowi" Widodo sought to minimize the pandemic's damage to his economic legacy. But propping up his legacy assuredly and unnecessarily cost the lives of tens of thousands of Indonesians (Setijadi 2021).

In the rice and rural sectors, Arifin's chapter demonstrates that, since the pandemic crisis has been less disruptive than the AFC, Jokowi's government has been less compelled to pursue major reforms. Many of the government's poverty alleviation policies, like subsidized rice assistance programmes (instituted in the aftermath of the AFC) and e-vouchers for basic commodities, were in place prior to the pandemic. Increasing domination of the rice trade, especially on Java, by large wholesale millers has continued apace and the reforms that Bulog should undertake—such as modernizing its warehouse systems and forging more commercial links with private sector actors—would have been pressing regardless of the pandemic. According to Arifin, a similar case can be made for productivity gains in paddy production through better seed development, improved extension services and irrigation maintenance. Even the controversial building of food estates in the country's outer island provinces has only been accelerated due to the pandemic; their development was already

TABLE 1.3
2020 Gross Domestic Product Rates

	2020
Indonesia	−2.1 per cent
Singapore	−5.4 per cent
Malaysia	−5.6 per cent
Thailand	−6.1 per cent
The Philippines	−9.6 per cent

Source: data.worldbank.org

underway prior to Jokowi's first term. (He was first elected in 2014.) Indonesian governments firmly believe that the success of these massive estates will bolster the country's food security. But the operative term here is "success"; there is little consensus on how it is to be measured. As the pandemic has revealed, access to food, especially that that is nutritious and affordable, can lag behind availability in bulk quantities.

THAILAND

In Thailand, a key change impacting the rice sector before the onset of the COVID-19 pandemic was the military's overthrow of Yingluck's elected government in 2014, which, as was noted above, stemmed from her administration's rice pledging fiasco, among other reasons. But owing to path dependency and certain structural conditions, including an abundance of rice farmers—their numbers are disproportionately large given Thailand's relatively high level of development (Ricks 2018)—the military, led by General Prayuth Chan-o-cha, found it frustratingly difficult to quit pledging rice prices to farmers. In part, this was because it made for good politics and lent political stability to the country. Having eliminated Yingluck's pledging programme, the junta subsequently offered generous subsidies to rice farmers. Then, in 2016, during a sharp fall in rice prices, it introduced another subsidy scheme by incentivizing growers to store their grain rather than sell it immediately. To many, this policy bore a close resemblance to rice pledging. The military government vehemently denied Yingluck's accusations that the new scheme was rice pledging in all but name (Watcharasakwet and Chaichalearmmongkol 2016;[17] Laiprakobsup 2017).

Eventually, Prayuth's leverage over the country's politically rambunctious farmers did improve. After years of delay, during which a new constitution in 2017 was promulgated, Prayuth's interim government won heavily engineered elections in 2019. The regime spent years crafting electoral rules that all but assured the former general's path to the prime ministership. Notably, the government banned offshoots of the TRT and Pheu Thai parties and determined that the Senate, which along with the House of Representatives selects the premier, would be fully appointed by the junta (McCargo 2019).

Thanapan Laiprakobsup and Manthana Noksawak detail in Chapter 5 that the country's rice farmers have suffered considerably since the outbreak of the 2020 pandemic. In addition to the restrictive mobility orders and the negative effects they have had particularly on off-farm economic activities, two additional factors have hurt rice farmers. The first was a devastating drought, the country's worst in decades that has caused hundreds of millions of US dollars' worth of economic damage. But Thanapan and Manthana caution that the governments' neglect of farming has exacerbated the drought's deleterious effects. Officials have been slow to invest in upgrading such infrastructure as irrigation works and water retention ponds—issues that the drought readily exposed. Governments have even diverted scarce water supplies for industrial and manufacturing usage, leaving farmers out to dry, so to speak. The second corresponding factor has been changes to the country's political dynamics. In short, they have shifted against farmers' interests. With electoral rule changes in place, Prayuth's government is now less dependent on the bloc votes of farmers. Accordingly, his Palang Pracharath-led government has been less pressed to funnel resources to them. Thanapan and Manthana point to the disappointing Rice Mega Farm programme as evidence. The programme was intended to consolidate farming operations to increase farmer leverage against traders and millers. But the coalition government's infighting, bureaucratic centralization and inertia as well as a lack of funding have contributed to the project's poor performance. Thanapan and Manthana go so far as to conclude that Prayuth's government has abandoned the country's rice farmers, returning the country to the period before the 1980s when government neglect of farmer welfare was conspicuous.

SINGAPORE

At first blush, including Singapore among the aforementioned country studies might seem misplaced. Unlike the cases above, due to the island-state's small size (724 square kilometres) and high population density (8,019 people per square kilometre), the republic produces none of its rice needs; dependence on the international market is total. But it is precisely this dependency and implications for policymaking that justifies its inclusion in this volume. After all, citizens and the country's sizeable non-citizen population still consume about 26 kilograms of rice per capita each year.[18] More importantly, not only does the country annually import about S$235 million worth of rice; but it also serves as a vital transshipment hub for the region's rice trade. Illustratively, its rice exports amount to about S$80 million each year, the majority of which is purchased by Indonesia.[19] The country's outsized role in the transshipment of rice and other agricultural commodities has been longstanding (Wong 1978).

Singapore's extreme dependency on the international market for food—estimated by the government at about 90 per cent[20]—was not preordained. To be sure, given obvious land constraints, the country would never fulfil its food (or rice) demand domestically. But as late as the 1960s, local farms did supply the city-state with about one-quarter of its vegetable needs. Remarkably, in the 1980s local production of hen eggs, poultry meat and chicken neared self-sufficiency levels (Ludher and Paramasilvam 2018, p. 3).

Deliberate government policies, however, shifted the country's economy aggressively toward export-oriented industrialization and as the population expanded so too did the government's building of housing and other infrastructure that extended into the country's former farming belt on the island's fringes. About four per cent of the agricultural land of the 1960s presently remains (Ludher and Paramasilvam 2018, p. 2). Still, open trade policies, the strong fiscal position of the government and purchasing policies such as diversification of supply sources helped to propel the country to the top of international rankings in food security, of which the tightly regulated domestic media is often proud to report.[21] While the prevalence of food insecurity among low-income households is less publicized (Nagpaul, Sidhu, and Chen 2020), the island-state's macro success seems to have vindicated its muscular neo-merchantalist strategy for agricultural trade policy and management.[22] Singapore's active promotion of increasing regional trade integration among members of the Association of Southeast Asian Nations (ASEAN) is well documented, as is its signing of bilateral free trade agreements with governments around the world to hedge against some ASEAN member intransigence (Terada 2009).

But as the COVID-19 pandemic hit the island-state in early 2020, as Jose Luis Montesclaros and Paul Teng chronicle in Chapter 6, Singapore's high import dependency strategy came under strain, along with its diversification approach. In the first half of 2020, with rice temporarily unavailable from Vietnam and with Thai rice prices soaring, Singaporean traders were forced to seek alternative suppliers like Pakistan and Cambodia that, prior to the pandemic, were known to export lower-quality rice at relatively high prices. As was noted above, subsequently international prices did begin to soften.

Similar to the cases surveyed above, a major decision regarding the food sector in Singapore was taken prior to the pandemic's outbreak. In 2019, the government announced its catchy "30 by 30" policy, aiming for 30 per cent of food demand to be produced domestically by 2030. Few doubt the ambitiousness of the target, although some experts have questioned its realism (Goh 2022). According to Montesclaros and Teng, the impetus behind the policy resided in the sector's failure to reach raised production targets following the 2008 rice crisis and attendant shortage fears. Learning from this middling performance, the government this time decided to throw its financial weight behind the new directive. Notably, it earmarked hundreds of millions of Singapore dollars for novel initiatives, including a S$144 million package for research grants. The government is leveraging its surfeit of highly skilled human capital and its proven track record in attracting foreign investment to promote the development of new technologies, from plant-based protein production to novel urban farming production techniques such as vertical systems where plants are grown in stacks of trays with minimal soil requirements and with computerized or robotic water infiltration techniques (Dean 2020). Still, Montesclaros and Teng, while appreciative of the government's efforts at bolstering internal food capacity—though arguably overdue—recognize that even the programme's complete success will still leave the city-state 70 per cent dependent on international food sources. To secure adequate levels of rice at affordable prices for future generations, Montesclaros and Teng suggest that Singapore, through technology transfer, aid and expertise, could do more in helping to improve rice productivity in neighbouring export countries in order to ensure adequate supply in the international market.

FUTURE DIRECTIONS

Before the COVID-19 pandemic, mounting threats to the well-being of the region's rice sector were well documented. Ageing farming populations, global warming that imperils reliable water supply, rapid conversion of productive lands out of agriculture, soil erosion exacerbated by deforestation, ecological degradation caused by chemically dependent production, limited farmer access to affordable credit, dwindling public finance for research and development (Anderson 2022, p. 7), changing consumer diets and tastes and the inexorable penetration of supermarkets number among these challenges. Facing an increasingly precarious future, the region's rice sector could hardly afford to have a "global pandemic" appended to the list. Fortunately, as the case studies that comprise this volume have underscored, the rice sector proved more resilient than many had feared. This pertains both to production and post-harvest marketing systems. The former performed better than the latter, although this was mostly due to the providence of beneficial weather. It was not wholly attributable to policy intervention and field implementation, although some governments would surely like to take credit for their "foresight". Governments did generously make available new monies during the height of the COVID-19 pandemic in the form of lost income supports, but these expenditures were not focused on productivity gains in the rice sector per se. Amid the intensity of implementing emergency measures of uncertain duration, longer-term planning is apt to be sidelined.

These insights did not stop observers from seizing the dramatic impact of the COVID-19 pandemic as an opportunity to advance certain policy positions. Put differently, has the crisis been a powerful enough shock to convince key actors to pursue structural reforms or to further strengthen status quo positions? Food sovereignty proponents have interpreted the disruption of global trade flows as a warning sign of the fragility of the neoliberal approach to food security with its over-reliance on large agro-multinationals and global logistics. For these scholar-activists, the pandemic has exposed the system's illogical and unjust practices and, as importantly, has presented a chance to shift the gravity of food systems to the local control of smallholder producers who prefer, if given proper resources, to grow healthy, nutritious food sustainably that is tailored for local markets and tastes. If the transformative pandemic has taught us anything, this argument goes, is that people, and not capital, should be at the forefront of food systems (Bello 2020).[23] On the other hand, the fears fostered by the pandemic did not dissuade trade enthusiasts of their own paradigmatic views on the matter. For them, the pandemic highlighted that further integration and opening of markets and accompanying logistic systems are still the most proven, reliable and cost-effective measures to overcome precisely those problems posed by the pandemic. Vulnerabilities and gaps in current global supply chains, as much as the pandemic itself, were what threatened food supplies, food safety, nutritious diets and livelihoods. Bolstering the resilience of the present globalized system to withstand future exogenous shocks should top policymakers' agendas, not the erection of more protectionist walls (FAO 2020; Fan et al. 2021; Anderson 2022).

Conflicting viewpoints lend difficulty to crisis planning. Assuredly, crises will happen, but their unpredictability in form, scope and timing are their defining features, even as some have already started to ponder a post-COVID world. This is especially pronounced in the rice sector. History has taught us that the next crisis is forthcoming. Preparing for it, however prudent, can be costly and fraught with predicaments. Increasing stockpiles, a common response to a crisis, adds burdens to scarce public resources, especially since rice cannot be stored indefinitely. But how we interpret the lessons learned from crisis governance or management complicates future planning as well. Are opening economies further truly the solution? What fair or objective indices of evaluation do we use to make this judgement? For example, questions have been raised about past studies' inadequate quantification of the environmental impact of global supply chains (Roberts and Lamp 2021). It is also relevant to ask about the extent to which vested interests lurk behind the push to open economies more widely to international trade and investment, or conversely, to close them more tightly.

For some countries this volume has surveyed, future paths are more settled than others, none more than Singapore. Given land constraints, it absolutely must pursue open policies, but more unsettlingly, also convince others that it is in their interests to follow its lead. Traditional rice exporters such as Thailand (and Vietnam) should follow suit, as they benefit from further agricultural trade integration, although key politicians and connected traders do so more than ordinary paddy producers. Yet, how far traditional exporters can be trusted in moments of crisis not to resort to trade-restricting measures is a pressing question. Notably, Vietnam slapped embargoes on rice exports during each of the past two major crises, while Yingluck's government, although unsuccessfully, sought to pass artificially high domestic rice prices onto international buyers. So, while Singapore, along with some business leaders, economists and technocrats in other ASEAN member states may trumpet regional multilateralism in food governance and crisis management—for example, risk-sharing through the bolstering of a regional rice reserve (Mujahid and Kornher 2016)—such cooperation is not ensured, especially under crisis conditions. When the chapters that comprise this volume are read closely, save for the Singapore case, the role ASEAN may play in future food crisis management hardly gains attention. This means that doubt is prevalent about the organization's effectiveness and reliability in such vital matters as food security. Although it was just noted that, in theory, rice exporters such as Thailand and Vietnam *may* support further agricultural trade integration, reports about the scheming of these two countries in particular to raise rice export prices ostensibly to help boost farmers' income amid inflationary pressures throw regional multilateralism into further doubt (*Straits Times*, 30 August 2022).[24]

The three net importers face knottier and more variable decision-making matrices. Reaching and sustaining complete self-sufficiency in rice in Malaysia is wildly optimistic. But this does not necessarily foreclose devoting more resources to boosting domestic production in order to ease dependence on foreign rice. There the ethnic dimensions of rice policy (and rural development) have upended cost-benefit analysis for decades. It will continue to do so for the foreseeable future, even if certain policies tend to favour Malay elites with connections over smallholders. We need not look further than the domination of the country's rice supply by a single businessman's corporation. Complex constraints also hound policymaking in Indonesia and the Philippines, both of which are more capable than Malaysia in achieving self-sufficiency in rice. Even though the Philippines recently liberalized its rice imports, new President Ferdinand Marcos Jr. could as easily reverse the reforms. He has hinted at the possibility. If his administration does not, given the incomparable strength of the executive in this country, a future president will still hold the power to do so. This specific reform is not set in stone. Nor is it predetermined that cheaper international prices will be fully transmitted to consumers amid traders' efforts to keep prices sticky. If this continues to be the case, the positive development outcomes might be more moderate than market reformers had championed. And in Indonesia, supporters and opponents alike agree that government rice-boosting programmes are costly, but disagree over the extent of costs governments should be absorbing. Should higher portions of the expenditures be spent in more productive ways? To the consternation of many, politics figures prominently in this determination, as attested by the integral role the military has played in the development and operation of new, massive food estates.

In terms of the nexus between food security and development, there are no easy solutions, under crisis conditions or otherwise. How has the COVID-19 pandemic affected our evaluations of the balance to be struck between access to rice and the grain's availability? The crisis has exposed considerable friction between availability and access. Should governments increase resources devoted to improving paddy production or should they concern themselves with broader or more robust development outcomes? What percentage of lands are to be converted (and at what costs) and whether efficient small-scale or large-scale farmers should benefit from any redistribution scheme? At what level does dependency on international trade become intolerable? At what point does subsidization of the sector become fiscally irresponsible? What are the viable employment alternatives for the hundreds of millions of denizens of rural Southeast Asia if industrial and manufacturing growth has stagnated? How should public investment be directed or reserved in anticipation of future crises? Given how the COVID-19 crisis has unfolded, boosting health sectors with enhanced public spending is warranted, but from where will the money come? Will governments risk spending less on agriculture, for example? The pandemic showed clearly that better outcomes in public health can indirectly bolster agriculture by keeping people healthier and able to work. More private sector participation can help fill the funding gap, but faced with variable rules of law environments and sensitive matters pertaining to land rights, poverty, ethnicity, rent-seeking by public officials and state ideologies extolling the virtues of rural life, the private sector has shied from making substantial investments in food crop production, especially in a staple commodity such as rice. Some of these are empirical questions, but at their core, they are political quandaries. So, intense struggles over resources and ideas, more than other influences in decision-making processes, will profoundly shape how these dilemmas unfold and are addressed, at least until the next crisis impacting the rice sector in Southeast Asia emerges.

Notes

1. This assumes rice price at US$400 per metric tonne, which was a rough pre-pandemic average from 2014 to 2019 (see https://fred.stlouisfed.org/series/PRICENPQUSDM).
2. For example, in 2007, the average retail prices of medium-quality rice in Indonesia was one and a half times more expensive than in Thailand; a decade later, it was two and a half times (Handayani 2017).
3. These are national averages. Research has shown that production costs in

select highly productive areas in the net importers can compare favourably to cultivating areas in the exporters (Bordey et al. 2016).
4. This pertained to these three countries for decades. Only recently, as discussed below, did the Philippines liberalize its rice import trade.
5. These figures are as of 2001 (http://www.knowledgebank.irri.org/ericeproduction/Importance_of_Rice.htm), except for Malaysia (Omar et al. 2019, Figure 6.3, p. 171).
6. In short, the Green Revolution package of technologies that led to double cropping and higher yields included a combination of: (1) modern, high-yielding seed varietals; (2) copious application of chemical fertilizers; and (3) improved water control (mostly through the construction and maintenance of modern irrigation systems).
7. On this point there is some overlap with the arguments of market advocates.
8. This also pertains to year-round jobs for marginal farmers or landless labourers who might benefit from shifting out of agriculture altogether. For a recent study of large-scale farmers earning nonfarming income on Java, see Ambarwati et al. (2017), especially pp. 285–87.
9. "The Pandemic's True Death Toll", economist.com, 6 May 2022 (accessed 7 May 2022).
10. In Asia, annual paddy production tripled from 200 to 600 million metric tons from 1960 to 2010 (Global Rice Science Partnership 2013, p. 80). For a recent study on the global macroeconomic gains of the Green Revolution (that also includes wheat and maize), see Gollin, Hansen, and Wingender (2021).
11. See www.ers.usda.gov/topics/crops/rice/rice-sector-at-a-glance/#Global (accessed 15 April 2022); Omar et al. (2019), p. 7, Table 1.1.
12. See https://fred.stlouisfed.org/series/PRICENPQUSDM (accessed 15 April 2022).
13. See the respective chapters of the volume.
14. It is worth noting that Indonesia and the Philippines are two of three top importers of Ukrainian wheat and protests in the former over rising food prices have grabbed the government's attention (Puma and Konar 2022; Faulder 2022; *Straits Times*, 4 March 2022; Imahashi and Phoonphongphiphat 2022). The country studies that comprise this volume were completed prior to the global inflationary impact of Russia's invasion in late February 2022.
15. These obligations, however, are not new. They were part of prior arrangements between BERNAS and the government.
16. In August 2021, Muhyiddin's government was replaced but the new government has not introduced any significant changes to the rice sector.
17. I thank Jacob Ricks for alerting me to this source.
18. https://www.statista.com/outlook/cmo/food/bread-cereal-products/rice/singapore (accessed 15 April 2022).

19. "Rice in the Husk (Paddy or Rough) in Singapore", oec.world, https://oec.world/en/profile/bilateralproduct/rice-in-the-husk-paddy-or-rough/reporter/sgp (accessed 15 April 2022).
20. https://www.sfa.gov.sg/food-farming/singapore-food-supply (accessed 15 April 2022).
21. For one example, see Koh (2018).
22. On neomerchantalism, see Helleiner (2021).
23. See also the dozens of short articles in the special issue of *Agriculture and Human Values* 37, Issue 3, September 2020.
24. I thank an anonymous reviewer for pointing to the lack of attention paid to ASEAN in these country case studies.

References

Akram-Lodhi, A. Haroon, Saturnino M. Borras Jr., and Cristóbal Kay, eds. 2007. *Land, Poverty and Livelihoods in an Era of Globalization: Perspectives from Developing and Transition Countries*. London: Routledge.

Alavi, Hamid R., Aira Htenas, Ron Kopicki, Andrew W. Shepherd, and Ramon Clarete. 2012. *Trusting Trade and the Private Sector for Food Security in Southeast Asia*. Washington, DC: World Bank.

Ambarwati, Aprilia, Ricky Ardian Harahap, Isono Sadoko, and Ben White. 2017. "Land Tenure and Agrarian Structure in Regions of Small-scale Food Production". In *Land and Development in Indonesia: Searching for the People's Sovereignty*, edited by Kathryn Robinson and John McCarthy, pp. 265–94. Singapore: ISEAS – Yusof Ishak Institute.

Anderson, Kym. 2022. "Trade-related Food Policies in a More Volatile Climate and Trade Environment". *Food Policy* 109: 1–18.

Anderson, Kym, and Will Martin, eds. 2009. *Distortions to Agricultural Incentives in Asia*. Washington, DC: World Bank.

Bello, Walden. 2020. *Never Let a Good Crisis Go to Waste: The COVID-19 Pandemic and the Opportunity for Food Sovereignty*. Amsterdam and Bangkok: The Transnational Institute and Focus on the Global South. https://focusweb.org/wp-content/uploads/2020/05/Covid19-Pandemic-Bello.pdf (accessed 15 April 2022).

Bordey, Flordelizah H., Piedada F. Moya, Jesusa C. Beltran, and David C. Dawe. 2016. *Competitiveness of Philippine Rice in Asia*. Science City of Muñoz and Manila: Philippine Rice Research Institute and International Rice Research Institute.

BPS (Badan Pusat Statistik; Central Bureau of Statistics). 2006. *Pengeluaran untuk Konsumsi Penduduk Indonesia* [Consumption Expenditures of the Indonesian Population]. 2006 and 2021. Jakarta: BPS.

Cullather, Nick. 2013. *The Hungry World: America's Cold War Battle against Poverty in Asia*. Cambridge, MA: Harvard University Press.

Davidson, Jamie S. 2016. "Why the Philippines Chooses to Import Rice". *Critical Asian Studies* 48, no. 1: 100–22.

———. 2018a. "Stagnating Yields, Unyielding Profits: The Political Economy of Malaysia's Rice Sector". *Journal of Southeast Asian Studies* 49, no. 1: 105–28.

———. 2018b. *Indonesia: Twenty Years of Democracy*. Cambridge: Cambridge University Press.

———. 2018c. "Then and Now: Campaigns to Achieve Rice Self-Sufficiency in Indonesia". *Bijdragen Tot de Taal-, Land- En Volkenkunde* 174, no. 2–3: 188–215.

Dawe, David, and Tom Slayton. 2010. "The World Rice Market Crisis of 2007–2008". In *The Rice Crisis: Markets, Policies and Food Security*, edited by David Dawe, pp. 15–28. London: Routledge.

———, Piedada F. Moya, and Cheryll B. Casiwan, eds. 2006. *Why Does the Philippines Import Rice? Meeting the Challenge of Market Liberalization*. Los Baños: International Rice Research Institute.

Dean, Michael. 2020. "Why AgFunder invested in Singrow". *AFN*, 2 June 2020. https://agfundernews.com/why-agfunder-invested-in-singrow (accessed 15 April 2022).

Department of Statistics Malaysia. 2019. *Household Expenditure Survey Report*. Putrajaya, Malaysia: Department of Statistics Malaysia.

Economic Planning Unit. 2020. *Household Income, Poverty and Household Expenditure Report*. Putrajaya, Malaysia: Prime Minister's Department.

Fan, Shenggen, Paul Teng, Ping Chew, Geoffry Smith, and Les Copeland. 2021. "Food System Resilience and COVID-19: Lessons from the Asian Experience". *Global Food Security* 28: 1–7.

Faulder, Dominik. 2022. "Asia Food Crisis: Ukraine War Triggers Chain Reaction of Shortages". *Nikkei Asia*, 18 May 2022. https://asia.nikkei.com/Spotlight/The-Big-Story/Asia-s-food-crisis-Ukraine-war-triggers-chain-reaction-of-shortages (accessed 20 May 2022).

Food and Agriculture Organization (FAO). 2020. *Why Export Restrictions Should Not Be a Response to COVID-19: Learning Lessons from Experience with Rice in Asia and the Pacific*. Bangkok: FAO. https://www.fao.org/policy-support/tools-and-publications/resources-details/en/c/1287457/ (accessed 15 April 2022).

Global Rice Science Partnership (GRSP). 2013. *Rice Almanac: Source Book for One of the Most Important Economic Activities on Earth*. Los Baños: International Rice Research Institute.

Goh, Yan Han. 2022. "Goal to Grow Local Agriculture Sector May Not Succeed, Says IPS Conference Panellist". *Straits Times*, 17 January 2022.

Gollin, Douglas, Casper Worm Hansen, and Asger Mose Wingender. 2021. "Two

Blades of Grass: The Impact of the Green Revolution". *Journal of Political Economy* 129, no. 8: 2344–84.

Graham, Collum. 2020. "Agro-Nationalism in Indonesia". *New Mandala*, 4 June 2020. https://www.newmandala.org/indonesias-agro-nationalism-in-the-pandemic/ (accessed 15 April 2022).

Griffin, Keith. 1974. *The Political Economy Agrarian Change*. Cambridge, MA: Harvard University Press.

Handayani, Oliviana. 2017. "Indonesian Rice Prices Double Global Average". *Indonesia Expat*, 3 July 2017. https://indonesiaexpat.id/news/indonesia-high-rice-price/ (accessed 15 April 2022).

Helleiner, Eric. 2021. *The Neomercantilists: A Global Intellectual History*. Ithaca: Cornell University Press.

Huff, Greg. 2020. "The Great Second World War Vietnam and Java Famines". *Modern Asian Studies* 54, no. 2: 618–53.

Imahashi, Rurika, and Apornrath Phoonphongphiphat. 2022. "Thailand Export Earnings Threatened by Rice Glut". *Asia Nikkei Review*, 25 July 2022. https://asia.nikkei.com/Spotlight/Market-Spotlight/Thailand-export-earnings-threatened-by-rice-glut (accessed 26 July 2022).

Ingram, James C. 1971. *Economic Change in Thailand, 1850–1970*. Stanford: Stanford University Press.

Kang, Yunhee, Anurima Baidya, Alec Aron, et al. 2021. "Differences in the Early Impact of COVID-19 on Food Security and Livelihoods in Rural and Urban Areas in the Asia Pacific Region". *Global Food Security* 31: 1–9.

Koh, Fabian. 2018. "Singapore Tops Global Index on Food Security, but Climate Change May Affect Food Supply". *Straits Times*, 17 October 2018. https://www.straitstimes.com/singapore/singapore-tops-global-index-on-food-security-but-climate-change-may-affect-food-supply (accessed 15 April 2022).

Laiprakobsup, Thanapan. 2017. "Inequality in Rice Farmers' Access to a Government Assistance Program in Rural Thailand". *Asian Politics and Policy* 9, no. 3: 442–61.

Ludher, Elyssa, and Thinesh Kumar Paramasilvam. 2018. *Food and the City: Overcoming Challenges for Food Security*. Singapore: Centre for Liveable Cities. https://www.clc.gov.sg/research-publications/publications/urban-systems-studies/view/food-and-the-city (accessed 15 April 2022).

McCargo, Duncan. 2019. "Southeast Asia's Troubling Elections: Democratic Demolition in Thailand". *Journal of Democracy* 30, no. 4: 119–33.

Montemayor, Raul. 2020. "Rice Traders Liberated, At Last!". *Philippine Daily Inquirer*, 25 August 2020. https://opinion.inquirer.net/132991/rice-traders-liberated-at-last (accessed 15 April 2022).

Mujahid, Irfan, and Lukas Kornher. 2016. "ASEAN Food Reserve and Trade: Review and Prospect". In *Food Price Volatility and Its Implications for Food Security and*

Policy, edited by Matthias Kalkuhl, Joachim von Braun, and Maximo Torero, pp. 413–33. Cham: Springer International.

Nagpaul, Tania, Dalvin Sidhu, and Jinwen Chen. 2020. *The Hunger Report: An In-depth Look at Food Insecurity in Singapore*. Singapore: Lien Centre for Social Innovation. https://ink.library.smu.edu.sg/lien_reports/15/ (accessed 15 April 2022).

Ocampo, Karl R. 2020. "Gov't Hits Disinformation on Farmgate Prices of Rice". *Philippine Daily Inquirer*, 5 October 2020. https://business.inquirer.net/308847/govt-hits-disinformation-on-farmgate-prices-of-rice (accessed 15 April 2022).

Omar, Sarena Che, Ashraf Shaharudin, and Siti Aiysyah Tumin. 2019. *The Status of the Paddy and Rice Industry in Malaysia*. Kuala Lumpur: Khazanah Research Institute. http://www.krinstitute.org/assets/contentMS/img/template/editor/20190409_RiceReport_Full%20Report_Final.pdf (accessed 15 April 2022).

Otsuka, Keijiro. 2021. "Strategies for Transforming Indonesian Agriculture". *Bulletin of Indonesian Economic Studies* 57, no. 3: 321–41.

Patashnik, Eric. 2008. *Reforms at Risk: What Happens After Major Policy Reforms Are Enacted*. Princeton: Princeton University Press.

Philippine Statistics Agency (PSA). 2009, 2018. *Family Income and Expenditure Survey: National and Regional Estimates*. Manila: PSA.

Puma, Michael J., and Megan Konar. 2022. "What the War in Ukraine Means for the World's Food Supply". *New York Times*, 1 March 2022. https://www.nytimes.com/2022/03/01/opinion/what-the-war-in-ukraine-means-for-the-worlds-food-supply.html (accessed 15 April 2022).

Rashid, Shahidur, Ashok Gulati, and Ralph Cummings, Jr., eds. 2008. *From Parastatals to Private Trade: Lessons in Agriculture*. Washington DC: International Food Policy Institute.

Ricks, Jacob. 2018. "Politics and the Price of Rice in Thailand: Public Choice, Institutional Change and Rural Subsidies". *Journal of Contemporary Asia* 48, no. 3: 395–418.

Rigg, Jonathan, Albert Salamanca, and Eric C. Thompson. 2016. "The Puzzle of East and Southeast Asia's Persistent Smallholder". *Journal of Rural Studies* 43: 118–33.

Roberts, Anthea, and Nicolas Lamp. 2021. *Six Faces of Globalization: Who Wins, Who Loses, and Why It Matters*. Cambridge, MA: Harvard University Press.

Sawit, M. Husein, and Erna Maria Lokollo. 2007. *Rice Import Surge in Indonesia*. Bogor: The Indonesian Center for Agriculture Socio-Economic and Policy Studies, in collaboration with ActionAid International.

Setijadi, Charlotte. 2021. "The Pandemic as Political Opportunity: Jokowi's Indonesia in the Time of COVID-19". *Bulletin of Indonesian Economic Studies* 57, no. 3: 297–320.

Siamwalla, Ammar. 1975. "A History of Rice Policies in Thailand". *Food Research Institute Studies* 14, no. 3: 233–49.
Straits Times. 2022a. "What Russia and Ukraine Export to The World". 4 March 2022, p. B10.
———. 2022b. "Thailand, Vietnam to Cooperate on Hiking Rice Prices Globally". 30 August 2022, p. A9.
Terada, Takashi. 2009. "Competitive Regionalism in Southeast Asia and Beyond: Role of Singapore and ASEAN". In *Competitive Regionalism: FTA Diffusion in the Pacific Rim*, edited by Mireya Solís, Barbara Stallings, and Saori N. Katada, pp. 161–80. London: Palgrave MacMillan.
Thailand Development Research Institute (TDRI). 2014. *The Demand of Rice Consumption in Thailand* (in Thai). Bangkok: TDRI.
Timmer, C. Peter. 1989. "Food Price Policy: The Rationale for Government Intervention". *Food Policy* 14, no. 1: 17–27.
———. 2010. "Reflections on Food Crises Past". *Food Policy* 35, no. 1: 1–11.
Walker, Andrew. 2012. *Thailand's Political Peasants: Power in the Modern Rural Economy*. Madison: Wisconsin University Press.
Watcharasakwet, Wilawan, and Nopparat Chaichalearmmongkol. 2016. "Ousted Thai Leader Likens Failed Rice-Subsidy Program to Junta's Current Policy". *Wall Street Journal*, 4 November 2016. https://www.wsj.com/articles/ousted-thai-leader-yingluck-shinawatra-likens-her-failed-rice-subsidy-program-to-governments-policy-1478245363 (accessed 15 April 2022).
Wong, Lin Ken. 1978. "Singapore: Its Growth as an Entrepot Port, 1819–1941". *Journal of Southeast Asian Studies* 9, no. 1: 50–84.
Wu, Friedrich. 1991. "The ASEAN Economies in the 1990s and Singapore's Regional Role". *California Management Review* 34, no. 1: 103–14.

2

The Role of Path Dependence in Malaysia's Paddy and Rice Policy under the Pandemic

Fatimah Mohamed Arshad

INTRODUCTION

Rice holds a special place in the socio-economic and political lives of Malaysians. It is a staple for almost the whole population and the first item in their food pyramid. Hence, rice is considered the major item in the "basket of food" for the country's food security. The paddy community is an important pool for political votes but more than 90 per cent of paddy farmers are in the bottom 40 per cent income bracket (Davidson 2018; MoA 2019b).

The sector only accounted for about 0.7 per cent of the Gross Domestic Product (GDP) in 1980, and was slashed in half by 2017 (Serin 2017). Its share of the agricultural GDP declined even faster, from 4.7 per cent in 1980 to 0.16 per cent in 2010. Paddy area accounted for about 20.5 per cent of agricultural land in 1970 but just 9.9 per cent in 2017 (MPIC 2018). The number of paddy farmers has declined from 208,000 in 1985 (MoA 2011) to 192,663 in 2019.[1] Paddy farms are mainly smallholders with an average size recorded at 1.2 hectares (ha) in 1970 and 2.0 ha in 2016 (Selvadurai 1978; MoA 2016a). After the Green Revolution[2] and purposive development support, absolute poverty among paddy farmers declined sharply from 88.1 per cent in 1970 to 48.3 per cent in 1990 and by 2015 the figure was significantly low.[3] However, the incidence of relative poverty among paddy farmers is still the highest in the agricultural sectors.

While abject poverty has been greatly reduced, the sector shows slow growth in terms of its ability to meet local consumption and limited value-added development (Mohamed Arshad et al. 2019a, 2019b). The self-sufficiency levels (SSL) which are proxies for food availability have remained in the range of 65 per cent to 75 per cent in the last four decades. The SSL dropped from 70 per cent in 2016 to 63 per cent in 2019 despite a quadruple increase in subsidy allocation and government expenditure on the sector accounting for about half of the budget of the Ministry of Agriculture and Agro-based Industry (MoA) for the period of 2015–17 (Ismail 2017).[4] A large portion of the budget went to input and output subsidies and irrigation maintenance. The local rice deficit is met by imports, a function of which has been monopolized by a state trading enterprise (STE) for more than fifty years.

The rice price crisis in the early 1970s set the trajectory of the policy on Malaysia's paddy and rice industry which has remained, to date, more or less intact. Before the 1970s, the sector was relatively competitive but highly vulnerable to price volatility in the international market. This was largely due to supply uncertainty and low exportable surplus at 3–4 per cent among rice exporters in the face of growing consumption. The crisis undercut the purchasing ability of poor consumers while market traders took advantage of the price swings through hoarding and speculative activities. These phenomena were perceived as detrimental to the industry's growth.

The crisis caused serious social disruption which posed a threat to the country's political stability, especially as it came so soon after the devastating May 1969 ethnic riots. Since rice was perceived as a political crop (the majority of paddy farmers were Malays who were crucial voters for the ruling party, the United Malays National Organization or UMNO), the government then decided to "protect" the sector. This was an important milestone for the paddy and rice industry as the country embarked on a comprehensive protectionist plan. The instruments implemented included price control (farm and retail), price zoning, the establishment of an STE, controlled movement, licensing of trading activities and provision of infrastructural, input and output subsidies. In 1971, the STE called the National Paddy and Rice Authority (NPRA) was set up to take charge of sector development and import activities.[5]

The sector continues to be challenged by a new order of the world economy (accelerated financial globalization in the 1990s), financial crises (1997 and 2009), rice price crisis (2008) and natural calamities (including a tsunami in 2004) and the latest—a coronavirus pandemic (since January 2020[6]) and repeated flash floods, most recently in December 2021 to January 2022. As in the 1971 crisis, the policy response to these challenges was fundamentally unchanged. The protectionist regime was upheld, but some instrument modifications were made. For instance, amidst the globalization trend in the 1990s, Malaysia embarked on privatizing the STE, from NPRA (a government body) to a new private entity called Padiberas Nasional Berhad (BERNAS). While BERNAS, like its predecessor, was empowered to be the sole importer of foreign rice, it was also responsible for administering several social responsibilities.

The political landscape of the country experienced radical change with the landslide victory of the opposition coalition (called Coalition of Hope, or Pakatan Harapan [PH]) in the 2018 elections. This short-lived government was taken over in 2020 by a new coalition called Pakatan Nasional (PN) even before new national elections were held. The PH campaign promise to open up the import market for a more competitive environment (PH 2017) was reversed under the PN government, and BERNAS's import monopoly concession was extended to 2030 with additional social responsibilities attached to the contract.

The 2008 rice price crisis was relatively severe for the country as it involved agricultural commodities worldwide, including wheat and soya bean, that may be directly or indirectly related to rice (Childs and Kiawu 2009). The crisis again prompted a government response, whereby more input and output subsidies and higher output subsidies were introduced in an attempt to induce a further increase in domestic production (Mohamed Arshad et al. 2019b). But their effectiveness in reaching targets has not materialized.[7]

Clearly, crises and the changing political landscape are important drivers in the policy matrix of the paddy and rice sector in Malaysia. The recent coronavirus pandemic crisis is unprecedented and incomparable to the previous crises in scale, impact and severity. Price crises are largely driven by the imbalance of supply and demand and the market tends to stabilize as the gap narrows. A pandemic by its name implies a health crisis that is global in scope. Like in other countries Malaysia implemented a number of mitigating measures to minimize the impact of COVID-19 which include lockdowns, area movement controls, Standard Operating Procedure (SOP)[8] requirements and a vaccination programme. The SOPs included physical distancing (of at least 1 metre), which was instituted to avoid infectivity, and the use of information communication technology mobile phone apps called MySejahtera to indicate the COVID-19 status of an individual. The latter was used widely as a certificate of health to be allowed entrance into any premises. As elsewhere, the impact of the pandemic on Malaysia has been monumental, multisectoral and devastating, involving economic slowdown, an increase in unemployment and poverty and increased food insecurity, among others (DOSM 2020, 2021b).

Given the unprecedented shock that shook the country and the world, this chapter examines Malaysia's policy response with regard to its paddy and rice sector during the COVID-19 pandemic. The literature on the industry shows that policy interventions over time have not digressed very much from the protectionism principle which suggests a strong path dependence behaviour (MARDITECH 2003; World Bank 1988; Davidson 2018; Mohamed Arshad et al. 2019a).

Broadly, path dependence refers to the causal relevance of preceding stages in a temporal sequence (Pierson 2000). This implies that preceding steps in a particular direction induce further movement in the same direction. Once a path is chosen, it is difficult to change because the processes become institutionalized and are reinforced over time with increasing returns. The underlying premise is that the relative benefits of the current activity compared with other possible options increase over time. The costs of exit or switching paths are high. Institutions are structural variables from which ideas, interests and powers are derived. They are the anchor of the activity of public policies in that institutions contribute to structuring them by either encouraging or constraining the organization and their actors and hence activities (Trouvé et al. 2010). Replicating the past reproduces almost similar impact.

To illustrate the path dependence hypothesis, I focus on the policy premises and actions in mitigating the rice price crisis in 2008 as a case study and later the COVID-19 pandemic to substantiate it. The chapter's structure is as follows. The following section briefly describes the status of the policy intervention in the sector. Malaysia's policy response to the 2008 rice price crisis and its impact on the paddy and rice economy are discussed in the subsequent paragraphs. This is followed by a discussion on the policy response to the pandemic and future policy implications. The last section concludes the paper.

CURRENT STATUS OF POLICY INTERVENTIONS IN MALAYSIA'S PADDY AND RICE SECTOR[9]

Malaysia's current market interventions in the paddy rice sector are rooted in its history. From the late nineteenth century to independence in 1957 the British government "left rice farmers to their own devices" (Hill 2012, p. xii). Only then did the industry receive government support, in the form of the Green Revolution project of the mid-1960s. The historical footprint of government intervention in the paddy and rice sector is depicted in Figure 2.1. The direct intervention started in 1971 when the world price of rice surged to its highest level compared to the 1960s. The crisis reinforced the interventionist moves in lieu of the structural weaknesses of the sector documented in Malaysia's First Five-Year Plan (1966):[10]

> the paddy marketing system was beset with a host of market imperfections which arise inter alia, from limited bargaining power, lack of market information, lack of grades and standards, middlemen monopsony, cartels and price fixing. The outcome of such a(n) imperfect structure was that farmers were open to exploitation and generally obtain a return which is incommensurate with their productive efforts ...

The above market behaviour was reaffirmed by several "market manipulations", particularly by the wholesalers and retailers at the peak of the crisis. Reported malpractices included hoarding and profiteering activities at the expense of consumers, especially the poor. To insulate the industry from market vagaries, the government envisaged that an STE was necessary to regulate the market through an import monopoly, price and physical movement control, and direct involvement in rice milling and trading. This industry framework was the backdrop of future policy interventions.

Similarly, it was during this era the government conceptualized the country's rice policy which is sustained till today. The rice policy objectives were as follows:

Path Dependence in Malaysia's Paddy and Rice Policy 39

FIGURE 2.1
Historical Timeline of the Paddy and Rice Industry in Malaysia, January 1961–December 2021

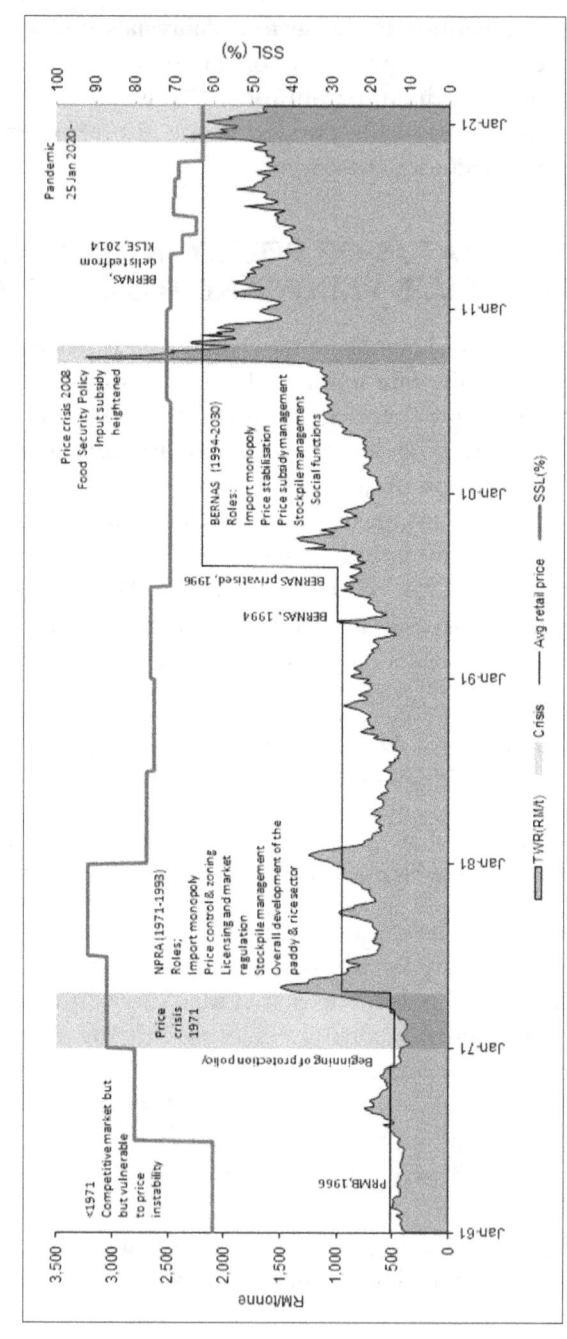

Source: TWR (Thai White Rice) 5 per cent from IMF 2021, retail rice price and SSL from Ministry of Agriculture and Agro-based Industries (various sources).

(i) to maintain a high price for paddy and hence income to the farmers;
(ii) to achieve a certain level of self-sufficiency; and
(iii) to ensure a stable and high-quality supply of rice to consumers.

The policy favoured protecting producers by offering a high and stable price which implied that consumers had to face higher prices. However, the value of the producer's surplus and consumer's transfer or indirect tax depends on the border price. As shown in Figure 2.1, except for crisis periods, the average retail price has been higher than the border price, implying the existence of indirect taxes on consumers (Mohamed Arshad et al. 2019a).

Objective (iii) was meant to ensure some level of rice "availability", a major pillar of food security. Over the years, the SSL has been used as a proxy for measuring the food security status of the country, particularly in relation to rice. As shown in Figure 2.1, the SSL levels were relatively high during the Green Revolution years but trended down afterwards; by 2019, they reached 63 per cent.

The above policy objectives necessitated protectionist measures in all dimensions to control production and price. Towards these ends, the government has implemented multiple interventions from the input subsector up to the consumer subsector. These measures are summarized in Figure 2.2 and described briefly below.

Input Subsector

Malaysia imports almost all inputs, particularly fertilizer, pesticides and weedicides and machines. To ensure that the farmers receive adequate input, the government has authorised sole distributorship to the National Farmers' Association (NAFAS)[11] which is the apex body of the Area Farmers' Associations (AFAs). NAFAS appoints AFAs as its farm-level distributors to producers. Its members include 14 State Farmers' Associations and 279 AFAs (Hill 2012) with a membership of over 921,000 in 2019 (NAFAS 2019). This system has been maintained for the last five decades. The monopoly and centralization of inputs such as fertilizer have constrained the development of the local input market. There is little investment in local input production and minimal new entrants into the industry as there are few opportunities for business and value addition (Mohamed Arshad et al. 2019a). The prolonged dependency means the country imports an

FIGURE 2.2
Market Interventions in Malaysia's Paddy and Rice Industry

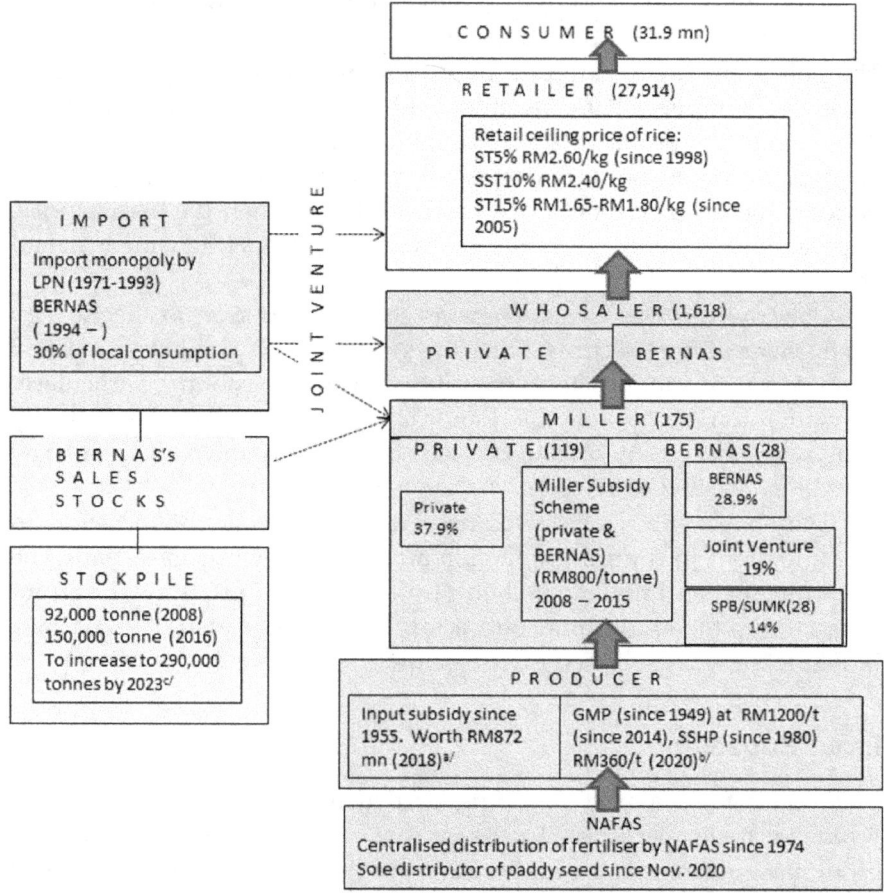

Source: a/, b/ and c/ are from MAFI (2021). Unless stated, all data refer to 2016. Adapted from Mohamed Arshad et al. (2019a).

inflationary effect from the international market especially during the pandemic while the development of the local input sector is impeded.

Farm Subsector

To insulate producers from the instability in the international market, the colonial British government instituted the Guaranteed Minimum Price

(GMP) of paddy in 1949 which was the floor price for paddy. To increase farmers' income, an output subsidy was introduced in 1980, in the form of cash transfers based on the paddy output sold by farmers, called the Paddy Price Subsidy Scheme (SSHP; Skim Subsidi Harga Padi). Its rationale was to increase the farmers' net receipt without further distorting the market. The history of the GMP and SSHP in Table 2.1 reveals a number of observations. First, the GMP has been in existence for almost eighty years. Second, the increase in the GMP revision was about 30 per cent between 1973 and 1997 compared to 118 per cent between 1997 and 2014. Third, before 1998, the paddy sold was graded into long, medium and short categories; later it was reduced to two (long and medium) and since 1998 there has been no grading. This shows that no premium is provided for long grains. Instead, a deduction system is used to grade the quality (Rusli, Mohamed Arshad, and Ibragimov 2017). Fourth, the longest market intervention was the SSHP (twenty-six years). Fifth, the GMP and SSHP increased by 141 per cent and 118 per cent respectively from 1980 to 2020. As for the SSHP, its share of the total subsidy allocation from 1979 to 2007 was 81.5 per cent and later reduced to 18.3 per cent, indicating a strong focus on input subsidy thereafter. These data indicate the deep-rooted pricing interventions in the farm sector since 1949.

The SSHP benefits the larger output producers—60 per cent of farmers received only 12 per cent of the total value of subsidies distributed while

TABLE 2.1
Paddy Guaranteed Minimum Price and SSHP, Selected Years (RM per MT)

Period	Paddy GMP (RM/mt)			Period	SSHP (RM/mt)
	Long	Medium	Short		
1949–19 July 1973	265	—	—	January–July 1980	33
20 July 1973	381	348	315	July 1980	165
29 January 1974	431	397	364	1990	248
2 August 1974	464	431	397	2016	300
1 January 1980	497	464	431	2019	360
1 June 1990	497	464			
1998–2005	550	—	—		
2006–8	650	—	—		
2009	750	—	—		
2014	1,200	—	—		

Source: Mohamed Arshad et al. (1991) for data before 1990 and MoA for data beyond 1990.

the top 2 per cent of farmers accounted for about 13 per cent of the total value (World Bank 1988; Mohamed Arshad et al. 1983, 2019b). In 1986 four-fifths of the farmers received more than half the total subsidies distributed while one-fifth received about half (Mohamed Arshad et al. 1991). BERNAS estimated that only 12.5 per cent of some 148,330 farmers who received the subsidies owned more than 4 ha of paddy area (about 60 per cent owned less than 2 ha).[12] The most recent data from the area under the auspices of Muda Agricultural Development Authority (MADA) show that only 7.3 per cent of the farms are more than 4.5 ha and 46.2 per cent are below 1.5 ha (MADA 2019).

Milling Subsector

The milling subsector transformed from a competitive industry in the 1960s to a highly concentrated one in the 1970s when NPRA and later BERNAS were introduced. The number of mills fell appreciably from 1,800 in 1968 to 295 in 1987—and kept falling. By 2015, their number had been reduced to 157 (private) and 30 (BERNAS) for about a reduction of 90 per cent between 1968 and 2015. Prior to NPRA's formation, about 60 per cent of the mills were cooperatives owned and run by farmers, indicating their involvement in value-added activities (Vokes 1978). As the industry became concentrated, farmers' bargaining power weakened and high entry barriers to participating in value addition were erected. After the STE's involvement in milling activities, paddy farmers became stuck as primary producers with limited room for vertical mobility.

Most private mills are not subsidized but their margins are more or less dictated by the difference between retail and farm prices which the government fixes. However, the price increases during the 2008 rice crisis affected BERNAS's profit and millers' margins as local prices increased in tandem with world market prices. To protect low-income consumers from the price hikes, the government provided subsidies which amounted to RM750 per metric ton (MT) to both private and BERNAS mills to produce low-quality 15 per cent broken rice (locally known as Super Tempatan or ST rice). The retail price was also set at RM1.65 to RM1.80 per kilogram according to geographical zone (NADM 2011). Despite the subsidy and price control, the ST15 per cent broken rice disappeared from the market because traders mixed it with higher-quality rice to take advantage of the price difference (NADM 2015). Due to the policy's poor performance and resulting abuses, the subsidy was withdrawn in 2015 (*Malay Mail*, 1 November 2015).

Retail Subsector

The rice price ceiling strategy was instituted to insulate consumers from world price instability. Before 1992 retail prices of selected rice were floated but by 1998, they were fixed thereon. As shown in Table 2.2, the price of ST15 per cent was between RM1.65 and RM1.80 while the price of Super Special Tempatan (SST) 5 per cent and SST10 per cent were RM2.60/kg and RM2.40/kg since 2008.[13]

Figure 2.3 indicates the deviations of local paddy and rice prices from the border price. It shows that the local price was higher than the border price which meant that consumers were indirectly taxed as they were paying more than they should under an open market. Yet the producer's price was set higher than the border price which implied that they received higher transfers, particularly during low price periods and vice versa (Mohamed Arshad et al. 2019a). Note that low-income consumers were paying relatively higher indirect tax than the rich because their share of expenditure on rice was relatively higher than the high-income group (Sahathavan, n.d.; Ali 2017).

Import Subsector

The NPRA, set up in 1971, was an STE in the rice distribution system. It lasted twenty-three years despite its heavy use of public money, inefficient and costly operations (milling and distributions) and minimal productivity improvement (Wong 1981; Tan 1987; Mohamed Arshad et al. 1983; World Bank 1988; Tamin and Meyanathan 1990; MIER 2010).[14] The wave of privatization starting in the 1980s as promoted by then Prime Minister Mahathir Mohamad led to the corporatization of NPRA into a new entity called BERNAS in 1994. It was created as a public limited company limited by shares registered under the Companies Act 1965 to carry out the relevant function for the government besides its own commercial activities. BERNAS was listed on the Kuala Lumpur Share Exchange in 1994 (Davidson 2018).

The three major duties of BERNAS are to ensure fair and stable prices, a sufficient supply of rice, and quality and standards. BERNAS's social

TABLE 2.2
Recommended Retail Price of Rice and Imported Rice Price, Selected Years (RM per kg)

Grade	Government Gazette 24 December 1992	Government Gazette 4 November 1998	Government Gazette 25 June 2001	2019, Reported by MAFI[a]	Imported Rice, 2019 Type	Imported Rice, 2019 2019
ST15	Floated	1.65–1.80/kg	1.65–1.80/kg	Terminated 2016	Basmathi rice	5.60–7.80
SST5 per cent	n.a.	n.a.	Floated	2.60/kg	Fragrant rice	3.80–5.00
SST 10 per cent	n.a.	n.a.	Floated	2.40/kg	Glutinous rice	4.40–5.00
Standard	0.98–1.04/kg	n.a.	n.a.	n.a.	White rice	3.00
Premium	1.04–1.11/kg	n.a.	n.a.	n.a.		

Note: The ceiling price for SST5% was set at RM2.60/kg, and SST10% at RM2.14/kg since 2008.
Source: MIER (2010), 2019 data from MAFI (2020).

FIGURE 2.3
Deviation of Farm and Retail Prices from the Border Prices, 1995–2016 (%)

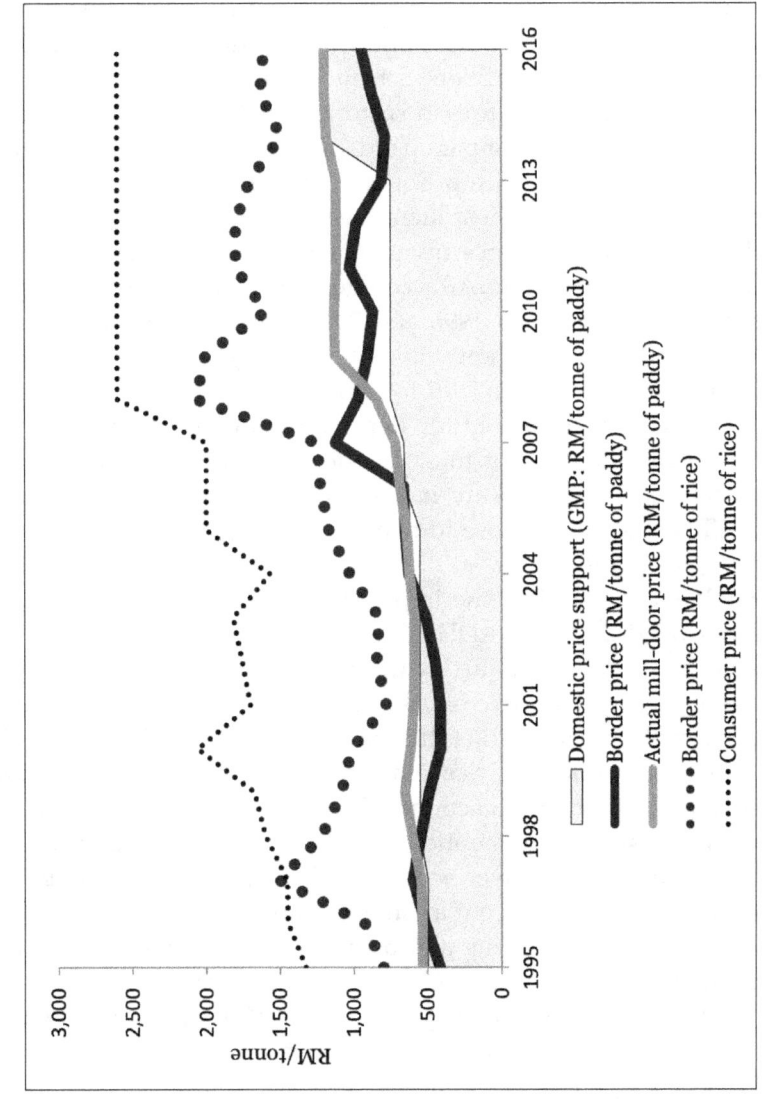

Note: Retail price of rice was floated before 2005.
Source: Mohamed Arshad et al. (2019a).

obligations include: (i) to conserve, maintain and manage the National Paddy/Rice Stockpile; (ii) to undertake the purchase of paddy from farmers at the GMP; (iii) to act as the Buyer of Last Resort for paddy farmers; (iv) to undertake the management of the disbursement of subsidies to paddy farmers under the SSHP; and (v) to undertake the management of the Bumiputera Rice Millers Schemes. Unlike the NPRA, BERNAS is not expected to play a role in sectoral development. The company's commercial activities encompass paddy seed production, paddy farming, paddy procurement and rice processing, distribution and trading of rice and its by-products and, most lucratively, rice importation.

The extent of BERNAS's involvement in supply chain activities is depicted in Figure 2.4. BERNAS accounted for 26 to 29 per cent of domestic rice procurement between 1996 and 2017. Private mills' share reduced from half to about 38 per cent while BERNAS's joint ventures with other mills rose from 4 per cent in 2002 to 14 per cent in 2017. By 2015, BERNAS (and its associates) accounted for 48 per cent of total paddy processed or approximately one-third of total rice demand nationally. Incorporating the 30 per cent market share it already possesses from imported rice sales, BERNAS controls close to two-thirds of the local market. By most measures, it is a monopoly.

Scholars have studied the impact of an STE on the paddy and rice industry (MIER 2010; MARDITECH 2003; World Bank 1984; Mohamed Arshad et al. 2019a). Combined with other protectionist strategies such as price controls, the distortive effect is very telling for Malaysia. Table 2.3 summarizes BERNAS's market share and the Herfindahl-Hirschman Index for milling, stockpile and rice wholesaling and distribution. Table 2.4 summarizes the market protection and comparative advantage indices for the sector. The subsectors mentioned earlier are highly concentrated with BERNAS as the major player across the chains. Its share is about half in the milling sector, 100 per cent in imports and stockpiling and about two-thirds in the rice wholesaling and distribution. As for market protection and comparative advantage indices, it is also clear that producers are highly subsidized as indicated by the Producer Subsidy Equivalent (PSE). The sector is also highly protected as reflected in the Effective Protection Coefficient (EPC) and other indicators.

FIGURE 2.4
Share of Paddy Buying by Institutions, 1996–2017 (MT)

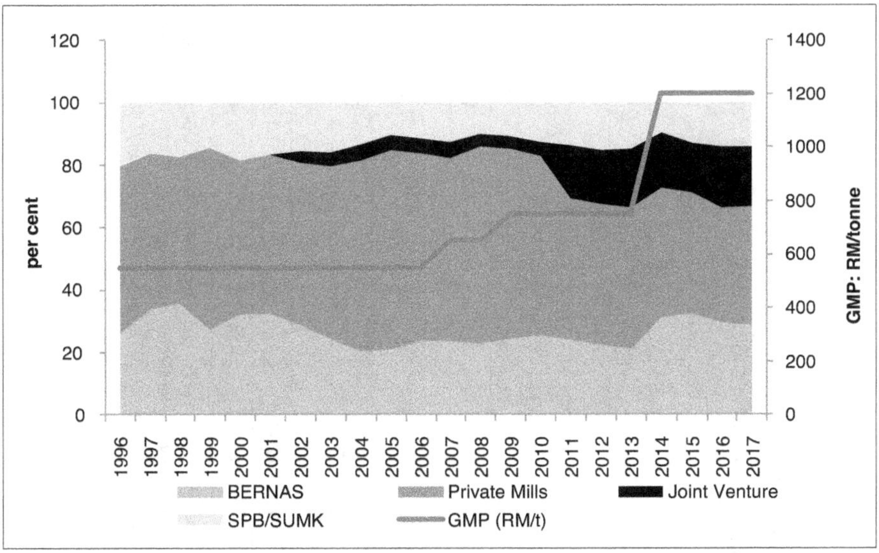

Source: Mohamad Arshad et al. (2019a). Data from BERNAS (2018).

TABLE 2.3
Concentration Ratios and HHI for Malaysia's Rice Market, 2018

Sector	BERNAS's Share of the Market	HHI
Milling	48%	2,304
Rice stockpile	100%	10,000
Rice importation	100%	10,000
Rice wholesaling and distribution	63.6%	4,945

Note: The United States Department of Justice defines a market with an HHI in excess of 2,500 points as highly concentrated.

POLICY RESPONSE TO THE 2008 CRISIS AND ITS IMPACT: A CASE STUDY

Figure 2.5 depicts the price spike of rice in the international market that defined the 2008 crisis between March and October 2008. Between January 2002 and December 2005, the price hovered between US$185 and US$231.

TABLE 2.4
Market Protection and Comparative Advantage Indices for Paddy and Rice Sector, Selected Years

Indicator/ Area	1980	1986	2007		2012			2015
	Malaysia		Granary	Non-granary	KADA	MADA	KETARA	BLS	Malaysia
EPC	1.1	4.6	2.0	2.0	–	–	–	–	4
NPCO	–	–	1.9	1.9	–	–	–	–	1.3
NPCI	–	–	1.1	1.1	–	–	–	–	0.3
DRC	0.4	3.4	0.9	0.6	0.9	0.8	1.1	0.8	3.6
SCB	–	–	0.9	0.6	0.9	0.9	1.1	0.9	–
PSE%	–	–	57.8	26.4	–	–	–	–	–
SRP	–	–	0.9	0.4	0.5	0.5	0.6	0.6	0.9
NCP	1	2.4	–	–	–	–	–	–	–
PNRL(RM)	–	–	–	–	2,842	3,380	2,101	4,239	–
SNRL(RM)	–	–	–	–	349	661	–307	891	–

Note: EPC: Effective Protection Coefficient; NPCO and NPCI: Net Protective Coefficient for Output and Input, respectively; DRC: Domestic Resource Cost; PSE% Producers Subsidy Equivalent (%); NPC: Nominal Protection Coefficient; PNRL: Private Net Return to Land; PNRL: Social Net Return to Land.
Source: 1986 figures are from World Bank (1988). 2007 figures are from Amin et al. (2010). Data for 2012 are from Ali (2017) and data for 2015 are from Abdul Fatah (2017).

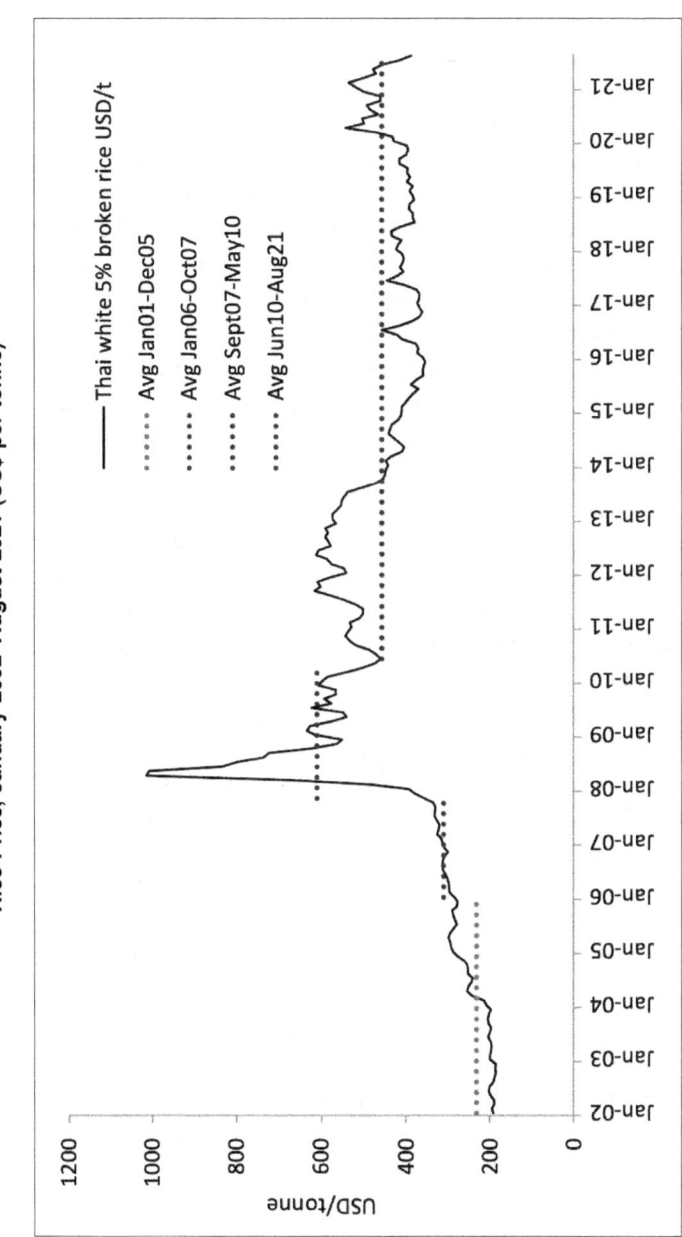

FIGURE 2.5
Rice Price, January 2002–August 2021 (US$ per tonne)

Source: IMF (2021).

The price soared to US$1,009 in May 2008, and later traded between US$354 and US$616 in the post-crisis phase. The price never reverted to its pre-crisis level.

The 2008 crisis was a case of a disruption in the cereal market complex comprising rice, wheat and corn as well as other technical variables that are interconnected in some way or another in a causal loop. The variables that orchestrated the crisis were: prices of cereals, demand for biodiesel, commodity futures, equity investment, exchange rate, herd behaviour and most importantly, policy response. A shock to the system resulted in some disequilibrium that caused it to react to restore stability.

The policy response of such exporters as Bangladesh and Vietnam was responsible for driving up the rice price beyond a normal band. Their response in part was motivated by the need to ensure adequate supply domestically, particularly for poor consumers. Exporters implemented protective policy measures, including export bans, taxes and quotas. Panic buying by importing countries accentuated the price spiral (Figure 2.6).

Malaysia was not spared the devastating effect of the crisis. In April 2008 for example, Malaysia through BERNAS attempted to secure 500,000 tonnes of rice from Thailand through a government-to-government arrangement. After difficult negotiations, BERNAS secured half this amount before the world price started to decline in May and the Vietnamese government lifted its export ban. The additional supplies were sourced from other countries as the price eased.

At the height of the crisis, Malaysia formulated its first-ever Food Security Policy (MoA 2008). Previously there was no specific document produced for this purpose except for the paddy and rice policy.

The objectives of the Food Security Policy (2008) were as follows:

(i) to increase productivity and hence the production of food to achieve self-sufficiency;
(ii) to ensure an adequate return to agricultural producers to sustain food production;
(iii) to ensure agricultural enterprises receive an adequate return to incentivize them to continue with food production;
(iv) to ensure adequate, high quality and safe food to consumers.

52 Fatimah Mohamed Arshad

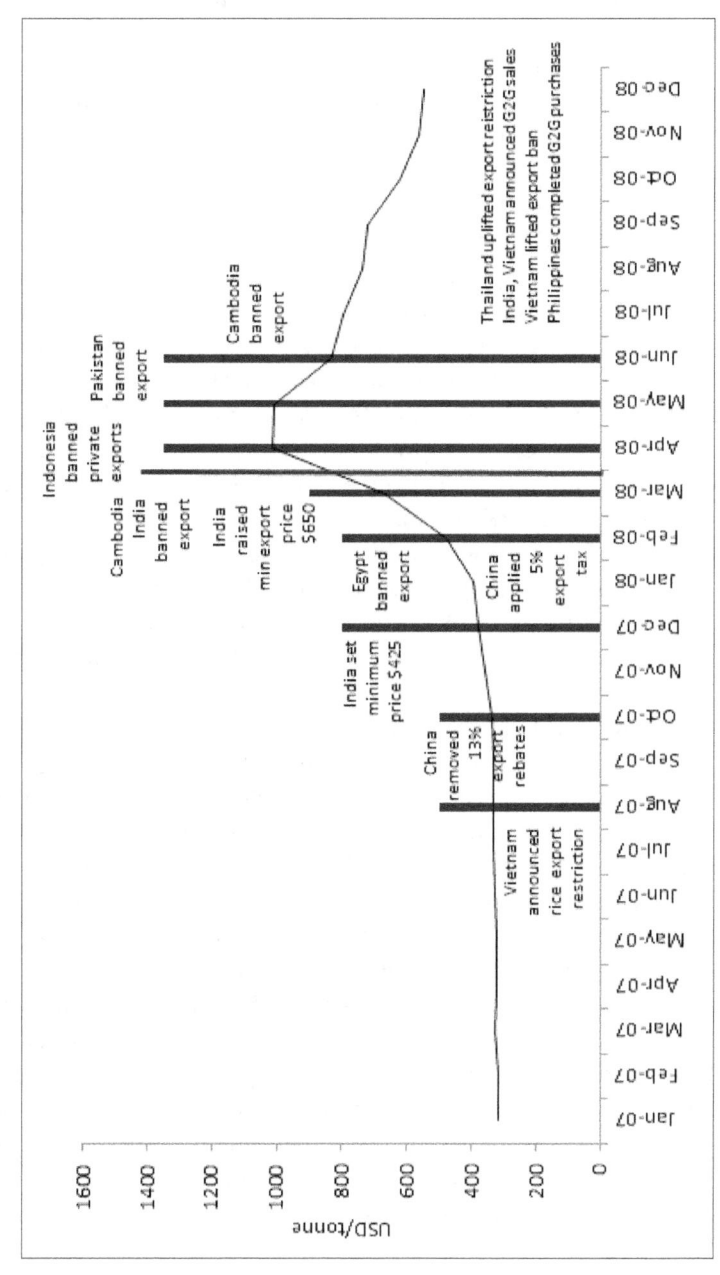

FIGURE 2.6
Policy Response to Rice Price Crisis in 2008

Source: Adapted from Brown et al. (2008).

Several initiatives were introduced and implemented to address the immediate impact of the crisis as well as for medium-term remedial. The list of policy interventions is shown in Table 2.5.

Table 2.5 indicates a protectionist response that strengthened state control over imports through a monopoly and maintained price control on producers and consumers. Malaysia continued its production support intervention programmes with infrastructural support, and incentives and subsidies to boost production at least in the short term.

After securing rice imports (at a high price), the government focused on revitalizing production by increasing input subsidies and incentives (Figures 2.7 and 2.8). The graphs summarize the following observations. First, the average value of input subsidies distributed before 2008 was RM112.84 million but ballooned to RM1.3 billion afterwards (until 2021). Second, the composition of input distributed diversified beyond the Federal Government Paddy Fertilizer Assistance Scheme (Skim Baja Padi Kerajaan Persekutuan, SBPKP) to include additional fertilizer, foliar, growth enhancers, pesticides, certified paddy seeds and incentive payment for higher yield as well as subsidies for hill rice. Reportedly, the paddy and rice sector expenditure accounted for about 40 per cent of the MoA's total allocation between 2015–2017. By 2021 the input subsidies were reduced to only SBPKP and the Fertilizer, Pesticide and Weedicides for Hill Paddy Scheme (Skim Subsidi Baja dan Racun Padi Bukit/Huma, SBRPB).

The yield impact showed minimal improvement. The value of all subsidies (input and output) increased fourfold in 2009 but yield increased by one per cent annually between 2009 and 2012. In fact, between 2012 and 2019 the yield trended downwards, reaching 3.6 tonnes/ha in 2019 compared to 4.2 in 2014. Meanwhile, the 80 per cent to 100 per cent SSL target failed to materialize; it remained almost stagnant at around 71 per cent between 2009 and 2011 and fell to 63 per cent in 2019.

Characteristically subsidies once given are hard to withdraw. Between 2008 and 2017, farmers enjoyed input subsidies amounting to RM1,914 per ha (Mohamed Arshad et al. 2019b). Attempts at subsidy withdrawal met strong resistance. Input subsidy accounted for about 30–50 per cent of farmers' total cost of production (COP) depending on productivity levels. High-yield farmers of 8 tonne/ha invested in their farms to ensure higher productivity. Hence the input subsidy accounted for about 30 per cent of COP. Low-yield farmers depended largely on subsidies to support input costs (Mohamed Arshad et al. 2019b).

TABLE 2.5
Food Security Strategies in 2008

Type	Response to Crisis
1. Domestic market-based measure	
Release stock (public or imported at subsidized price)	Stockpile inventory for emergency purposes was set at 92,000 MT before the crisis. It could sustain 15 days of supply of rice to the public. Given the crisis, the stock coverage was increased to 552,000 tonnes. A total of RM1.75 billion was allocated to buy rice for the stockpile, construction of godown and maintenance costs of RM103.8. BERNAS was responsible for managing the stockpile.
Suspension/reduction Value Added Tax and other taxes	NA
Admin. price control or restricted private trade	The Guaranteed Minimum Price has been maintained at RM550/tonne. To increase amidst the crisis would reinforce the price spiral. However, the farmers are paid a higher price than GMP
2. Trade-based measure	
Reduction of tariffs and customs fees on imports	NA
Restricted or banned export	NA
3. Non-market-based production support measures	
Production support intervention programmes (Objectives: • to improve yield from 3.7/ tonne (2007) to 4.48 t/ha in 2021; • to increase cropping intensity in granary area from 193% to 199%; non-granary from 112% to 120%; and • to increase SSL to 100%.)	Improvement in drainage and irrigation infrastructure in Sabah and Sarawak to increase paddy production. Allocation: RM1 billion. Improvement in farm mechanization and help farmers to buy machines. Allocation: RM305 million. To increase in paddy transplanting method. Allocation: RM60 million. Pest and disease management. Allocation: RM276 million. Infrastructural development (irrigation, drainage, farm roads). Allocation: RM6 billion (RM2.5 billion for the granary area, RM1 billion for non-granary areas, and RM1.5 billion for Sabah, and RM1 billion for Sarawak). Allocation for maintenance of drainage and irrigation amounting to RM190 million/yr for all paddy areas. Promotion of paddy production through estate model of management for efficient production and hence better yield and income.

Productive safety nets Fertilizers and seeds programmes	Input subsidies as per above and below. An increase in compound fertilizer subsidies from an average of RM150 million to RM255 million.
4. Market-based production support measures	
Safety net programmes Cash transfer	Since 1980 the government provides a cash subsidy amounting to RM350 per tonne on paddy sold.
Food assistance	NA

Note: NA: Not available.

PADDY AND RICE SECTOR DURING THE PANDEMIC

Malaysia's first COVID-19 case was reported on 25 January 2020. After the first wave crested, Malaysia reported zero cases in July 2020. A second wave emerged in August, when daily cases peaked at nearly 25,000 cases, which then fell gradually to under 6,000 by November 2021. The emergence of the Omicron variant spurred a larger third wave; daily cases reached some 30,000 in March 2022. Total positive cases (3.68 million) as of 8 March 2022 slightly surpassed 10 per cent of the country's population. At this time an estimated 33,000 Malaysians had died because of COVID-19.

World Market Situation

Fortunately during the pandemic years of 2020 and 2021, the rice market was ample. World rice production in 2020/21 increased slightly from its total of about 500 million MT (milled equivalent) in 2017/18 and was expected to increase to 519 million MT in 2021/22. According to the Food and Agriculture Organization (FAO), increases were expected from Bangladesh, Brazil, Indonesia and Sri Lanka (Figure 2.9).

The early period of the pandemic caused exporters to be protective while net importers indulged in panic buying. This behaviour triggered a price surge despite abundant supply. As shown in Figure 2.10, during the first half of 2020, the price rose from US$428/MT in January 2020 to US$508/MT in June. The world rice stock-to-use ratio[15] which indicates the percentage of carryover stock for rice to total use was about 37 per cent in 2018 but fell to 35.5 per cent in 2022. This means that the world has enough rice in stores to meet 35.5 per cent of a year's demand. The

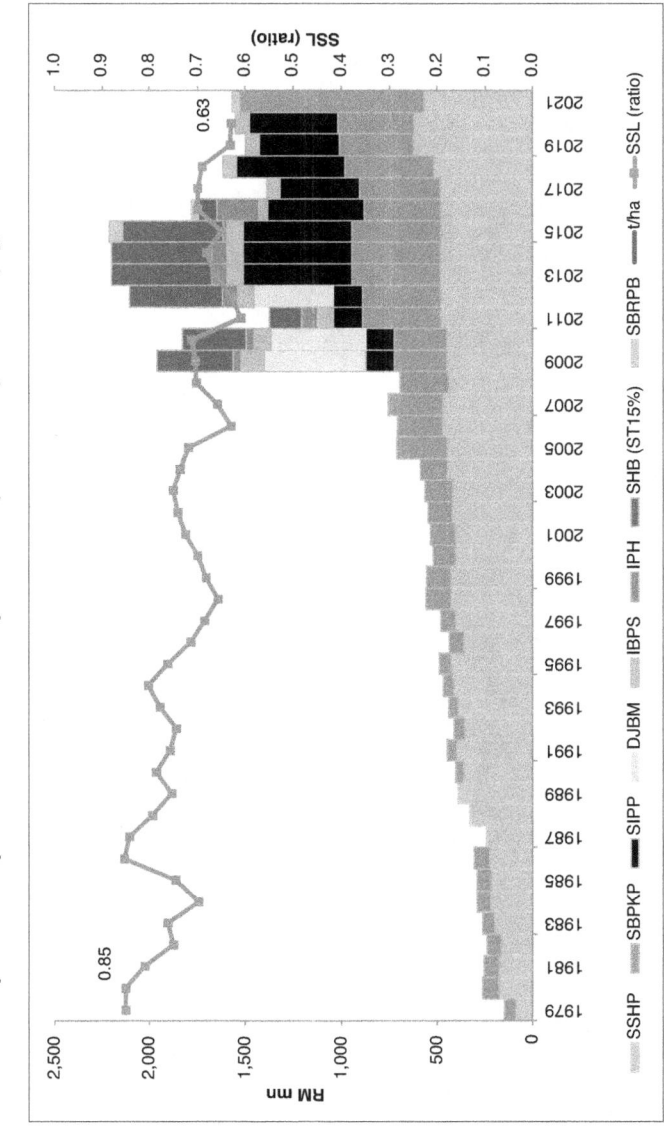

FIGURE 2.7
Input and Output Subsidies for Paddy and Rice (RM million) and SSL (%), 1979–2021

Note: SSHP: Skim Subsidi Harga Padi, or Paddy Price Subsidy Scheme; SBPKP: Skim Baja Padi Kerajaan Persekutuan, or Federal Government Paddy Fertilizer Assistance Scheme; SIPP: Skim Insentif Pengeluaran Padi, or Paddy Production Incentive Scheme; DJBM: Dasar Jaminan Bekalan Makanan, or Food Security Policy; IBPS: Insentif Benih Sah Padi Sah, or Certified Paddy Seeds Incentive; IPH: Insentif Peningkatan Hasil, or Incentive for Yield Improvement; SHB (ST15%): Subsidi Harga Beras ST15%, or Rice Price Subsidy (ST15%); SBRPB: Skim Subsidi Baja dan Racun Padi Bukit/Huma or Fertilizer, Pesticide and Weedicides Subsidies for Hill Paddy Scheme.
Source: MoA and MAFI (various years).

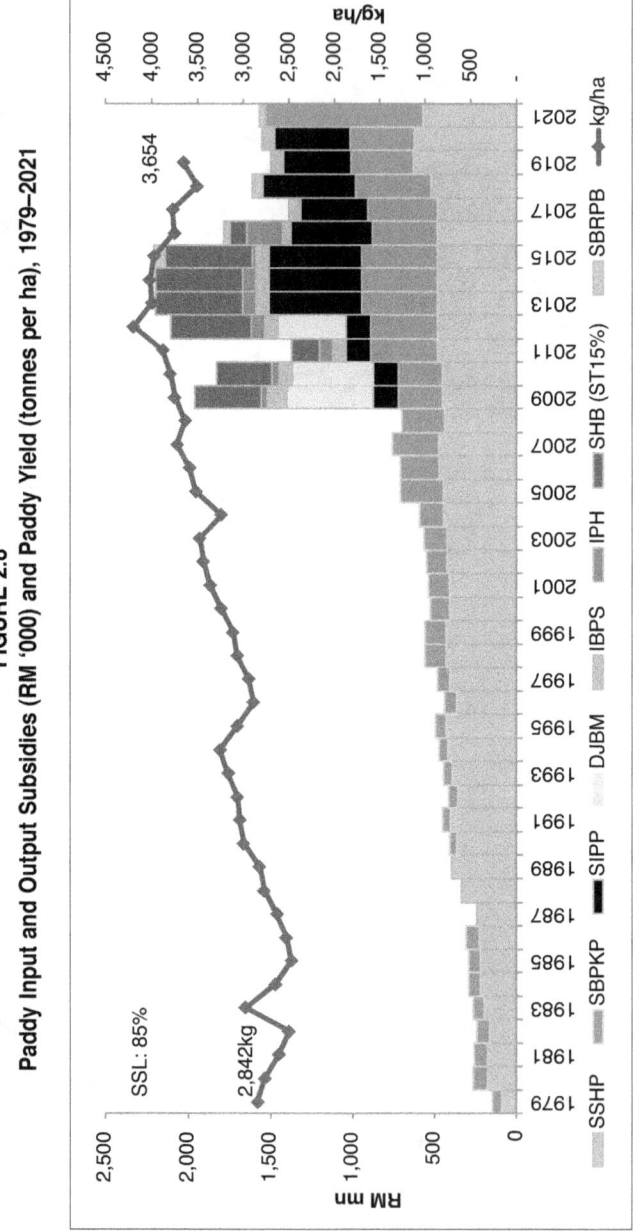

FIGURE 2.8
Paddy Input and Output Subsidies (RM '000) and Paddy Yield (tonnes per ha), 1979–2021

Note: Refer to Figure 2.7 for the abbreviations.
Source: Mohamed Arshad et al. (2019b); NADM (2019) for data 2017 and 2018; and MoA (2019b) for data 2019.

FIGURE 2.9
World Rice Stock-to-Use Ratio (%), Production and Utilization (million MT)

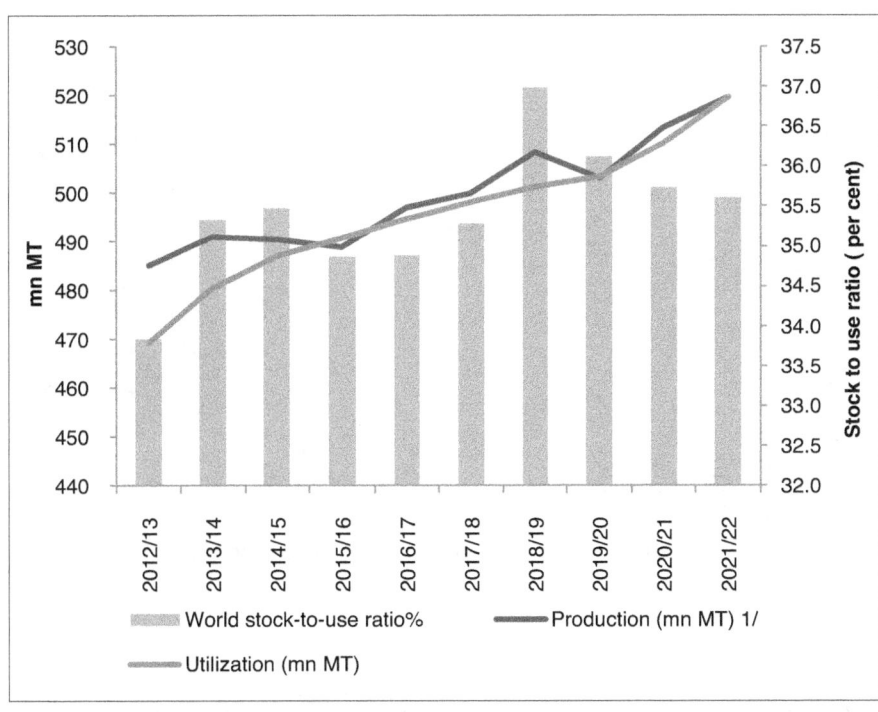

Notes: 1. Production data refer to the calendar year of the first year shown. Rice production is expressed in milled terms.
2. Production plus opening stocks.
3. Trade data refer to exports based on a July/June marketing season for wheat and coarse grains and on a January/December marketing season for rice (second year shown).
4. May not equal the difference between supply and utilization due to differences in individual country marketing years.
5. Stocks-to-use ratio indicates the level of carryover stock for any given commodity as a percentage of the total demand or use.
Source: http://www.fao.org/worldfoodsituation/csdb/en/

amount may be considered "safe" as during the 2008 crisis the figure was 10.9 per cent (Childs 2008).

In response to the COVID-19 outbreak, major exporters implemented policies to ensure adequate domestic supply. Vietnam suspended new export contracts in April 2020. In India, mobility and logistics were challenged due to social distancing while regulations reduced the availability of rice

FIGURE 2.10
Rice Prices, January 2015–August 2021 (US$ per tonne)

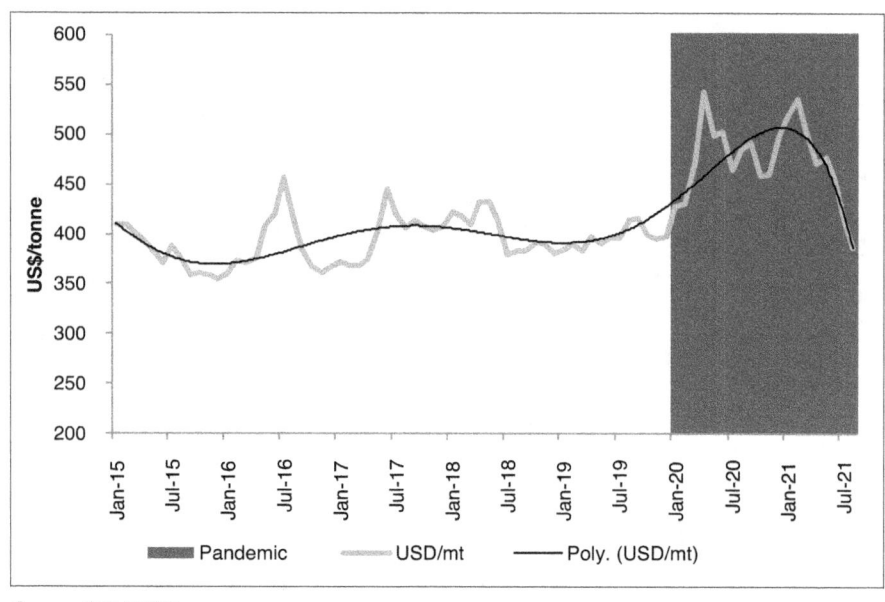

Source: IMF (2021).

domestically which contributed to lower export volumes. These reactions led to the aforementioned price rises. However, prices eased subsequently but remained high compared to the pre-pandemic period, despite high supply primarily led by consecutive year-on-year production increases in India. The eruption of COVID-19 cases in the first half of 2020 pushed up the demand for rice. As lockdown measures across the globe eased, demand eased too. Nevertheless, Thai and Vietnamese rice prices remained elevated in the subsequent months; they were on average 22 per cent and 28 per cent higher, respectively (Schmidt, Dorosh, and Gilbert 2021).

The Rice Price Index estimated by the FAO indicates a declining trend from August 2020 to August 2021 for the reasons discussed above. The All Rice Price Index (where the base equals 100) declined from 117.5 in August 2020 to 102 a year later; white rice prices declined from 113 to 98 in the same period.

Based on estimates, production was expected to increase from 2.35 to 2.93 million MT between 2019 to 2020 but dipped to 2.49 million in

2021. Due to panic demand and an increase in rice consumption, import estimates grew from 0.89 million in 2019 to 1.1 million in 2020 and 1.2 million in 2021 (EPU 2022; FAO 2021b). Correspondingly, the estimated SSL was expected to drop from 63 per cent in 2019 to 57 per cent by the end of 2021 (Figure 2.11).

Domestic Capacity in Absorbing Pandemic Shock

Government pandemic mitigation measures devastated the economy. Real GDP declined by 5.6 per cent in 2020 compared to 4.4 per cent growth in 2019; expansion in 2021 was expected to mirror the 2019 figure (OECD 2021). Other indicators of the impact included a decline in private consumption by 4.3 per cent, exports by 8.9 per cent and imports by 8.4 per cent. The

FIGURE 2.11
Malaysia: Rice Production, Consumption and Import ('000 tonnes), and SSL (%)

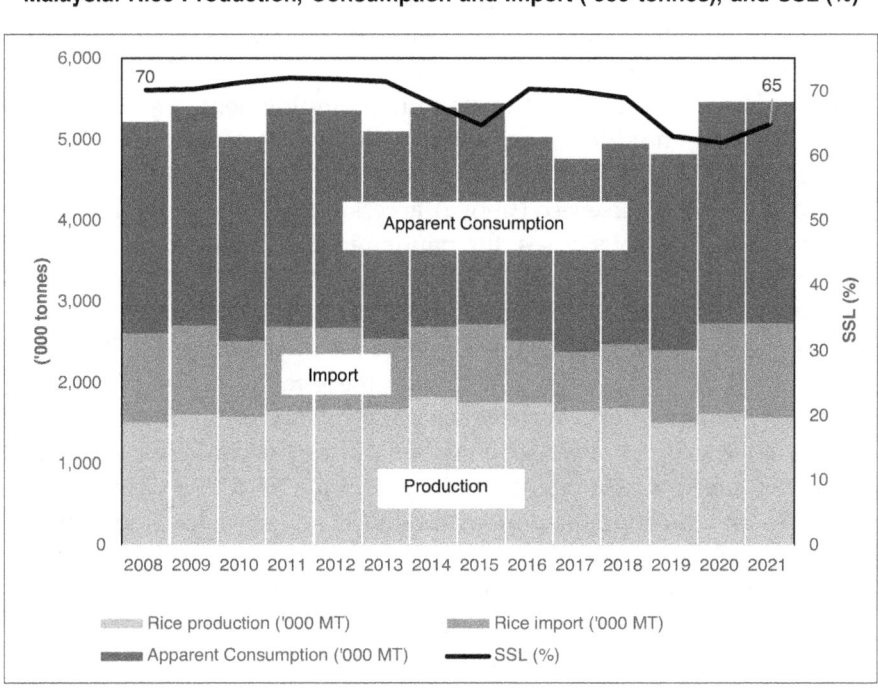

Source: Production, import before 2020 from DOSM (2021a) and EPU (2022), production in 2021 from FAO (2021b). Import and consumption beyond 2020 from KNOEMA (2022).

federal government's gross debt stood at 62.1 per cent in 2020 compared to 52.4 per cent in 2018 and was projected to reach 63.5 per cent in 2022.

The labour market was hit particularly hard. In June 2021, 768,700 Malaysians were unemployed, or 4.8 per cent up from 3.3 per cent in 2019. The incidence of absolute poverty increased from 5.6 per cent in 2019 to 8.4 per cent in 2020. Hardcore poverty was estimated to have increased from 0.4 per cent in 2019 (27,200 households) to 1 per cent (78,000 households) (DOSM 2021b).

The pandemic has restructured society: 20 per cent of households from the middle 40 per cent income group (M40, or income between RM4,850 and RM10,959 per month) have moved down to the bottom 40 per cent income group (B40). Meanwhile, about 12.8 per cent of the households in the T20 (top 20 per cent income) slid to the M40 group.

Consequently, the inequity gap widened. The T20 group now owned 47.2 per cent of income, up by 0.4 per cent from 2019. From 2019 to 2020, monthly household gross income decreased by 10.3 per cent to RM7,089. Contributing to this decline disproportionately were households or individuals with the status of employee, self-employed or others. Income reduction was not only caused by job loss but also by a reduction in working hours and an increase in skill-related underemployment.

At the household level, serious food insecurity incidence especially among the poor (urban and rural) emerged. While availability was not much of an issue (as discussed above), accessibility and affordability were. Unlike during previous crises, the pandemic resulted in job and income losses, and the consequent fall in purchasing power to buy food.

Based on a study on Kuala Lumpur flat dwellers, the average income is RM1,650 per month for a household of 5.8 members and 2.5 children (UNICEF 2020). The poverty rate among these families using UNICEF's threshold remains very high at 42 per cent.[16] One in four heads of households was unemployed at one point during the pandemic and 60 per cent experienced a reduction of monthly income by RM700. Households spent less on education (84 per cent), rent (39 per cent), transport (39 per cent) and food (4 per cent).

According to the same study in terms of food intake, on average, households consumed more eggs (an increase of 50 per cent), rice (40 per cent) and instant noodles (40 per cent), but fewer snacks and sweets (a reduction of 62 per cent) and fruits (40 per cent). Note that rice consumption increased as well as instant noodle consumption.

A pre-pandemic study indicated that one in ten Malaysian children ate less than three meals a day, one in five was stunted and one in ten was underweight (UNICEF 2018). In other words, even before the pandemic malnourishment among low-income children was already a problem. The pandemic in all likelihood has exacerbated this bourgeoning health crisis.

The above data indicate that the COVID-19 pandemic has had only a modest impact on food availability but greater consequences for food affordability, particularly among the poor. During the MCO food including rice was considered an essential item. Hence access to food was assured although labour and input movement was restrictive. Rice, egg and instant noodle consumption has increased as these are cheaper food items. Eggs cost less than chicken, beef and fish. The food insecurity the low-income have been experiencing is a continuation of their past situation, now worsened by the pandemic.

POLICY RESPONSE UNDER PANDEMIC

Since 2020 Malaysia has issued seven stimulus packages, totalling US$91 billion, to mitigate the economic impact of the pandemic (ASEAN Briefing 2021). The first major package was worth RM250 billion, another in 2021 amounted to RM150 billion and RM10 billion in direct fiscal spending in the form of wage subsidies, unemployment assistance and cash aid.

Support for the paddy and rice industry has been indirect through easing labour and input restrictions, assistance to micro, small and medium food enterprises and the informal sector (food distributors and retailers) and cash handouts to the poor.

The government allocation of RM1 billion to the Food Security Fund aims to aid farmers and fishermen and boost domestic production and improve supply chains. The government also allocated RM300,000 to each member of parliament for food basket assistance to help affected groups in their respective constituencies and RM10 million for a food basket programme for indigenous peoples.

Paddy and rice industry support took the form of additional market interventions. Notably, the government signed a contract with BERNAS in December 2020 to continue its import monopoly concession until 2030. (Recall the PH's contrasting desire to deregulate imports.) The policy reversal is purely political; it disregards the socio-economic cost of the monopoly and other protectionist measures on the industry. The government has also decided to increase the mandatory stockpile to reach 290,000 MT by 2023 to ensure preparedness for future shocks. The cost of the stockpile, estimated at RM250 million,[17] will be borne by BERNAS.

In the 1970s, NPRA stockpiles were between 260,000 and 300,000 MT (Caballero-Anthony et al. 2016). When BERNAS was established, the stockpile reportedly was reduced to 92,000 MT. After all, BERNAS was a for-profit firm and stockpiling is a heavy expense on company books. Since the 2008 rice crisis, the quantity re-increased between 239,000 and 292,000 MT. A decade later it declined to the current level of 150,000 MT.[18] Based on 2018 consumption figures, this quantity is able to support twenty-two days of rice consumption (Mohamed Arshad et al. 2021).

The trade-off of this policy is between the stock coverage (number of days it can support) versus the cost of stockpile management. The estimated cost of storage is RM150 per MT.[19] The higher the stockpile, the higher the storage cost. Under such a situation BERNAS may pass on the high cost to farmers through a higher deduction rate[20] and higher imported rice prices to consumers. BERNAS has estimated that the total trade inventory (stockpile plus private sector inventories) which is estimated at 550,000 MT is adequate to feed the country for about three months. A study on stockpiling has found that the current stockpile system is robust and resilient and handles shocks reasonably well (Mohamed Arshad et al. 2021). The system is able to normalize or recover from shock (be it production of import shocks) within two to three months. Nevertheless, experience under the pandemic shock indicates that even with active international trade the major impediment is not rice accessibility but affordability as the pandemic crippled producers and consumers alike through income loss. Importantly this means that providing rice availability is not enough without adequate consumer purchasing power.

As in earlier rice crises, the import of rice increased beyond the normal market level (Figure 2.12). At the peak of Malaysia's COVID-19 caseload in May 2020, RM340 million worth of rice was imported compared to RM230 million in the same month a year earlier. However the import value was lower than the highest value recorded in 2008 at RM511 million. Note that the rice trade deficit more than tripled from about RM60 million in the 2000s to RM186 million in 2021.

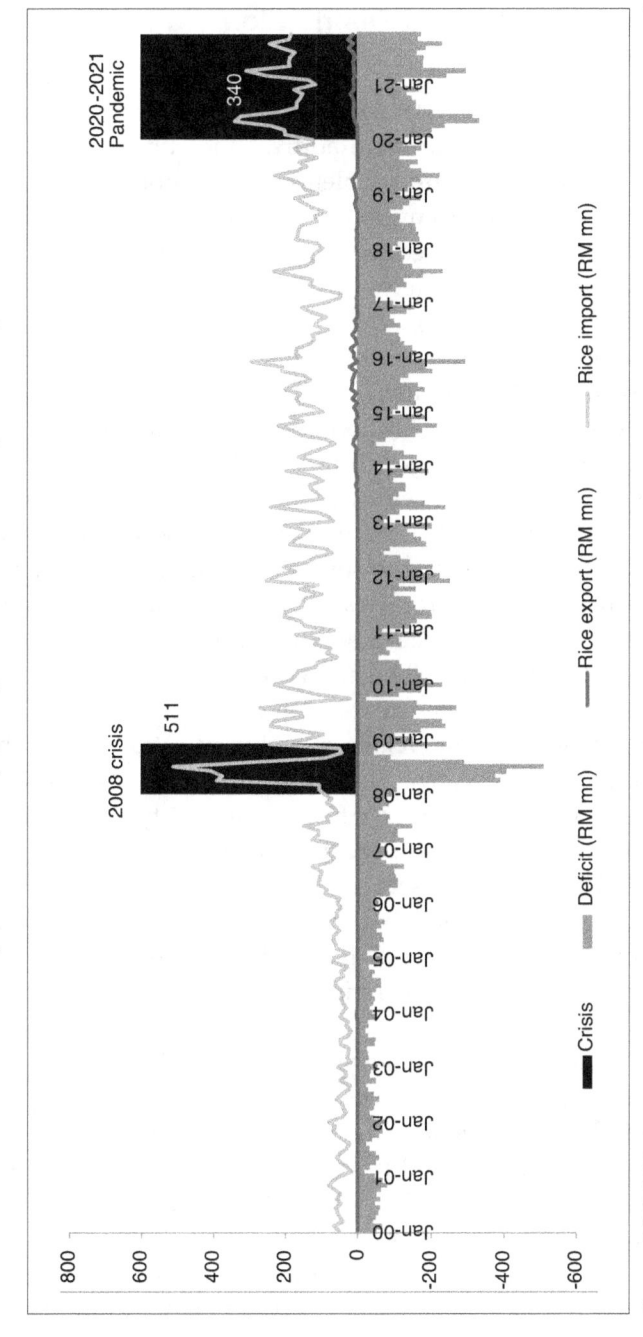

FIGURE 2.12
Malaysia's Rice Trade, January 2000–December 2021 (RM million)

Source: DOSM (2022).

Centralized Paddy Seed Distribution

Another policy intervention introduced during the pandemic was the appointment of NAFAS as the sole distributor for certified paddy seeds. This move was meant to address the supply chain issues of the previous system beset with problems such as poor quality, high price, a non-competitive market environment and slow release of seeds due to lengthy bureaucratic procedures (Omar, Shaharudin, and Tumin 2019). Late delivery and poor-quality seeds reduce farmers' harvest and return (*Berita Harian*, 3 May 2021).

In support of the new centralized move, several policy measures were implemented. They include: (1) a ceiling price for certified seeds at RM35 per bag (20 kg); (2) licences and distribution permits only for those registered with the government; (3) only licensed seed producers are allowed to produce several varieties; and (4) a buffer stock for seeds.

NAFAS has been entrusted with this function based on the premise that it has strong financial resources and experience in the nationwide distribution of SBPKP (*Borneo Post*, 4 November 2020). Adding seeds to its range of services would incur lower marginal costs due to its experience, business scale and established network. These arguments belie several structural problems it may create as in the case of a centralized fertilizer system such as frequent delays in delivery estimated in the range of 20–200 days (NADM 2019). This problem is exacerbated further by the folly of providing one fertilizer formula for all types of soil nationwide since 1980 and frequent rent-seeking practices by NAFAS executives. It is estimated that the rent-seeking index in the input and rice market is high, at 1.8. This indicates that for every RM1 received by farmers, the distributors (BERNAS, NAFAS and traders) would gain an equal amount without incurring any cost or risk-bearing (Aiman 2018). Incidences of corruption are rampant too.

Barely one year old, the new system has suffered serious distribution issues: Some 55,000 farmers reported delays in seed delivery (Mohd Noor 2021). Supply shortages have driven up the price by 20 per cent to RM42 per bag, rendering the fixed price policy ineffective. Farmers report that a competitive market should yield RM25 per bag. Meanwhile, fertilizer costs have risen by 20–40 per cent (Tan 2021).

The centralization of seed distribution would probably yield a similar impact as in the case of fertilizers. The new policy encourages rent-seeking practices, non-competitive markets and high barriers to entry (in particular for farmers); the outcome has been low investment and innovations in the seeds industry.

Smart Padi Field Programme

Another programme introduced during the pandemic is a farming project called Smart Paddy Field Programme (Smart Skel Berskala Besar or Smart SBB). Smart SBB is a large-scale paddy land consolidation programme which aims to increase productivity through optimal and efficient resource management and to increase the income of farmers and entrepreneurs through smart and strategic public-private partnerships (PPPs). The Ministry of Agriculture and Food Industries (MAFI) signed a Memorandum of Understanding with eleven companies for implementation, including contract farming and renting.[21]

The project is expected to reduce the government's financial liabilities in terms of subsidized agricultural input in the long term, as well as introduce a new approach through modernizing agriculture. The justifications include increasing efficiency through large-scale paddy farming, reducing dependency on middlemen and improving efficiency through the use of such advanced technologies as drones, artificial intelligence, Internet of Things and other smart agriculture applications.

Expected outcomes include:

1. improving SSL to 75 per cent under the Twelfth Malaysia Plan (2021–25).
2. involving private companies in supply chains.
3. reducing farmers' risk through contract farming, lowering their costs and hence producing higher margins.
4. raising farmers' income by 47 per cent or RM2,521/ha/season, and offering fragrant paddy crops a return of RM1540/MT compared to ordinary paddy at RM1,200/MT.
5. doubling the yield to 7 MT/ha under the Twelfth Malaysia Plan.

This policy is a continuation of earlier farm consolidation efforts. The government established two Entry Point Projects (EPPs) under the country's Economic Transformation Plan of 2020.[22] Under these projects, paddy farms were consolidated by farmers surrendering management of their land to a Special Purpose Vehicle (SPV). The SPV in many cases were local AFAs, but in principle, it could be any organization, cooperative or business entity.[23] One project was implemented in the MADA area and another in the Kemudu Agricultural Development Area (KADA). The cost of the former was RM2.7 billion for the duration of the project. It achieved its area target but yield growth fell short. The cost of the KADA project was RM1.8 billion but it also covered other granary areas known as Integrated Agricultural Development Authorities (IADAs) (KADA 2016).

Major project digressions were the deployment of project funds towards irrigation and physical infrastructure, rather than establishing a production supply chain of paddy and rice system. For example, the MADA project earmarked 78 per cent of project funds for developing tertiary infrastructure (irrigation canals and farm roads), 18.5 per cent for farmer incentives, 2.5 per cent for seed grants to support consolidation, 0.5 per cent for R&D and 0.3 per cent for developing a rice trading centre (MoA 2018). Sizeable resources dedicated to connecting small farms to irrigation and farm infrastructure suggest that EPPs have yet to embrace large-scale farming as a new model. Yet before these models had been diagnosed critically and rectified, the SBB estate programme was introduced.

Besides scale and production practices, what separates the Smart SBB farms from small paddy farms is the orientation of the enterprise. The former is capital-oriented with a focus on capital return. The latter's objective function is livelihood and hence a focus on returns to land, labour and capital. Empowering small farms with knowledge, technology and support yield more than just higher returns but an equitable and dynamic rural community, ecological services and environmental benefits, which are not the priorities of large enterprises. Studies have shown that small farms are better custodians of the countryside, ensuring varied landscapes, sustainable use of natural resources and better provision of public goods than larger farms do (Rigg, Salamanca, and Thompson 2016; Rosset 2000; Giller et al. 2021). Rigg and his colleagues indicate that more than 95 per cent of agricultural farms in Asia including paddy farms are small scale having persisted for decades despite technological advances (Rigg, Salamanca, and Thompson 2016). Based on economic theory, the benefits of economies of scale would encourage the merging of farms into large scales such as an estate. However such evolution has not materialized as small scales offer socio-economic benefits which have made them sustainable and resilient as proven in some countries like China, Japan, Korea and Thailand. Simply put, scale is not a barrier to efficiency and productivity.

According to farmers the estate model may not be sustainable as SPVs come and go while farmers remain steadfast, as paddy farming has been their source of income for generations. Hence equipping the farmers with modern technology will ensure the sustainability of paddy farming in the future. Farmers are also of the opinion that the provision of modern technology should be provided to them rather than the selected few SPVs as the returns are distributed to a large number of farmers and their families. Moreover they contend that improved infrastructure especially irrigation particularly outside granary areas (or IADAs) would improve productivity. The SBB project has been a top-down effort with minimal engagement of stakeholders particularly the farmers, nor were trial runs implemented to gauge feasibility.[24] Notably, an SPV for an SBB project in Kelantan failed to deliver its promise to farmers who suffered losses amounting to RM200 million (*The Sun Daily*, 18 October 2021).[25] This implies the shoddiness of the planning and hence monitoring and evaluation (Dialektika TV 2022).

CONCLUSIONS AND POLICY IMPLICATIONS

This analysis points to the significant role of path dependence in Malaysia's paddy and rice policy. Starting with the critical juncture in 1971 when the country adopted protectionist policies, this path has endured. Little effort has been made to deregulate the sector (except for the PH's promise to deregulate the import market). In crisis upon crisis, the government has not only maintained this historical path, but it has strengthened relevant institutions including: (1) continuing the import monopoly; (2) consolidating the centralization of input distribution by adding paddy seeds into the list of NAFAS functions; (3) promoting PPPs in large scale paddy farming; (4) massively increasing input and output subsidies; (5) continuing with price control and licensing programmes; and (6) increasing the government's stockpile. The steadfast policy objectives are to improve production to realize 80 per cent SSL by 2030 while maintaining high prices for producers and a stable supply to consumers.

The market is distortive. It exhibits inefficient use of resources, slow growth and a heavy fiscal burden on the government. The strengthening of current institutions and their structure exacerbates the problems. For instance, import monopoly and centralization of input distribution have resulted in a big divide between the upstream sector (paddy production) and input (agribusiness) and downstream sectors (rice). The former is plagued with low returns with little market power while the latter two are highly concentrated and integrated through joint venture moves (importer, miller, wholesaler) in paddy procurement and rice distribution. The two subsectors, input and downstream, are non-competitive with high barriers to entry.

The divide has far-reaching consequences. Divides deter the entry of new entrants such as new farmers, entrepreneurs and start-ups due to low returns in paddy farming and high barriers to entry in the agribusiness and downstream sectors. The overall impact is low investment in the sector and minimal value-added activities which impede industry development. Value-added products are necessary to increase the value of paddy to producers besides other multiplier effects. A similar argument applies to the input market. Its centralization hinders new entrants, limits investment and leaves the local input market underdeveloped. This has resulted in the continuous dependence on imports of inputs and any inflationary effect that comes with it. This explains the untapped competitive advantage of the agricultural sector at large and rice specifically.

The injection of large subsidies thus far has failed to produce a commensurate increase in paddy yield. Instead, the latter has fallen albeit at a slow declining rate. Producers' incomes have shown a minimal increase. That nearly 90 per cent of producers were in the bottom 40 per cent income category in 2019 proves these points. Subsidies are deeply entrenched in the production system, so their withdrawal may lead to the system's disruption and related socio-political repercussions.

The Smart SBB programme is another path-dependence strategy where prior large-scale farming is modified by involving PPPs while farmers function as mere contractees. The private sector holds the capital and technology, not the farmers who need them most. The project privileges the corporate sector instead of enhancing the full potential of small farms as advocated by the European Union and International Fund for Agricultural Development (IFAD 2021; FAO 2021a). Farm institutions have not kept up with the times, particularly in terms of improvements in extension services, farming technology, infrastructure, climate change mitigation and strengthening of collective efforts, particularly cooperatives.

The path dependency is deep; future variables and concerns are not fully encapsulated in the policy agenda, including technological advancement, future shocks and climate change and domestic capacity-building. The embodiment of future variables will open up new policy horizons and opportunities. For instance, Internet technology allows direct marketing from producers to consumers without the need for a monopoly agency and some farm processes can be automated, which reduces labour requirements. The ecological and climate change challenges demand a new ecosystem. The 2021 Food Summit called for systems thinking in food policy and programme, to incorporate ecological, climate and other structural and institutional factors in policy-making to ensure saliency.[26] The Malaysian government however shows policy resistance despite the growing complexity of the system. Structurally successful models of deregulation have been convincing in countries such as China, Thailand, Vietnam and Bangladesh, but Malaysia has chosen to be inward-looking and chart its own path. In this case, path dependence policy has not resulted in "increasing returns" (Pierson 2000). It has brought stability but at the cost of stagnation and inequity.

Nevertheless the government should be commended for placing rice at the top of its agriculture agenda every year to ensure rice availability before anything else at all costs. This seems to be the order of the day. Treading the historical path gives a sense of stability as one can predict the outcome compared to a structural shift clouded with uncertainty and risk. This is understandable as disruption has high political costs. However the strength of the government's commitment and resources can be mobilized towards a more productive, equitable, economically and ecologically sustainable industry. Some degree of market deregulation is needed for the following: (1) to unleash the creativity of producers in making their own decisions (after decades of being dictated) to improve productivity and efficiency; (2) to increase producers' income by allowing them to participate in value-added activities by innovating small machines and mills for small farms; (3) to create Micro, Small and Medium Enterprises in the paddy and rice-based industry for value-addition; (4) to expedite development of technological applications in smart agriculture; (5) to produce innovations in sustainable farming; (6) to develop local input production to create local input markets and boost competitive advantage; and (7) to support a strong cooperative model to encourage collective effort among farmers to improve their market position, among other advantages. In short, all resources should be channelled towards domestic capacity-building to achieve self-reliance in paddy and rice production. As seen in other countries such as Thailand, Vietnam, Bangladesh and China, some degree of deregulation, along with strong institutional support, enhances growth and economic sustainability.

Notes

1. About 9 per cent and 1 per cent of the agricultural and total labour, respectively (MoA 2019b).
2. The Green Revolution refers to the incorporation of scientific advances in plant breeding with technological packages that have allowed the yield potential of the crops to be realized more fully and under conditions experienced by farmers from developing countries. The Green Revolution was initiated in the 1960s in developing countries in Asia including Malaysia (FAO 1996).
3. As of October 2015, the new global poverty line was updated to US$1.90/day (World Bank 2015). Based on this measurement, the percentage of farmers in this category is very small.
4. The average allocation for the period 2011–16 was RM2 billion to RM2.5 billion.
5. National Paddy and Rice Authority (1971): Act 1971 (Act 47: Section 4 "Objectives of Establishment").
6. Malaysia recorded its first COVID-19 case on 25 January 2020 (https://covid-19.moh.gov.my).
7. MoA, Agro-food Statistics, various years.
8. Ministry of Health Malaysia, https://covid-19.moh.gov.my/
9. Some parts of this section are drawn from Mohamed Arshad et al. (2019a).
10. "First Malaysia Plan, 1966–1971", p. 120.
11. NAFAS was inaugurated in 1972.
12. Personal communication, 2018. Data was provided by a senior BERNAS official.
13. There are currently three major grades of local white rice in Malaysia: (i) ST15% is Super Tempatan 15% rice, which means 15 per cent of the rice is broken rice; (ii) SST10% is Super Special Tempatan 10% rice, which means 10 per cent of the rice is broken rice; (iii) SST5% contains 5 per cent of broken rice accordingly (MAFI 2020).
14. Note that NPRA was entrusted with overseeing the overall development of the paddy and rice sector.
15. Stock-to-use ratio indicates the level of carryover stock for any given commodity as a percentage of the total demand or use. This ratio can then be used to indicate whether current and projected stock levels are critical or plentiful (www.oecd-ilibrary.org).
16. Absolute poverty rates for all types of households are derived based on the threshold of RM2,216, Kuala Lumpur's absolute poverty line (UNICEF 2019).
17. This is a one-off cost of an increase of the stockpile quantity from the current

150,00 MT to 200,000 MT in 2021, 250,000 MT (2022) and 290,000 (2023) (personal communication, in 2022 with the Paddy and Rice Section or IPB, MAFI, 2022). Data was provided by a senior official, Paddy and Rice Section, Ministry of Agriculture and Food Industry, Putrajaya.
18. Under the new agreement between MAFI and BERNAS signed on 3 December 2020 (*Sinar Harian*, 3 December 2020), the stockpile level has been reduced to 140,000 MT.
19. This figure is estimated by IPB, MAFI (personal communication 2021). Data was provided by a senior official of the Paddy and Rice Section, Ministry of Agriculture and Food Industry, Putrajaya.
20. One way of maintaining receipts from paddy purchase is by imposing a high deduction rate (for immature paddy, moisture contents, foreign matters, etc.) from the gross paddy price paid at the farm gate. The average deduction rate reported by farmers were 20 per cent and maximum reported ranged from 45 per cent to 75 per cent (Mohamed Arshad 2019b).
21. MAFI, Smart SBB, 2021, www.mafi.gov.my.
22. "Economic Transformation Programme: A Roadmap for Malaysia", 2010, Economic Planning Unit, Prime Minister Department, Putrajaya.
23. Three management models have been used to facilitate large-scale farming in EPPs without requiring physical land consolidation. These are: fee-based management, fixed rental and profit sharing (Md Zuki et al. 2015).
24. See also Padi Rescue, Badan Bertindak Selamatkan Industri Padi, and https://www.facebook.com/selamatkanpadiberas/
25. The losses are an aggregative figure for 200 farmers for one season of paddy production from various areas in Kelantan (Dialektika TV 2022).
26. United Nation Food Systems Summit 2021, https://www.un.org/en/food-systems-summit

References

Abdul Fatah, Fadzleen. 2017. "Competitiveness and Efficiency of Rice Production in Malaysia". PhD dissertation, Georg-August-Universität Göttingen.

Aiman, Ainaa, 2018. "Ahli Akademik Dedah Masalah Struktur Dalam Industri Padi". *Free Malaysia Today*, 8 December 2018. www.freemalaysiatoday.com/category/bahasa/2018/12/08/ahli-akademik-dedah-masalah-struktur-dalam-industri-padi/ (accessed 20 June 2022).

Ali, Roslina. 2017. "Economic and Policy Evaluations and Impacts of the National Rice Development Policy Strategies in Malaysia: Self-Sufficiency, International Trade, and Food Security". PhD dissertation, University of Arkansas.

ASEAN Briefing. 2021. "Malaysia's Pemulih Stimulus Package: Supporting Businesses and Individuals". 30 June 2021. www.aseanbriefing.com/news/

malaysias-pemulih-stimulus-package-supporting-businesses-and-individuals/ (accessed 30 June 2022).

Berita Harian. 2021. "10,000 Petani Belum Terima Benih Padi Sah". 3 May 2021. https://www.bharian.com.my/berita/nasional/2021/05/813368/10000-petani-belum-terima-benih-padi-sah (accessed 30 June 2022).

BERNAS. 2018. "Data on Rice Distribution and Import". Selangor Darul Ehsan, Malaysia.

Borneo Post. 2020. "Nafas Appointed as Sole IBPS Agent — Kiandee". 4 November 2020. https://www.theborneopost.com/2020/11/04/nafas-appointed-as-sole-ibps-agent-kiandee/ (accessed 20 June 2022).

Brown, N., J. Laffan, and M. Wright. 2008. "High Food Prices, Food Security and the International Trading System". Paper presented to the Informa National Food Pricing Summit, Sydney, 29–30 September 2008. Canberra: Australian Government Department of Foreign Affairs and Trade.

Caballero-Anthony, Mely, Paul Teng, Jonatan Lassa, Tamara Nair, and Maxim Shrestha. 2016. "Public Stockpiling of Rice in Asia Pacific". NTS Report No. 3, April 2016. Rajaratnam School of International Studies, Singapore.

Childs, Nathan. 2008. "Rice Situation and Outlook Yearbook". RCS-2008, February 2009. United States Department of Agriculture. https://downloads.usda.library.cornell.edu/usda-esmis/files/7s75dc36z/k930bx62t/1c18dg59n/RCS-yearbook-02-17-2009.pdf (accessed 20 June 2022).

———, and James Kiawu. 2009. "Factors Behind the Rise in Global Rice Prices in 2008". RCS-09D-01, May 2009. United States Department of Agriculture.

Davidson, Jamie S. 2018. "Stagnating Yields, Unyielding Profits: The Political Economy of Malaysia's Rice Sector". *Journal of Southeast Asian Studies* 49, no. 1, 105–28.

Department of Statistics, Malaysia (DOSM). 2020. "Report of Special Survey on Effects of COVID-19 on Economy & Individual (Part 1)". www.dosm.gov.my/v1/index.php?r=column/cone&menu_id=d3pnMXZ4ZHJjUnpnYjNyUnJhek83dz09 (accessed 20 June 2022).

———. 2021a. "Time Series: Paddy Statistics". https://www.dosm.gov.my (accessed 20 June 2022).

———. 2021b. "Labour Force Malaysia". June 2021. https://www.dosm.gov.my/v1/index.php?r=column/cthemeByCat&cat=124&bul_id=SkFRMTJ0d1RIR3BrdG1aUTBsUmw2Zz09&menu_id=Tm8zcnRjdVRNWWlpWjRlbmtlaDk1UT09 (accessed 20 June 2022).

———. 2022. "Time Series: Paddy Statistics". https://www.dosm.gov.my (accessed 20 June 2022).

Dialektika TV. 2022. "Anekdot: Smart SBB: Janji@Realiti". https://www.facebook.com/dialektikatv/videos/274800534625376 (accessed 20 June 2022).

Economic Planning Unit (EPU). 1975. *Second Malaysia Plan, 1971–1975*. Kuala Lumpur: Prime Minister's Office, Malaysia.

———. 2022. "Data Sosio-Ekonomi". https://www.epu.gov.my/ms (accessed 20 June 2022).
Food and Agriculture Organization (FAO). 1996. "World Food Summit: Food for All". https://www.fao.org/3/x0262e/x0262e00.htm#TopOfPage (accessed 20 June 2022).
———. 2021a. "Empowering Smallholders, Family Farms and Youth". FAO Regional Office for Europe and Central Asia. https://www.fao.org/europe/regional-initiatives/smallholders-family-farms/en/ (accessed 20 June 2022).
———. 2021b. "Food Security Snapshot". https://www.fao.org/giews/countrybrief/country.jsp?lang=es&code=MYS (accessed 20 June 2022).
Giller, Ken E., Thomas Delaune, Joâo V. Silva, Katrien Descheemaeker, Gerrie van de Ven, Antonius G. T. Schut, et al. 2021. "The Future of Farming: Who Will Produce Our Food?". *Food Security* 13: 1073–99.
Hill, R.D. 2012. *Rice in Malaya: A Study in Historical Geography*. Singapore: NUS Press.
IFAD. 2021. "Rural Development Report 2021: Transforming Food Systems for All". https://www.ifad.org/en/rural-development-report/ (accessed 20 June 2022).
International Monetary Fund (IMF). 2021. "IMF Commodity Prices". https://www.imf.org/en/Research/commodity-prices (accessed 20 June 2022).
Ismail, Shamsuddin. 2017. "Dasar Dan Polisi Industri Padi dan Beras". Persidangan Padi Kebangsaan, Dorsett Grand Subang, Selangor. http://padi.mardi.gov.my/dokumen/slide/L1%20Dasar%20dan%20Polisi%20Industri%20Padi%20dan%20Beras_Shamsuddin%20Ismail%20(MOA).pdf (accessed 20 June 2022).
KADA. 2016. "Laporan Tahunan KADA 2016". https://www.parlimen.gov.my/ipms/eps/2017-11-29/ST.150.2017%20-%20Laporan%20Tahunan%20KADA%202016.pdf (accessed 20 June 2022).
KNOEMA. 2022. "Malaysia Rice Import". https://knoema.com/atlas/Malaysia/topics/Agriculture/Trade-Import-Value/Rice-imports (accessed 20 June 2022).
MADA (Muda Agricultural Development Authority). 2019. "Perangkaan MADA, 2018". https://www.mada.gov.my/FLIPBOOKMADA1/index.html (accessed 20 June 2022).
Malay Mail. 2015. "Government Abolishes Subsidy for Super Tempatan Rice". 1 November 2015. https://www.malaymail.com/news/malaysia/2015/11/01/government-abolishes-subsidy-for-super-tempatan-rice/997255 (accessed 20 June 2022).
Malaysian Institute of Economic Research (MIER). 2010. "Economic Study on the Development of the Paddy and Rice Industry towards Achieving the Objectives of the National Food Security Policy". Policy report submitted to the Economic Planning Unit, Prime Minister's Department, Malaysia.
MARDITECH. 2003. "The Review of Paddy and Rice Industry in Malaysia". Policy report submitted to the Ministry of Agriculture, Malaysia.

Md Zuki, I., A. Fouzi, D. Kamarudin, and O. Ernnie. 2015. "Strategies Towards National Self-Sufficiency Level: Estatization Initiative as Model to Increase Rice Productivity". Paper presented at NAPICEX 2015, 28–30 September 2015, Kota Kinabalu, Sabah. http://www.iipm.com.my/wp-content/uploads/2016/05/TN.-HJ.-KAMARUDDIN-DAHULI.pdf (accessed 17 July 2022).

Ministry of Agriculture and Agro-based Industry (MoA). 2008. *Polisi Jaminan Bekalan Makanan*. Putrajaya: Kementerian Pertanian dan Industri Agro Makanan.

———. 2011. *Agriculture Statistics Handbook, 1980–2010*. Putrajaya: Kementerian Pertanian dan Industri Agro Makanan.

———. 2016a. *Data on Paddy and Rice, Paddy and Rice Section*. Putrajaya: Kementerian Pertanian dan Industri Agro Makanan.

———. 2016b. *Laporan Tahunan Dan Penyata Kewangan Yang Telah Diaudit Bagi Tahun 2018*. Lembaga Kemajuan Pertanian Muda or Muda Agricultural Development Authority.

———. 2018. *Laporan Tahunan Dan Penyata Kewangan Bagi Tahun 2018*. Putrajaya: Policy and Strategic Planning Division, Ministry of Agriculture and Agro-based Industries.

———. 2019a. "Teks Ucapan Menteri Pertanian". http://www.moa.gov.my/documents/20182/139717/Teks+Ucapan+Majlis+Pelancaran+Hala+Tuju+MOA+YBM+-+MASTERCOPY+FINAL+.pdf/b27792b2-0f6a-479b-8e18-fd5c619ba3ee (accessed 20 June 2022).

———. 2019b. *Agrofood Statistics 2018*. Putrajaya: Policy and Strategic Planning Division, Ministry of Agriculture and Agro-based Industries.

Ministry of Agriculture and Food Industry (MAFI). 2018, 2019, 2020, 2021, 2022. *Data on Paddy and Rice, Paddy and Rice Section*. Putrajaya: Kementerian Pertanian dan Industri Makanan.

Ministry of Plantation and Industrial Commodity (MPIC). 2018. *MPIC Annual Report 2017*. Putrajaya: MPIC.

Mohamed Arshad, Fatimah, Mohd Ghazali Mohayidin, Ahmad Mahzan Ayub, and Madinah Husin. 1983. "The Impact of Paddy Subsidy Schemes on Malaysian Farmers". Consultancy report submitted to the Ministry of Public Enterprise, Kuala Lumpur, November 1983 (in Malay).

———, Bustanul Arifin, and Yeong Sheng Tey. 2019a. "Effectiveness of State Trading Enterprises in Achieving Food Security: Case Studies from BERNAS in Malaysia and BULOG in Indonesia". *Malaysia Agriculture Report, 2019*. Kuala Lumpur: Institute of Democracy and Economic Affairs (IDEAS).

———, Kusairi Mohd Noh, and Allia Farhana Rosmanshah. 2019b. "Empirical Study on the Impact of Subsidies on Paddy Production and Income". Policy report submitted to the Paddy and Rice Industry Division, Ministry of Agriculture and Agro-based Industry, Malaysia.

———, Kusairi Mohd Noh, and Emmy Farha Alias. 2021. *Paddy and Rice Sector*

Policy Roadmap: Towards Equity and Sustainability. Institute for Democracy and Economic Affairs. Kuala Lumpur: IDEAS Policy Research Berhad.

———, Mohd. Ghazali Mohayidin, and Ahmad Zubaidi Baharomshah. 1991. "Kesan Skim Subsidi Harga Padi ke atas Pengusahaan and Pemasaran Padi". Report to Paddy and Rice Agency (LPN), Kuala Lumpur, Malaysia (in Malay).

Mohd Noor, Zaid. 2021. "Lebih 50,000 Pesawah Kecewa Bekalan Benih Padi Lewat". *Utusan Melayu*, 19 October 2021. https://www.utusan.com.my/terkini/2021/10/pesawah-kecewa-bekalan-benih-padi-lewat/ (accessed 20 June 2022).

NAFAS. 2019. "Farmers' Association data". (In author's possession.)

National Audit Department (NADM). 2011, 2015, 2019. *Laporan Ketua Audit Negara 2011, 2014, 2018*. Putrajaya: Jabatan Audit Negara.

OECD. 2021. *OECD Economic Surveys: Malaysia 2021*. www.oecd.org/publications/oecd-economic-survey-malaysia-2021-cc9499dd-en.htm (accessed 20 June 2022).

Omar, Sarena Che, Ashraf Shaharudin, and Siti Aiysyah Tumin. 2019. *The Status of the Paddy and Rice Industry in Malaysia*. Kuala Lumpur: Khazanah Research Institute.

Pakatan Harapan (PH). 2017. *Buku Harapan: Building Our Nation Fulfilling Our Hopes*. Kuala Lumpur: Pakatan Harapan.

Pertubuhan Peladang Kebangsaan (NAFAS). 2019. "Sejarah & Latar Belakang NAFAS". http://nafas.com.my/v2/index.php?option=com_content&view=article&id=442&Itemid=408&lang=my (accessed 20 June 2022).

Pierson, Paul. 2000. "Increasing Returns, Path Dependence, and the Study of Politics". *American Political Science Review* 94, no. 2: 251–67.

Rigg, Jonathan, Albert Salamanca, and Eric C. Thompson. 2016. "The Puzzle of East and Southeast Asia's Persistent Smallholder". *Journal of Rural Studies* 43: 118–33.

Rosset, Peter. 2000. "The Multiple Functions and Benefits of Small Farm Agriculture in the Context of Global Trade Negotiations". *Development* 43, no. 2: 77–82.

Rusli, Rawaida, Fatimah Mohamed Arshad, and Abdulla Ibragimov. 2017. "The Causal Structure of Paddy Deduction System in the MADA Granary Area: A System Dynamics Approach". *Economic and Technology Management Review* 12: 1–10.

Sahathavan. N.d. *The Welfare Cost of the Malaysian Rice Policy under Alternative Price Regime*. Kuala Lumpur: University of Malaya.

Selvadurai, S. 1978. *Agriculture in Peninsular Malaysia*. Kuala Lumpur: Ministry of Agriculture.

Serin, Tapsir. 2017. "Senario Ekonomi Pengeluaran Padi di Malaysia". Persidangan Padi Kebangsaan, Dorsett Grand, Subang, Selangor.

Schmidt, Emily, Paul Dorosh, and Rachel Gilbert. 2021. "Impacts of COVID-19

Induced Income and Rice Price Shocks on Household Welfare in Papua New Guinea: Household Model Estimates". *Agricultural Economics* 52, no. 3: 391–406.
Sinar Harian. 2020. "Bernas Terus Diberikan Mandate". 3 December 2020. https://www.sinarharian.com.my/article/113121/berita/nasional/bernas-terus-diberikan-mandat
Sun Daily, The. 2021. "Govt to Resolve Problems Faced by Fragrant Rice Padi Farmers in Kelantan Soon: MAFI". 18 October 2021. https://www.thesundaily.my/home/govt-to-resolve-problems-faced-by-fragrant-rice-padi-farmers-in-kelantan-soon-mafi-AD8476301 (accessed 20 June 2022).
Tamin, M., and S. Meyanathan. 1990. "Rice Market Intervention System in Malaysia: Scope, Effects and the Need for Reform". Faculty of Economics & Administration, Universiti Malaya.
Tan Siew Huey. 1987. *Malaysia's Rice Policy: A Critical Analysis*. Malaysia: ISIS.
Tan Siew Mung. 2021. "Spike in Fertiliser Price will lead to Higher Production Cost for Planters in 2022, says UOB KayHian". *The Edge Markets*, 10 November 2021. www.theedgemarkets.com/article/spike-fertiliser-price-will-lead-higher-production-cost-planters-2022-says-uob-kayhian (accessed 20 June 2022).
Trouvé, Hélène, Yves Couturier, Francis Etheridge, Olivier Saint-Jean, and Dominique Somme. 2010. "The Path Dependency Theory: Analytical Framework to Study Institutional Integration. The Case of France". *International Journal of Integrated Care* 10: 1–9.
UNICEF. 2018. "Children Without: A Study of Urban Child Poverty and Deprivation in Low-cost Flats in Kuala Lumpur". https://www.unicef.org/malaysia/sites/unicef.org.malaysia/files/2019-04/UNICEF-ChildrenWithout-EnglishVersion-Final%2026.2.18_0.pdf (accessed 20 June 2022).
———. 2020. "Families on the Edge". https://www.unicef.org/malaysia/media/1441/file/Families%20on%20Edge% 20part% 201.pdf (accessed 20 June 2022).
Vokes, R.W.A. 1978. "State Marketing in a Private Enterprise Economy: The Paddy and Rice Market in West Malaysia, 1966–1975". PhD dissertation, University of Hull.
Wong, D. 1981. "Rice Marketing in Kedah, Malaysia". Working Paper, University of Bielefeld, Faculty of Sociology, Sociology of Development Research Center, Germany.
World Bank. 1984. *Sector Report. Malaysia: Incentive Policies in Agriculture* (3 volumes). Country Programs Department, East Asia and Pacific Regional Office.
———. 1988. *The World Bank Annual Report 1988*. http://documents.worldbank.org/curated/en/267711468779986991/pdf/multi0page.pdf (accessed 20 June 2022).

3

Impact of COVID-19 on the Philippine Rice Sector

Roehlano M. Briones and Isabel B. Espineli

INTRODUCTION

Paddy rice is the most widely grown crop in the Philippines, the thirteenth most populous country in the world, and a world top-ten producer of the commodity. Milled rice is likewise the nation's main staple, accounting for 35 per cent of the average calorie intake of the population. Historically, rice has played a significant role in the culture of most Filipinos; the word "rice" is the same as the word "eat" in some of the country's major languages. It was perhaps inevitable that the commodity would become heavily politicized: maintaining its affordability for the consumer while safeguarding the livelihoods of the paddy rice farmer are seen by the populace as key benchmarks of a competent government.

The Philippines has also been historically a rice importer. A net rice exporter engaging in a few thousand tons of external trade in the 1850s and 1860s, the nation became a chronic rice importer since the 1870s. Net annual imports were typically in the 50,000 to 100,000-ton range in the 1880s and 1890s (with an interregnum due to the Philippine Revolution and Philippine-American War from 1896 to the early 1900s). In the 1900s net annual imports ranged from 100,000 to 300,000 tons. One reason for the rice deficit in the country is inconsistent rainfall in Luzon, the northern island group that hosts the country's "rice bowl", in contrast to the "great river deltas of the Southeast Asian mainland" (Doeppers 2016, p. 64). By the late twentieth century average annual imports were 380,000 tons, and by the twenty-first century the average was 1.4 million tons (FAO 2022). Such a persistent trade tendency can only be explained not by vagaries of policy, governance, land use, and so on, but rather by the fundamental features of geography (Dawe 2006).

Rather than accepting economic reality, successive governments since the 1930s have instead acted to reserve the local market for domestically produced rice, placing imports under strict government control, while supporting paddy rice production with public funds (Briones 2018). The regime of import control intensified in the 1970s and successfully withstood all efforts at reform; it was only in 2019 that the government finally liberalized the rice industry, including the decision to import rice, albeit still subject to high tariffs.

Within a year of the reform, the country fell under the deadly pall of the COVID-19 pandemic. This remarkable (and entirely fortuitous) conjunction raises the following questions: How was the rice market affected by the policy reform, and later by the disruptive effects of the COVID-19 crisis? What was the role of the reform in worsening—or mitigating—the impact of the crisis? This chapter seeks to answer these questions, first by providing a background on the COVID-19 pandemic in the Philippines; followed by a description of the rice industry and the evolving policy regime; then undertaking a before-after assessment of the rice industry liberalization; and finally drawing implications for the future of rice policy reform.

THE COVID-19 PANDEMIC IN THE PHILIPPINES

When the first case of COVID-19 local transmission was detected on 7 March 2020, a state of public health emergency was declared the next day; schools were closed, and large public gatherings were banned. Less than two weeks later, President Rodrigo Duterte instituted an enhanced community quarantine (ECQ) throughout the National Capital Region (NCR) and the whole of Luzon, which prohibited work and movement except for "essential sectors", which were themselves subjected to work restrictions.[1]

Essential sectors included: agriculture; manufacture of basic food products, essential products, medicine, and medical supplies; retail establishments (related to essentials); logistics service providers; delivery services; hospitals and medical clinics; banks; power, energy, water, information technologies, and telecommunications; and export and business product outsourcing. Subsequently, the ECQ was enforced throughout the country.

By 23 March, Congress had expedited the passage of Republic Act No. 11469, or the Bayanihan to Heal as One Act, signed into law by the President the next day. It provided for temporary emergency measures in response to the pandemic, including implementation and enforcement of community quarantine rules, social protection subsidies, penalties for illegal business practices such as hoarding and profiteering, and extension of a grace period for lease and interest payments.

The ECQ, originally scheduled to end on 12 April, was twice extended until 1 June 2020. The government has since eased movement restrictions to varying degrees by geographic zone. By early 2022, most restrictions had already been lifted, but by then tremendous economic damage had been inflicted. The Philippines is considered to have applied one of the most stringent responses to the pandemic worldwide (Hapal 2021). In the first month of the ECQ, mobility declined by 80 per cent nationwide; four months later, workplace mobility was still down by 60 per cent relative to pre-pandemic levels, according to the Food and Agriculture Organization (FAO 2021).

Mostly as a result of mobility and related restrictions, the COVID-19 crisis inflicted severe hardship on the economy. In 2020, the country's gross domestic product (GDP) fell by 9.6 per cent (Figure 3.1). This has been the steepest one-year drop in GDP ever recorded (since the start of official national accounts in 1948).

Grave challenges confronted agriculture during the pandemic. Some farmers reported not going to their fields for fear of infection. Different local government unit (LGU) quarantine regulations limited the movement of products and personnel, despite national government exemptions. Some LGUs required health certifications before allowing movement into or out of their jurisdiction, temporarily curtailing the movement of agricultural workers, and traders attempting to access farms and purchasing stations. Operating hours for purchasing stations, trade centres and wet markets were limited, narrowing the window time for deliveries.

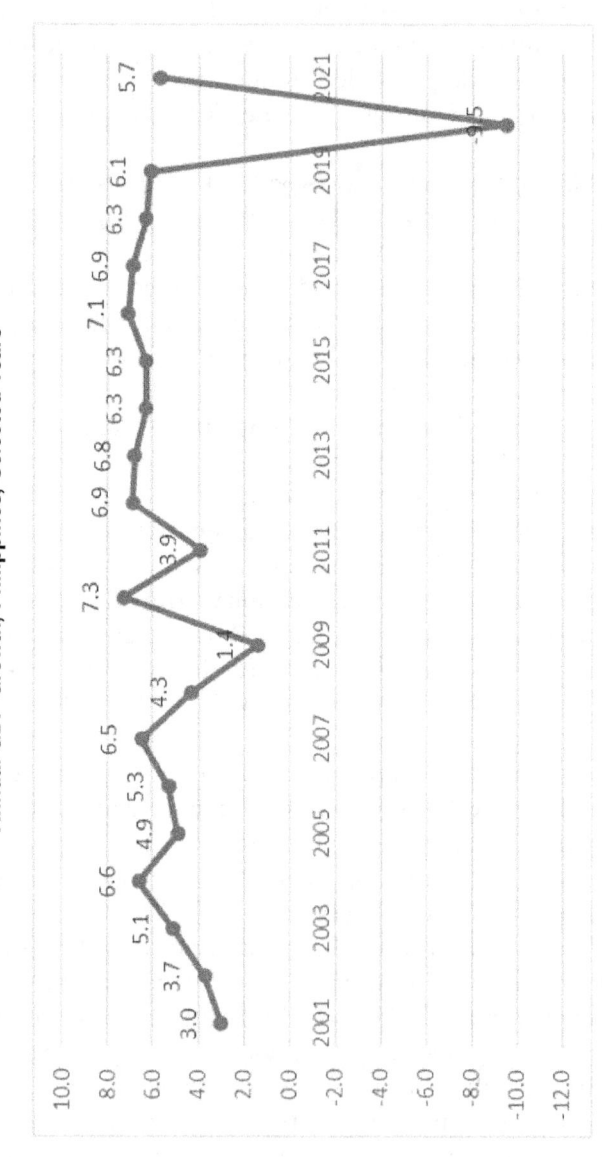

FIGURE 3.1
Annual GDP Growth, Philippines, Selected Years

Source: PSA Openstat.

Even before ECQ was implemented, COVID-19 emergency measures were expected to adversely affect agricultural market chains and food security. To ensure that agriculture and food systems remain exempted from ECQ restrictions, a Food Lane Pass scheme under the Department of Agriculture (DA), in place since 2018, was significantly expanded, starting in March 2020. Despite the challenges encountered during the pandemic, authorities managed to resolve most of the outstanding issues. Hence, agriculture managed to grow in the second and third quarters (Figure 3.2). Agriculture, food production and logistics were allowed to operate with relatively fewer restrictions than manufacturing and services, which bore the brunt of the lockdowns.

The full-year decline in GDP was 13.2 per cent for industry and 9.2 per cent for services, but only 0.2 per cent for agriculture. The economic upturn had to wait until the second quarter of 2021; for the full year, the growth rate recovered to 5.7 per cent. Consumer demand certainly fell as a result of the overall income decline. Fortunately, agriculture appeared to be the sector best positioned to avoid the worst effects of economic contraction. As household income shrank, households preferred to prioritize food purchases over shopping for durables or travelling, given their tight budget.

From the second quarter of 2021, the economy began recovering, with year-on-year GDP growth reaching 12 per cent, powered by the 21 per cent expansion of industry and followed by the 9 per cent gain in services. Yet during the 2021 recovery, agriculture missed the boat, rising by a measly 0.01 per cent, owing to coincident disasters, namely typhoons, floods (affecting crops and fisheries) and African swine fever (decimating swine inventories). They weighed down the sector. By the end of the year, agriculture's coverage quarterly growth was down to 1.5 per cent.

The most recent poverty statistics available are only for the first semester of 2020 (PSA 2022). Poverty incidence as of the first semester of 2021 (one year into the pandemic) was estimated at 23.7 per cent, or 2.6 percentage points higher than its level in 2018. Notably, from 2006 to 2015, the first-semester poverty incidence averaged 2.6 percentage points greater than the full-year incidence, leading to an estimate of 26.3 per cent full-year poverty incidence, a reversal of a decade's worth of poverty reduction, as that level was last observed back in 2009.

Although economic recovery is well underway, the economic climate remains uncertain both domestically and worldwide. Escalation of the

FIGURE 3.2
Quarterly GDP Growth, Philippines, Selected Years

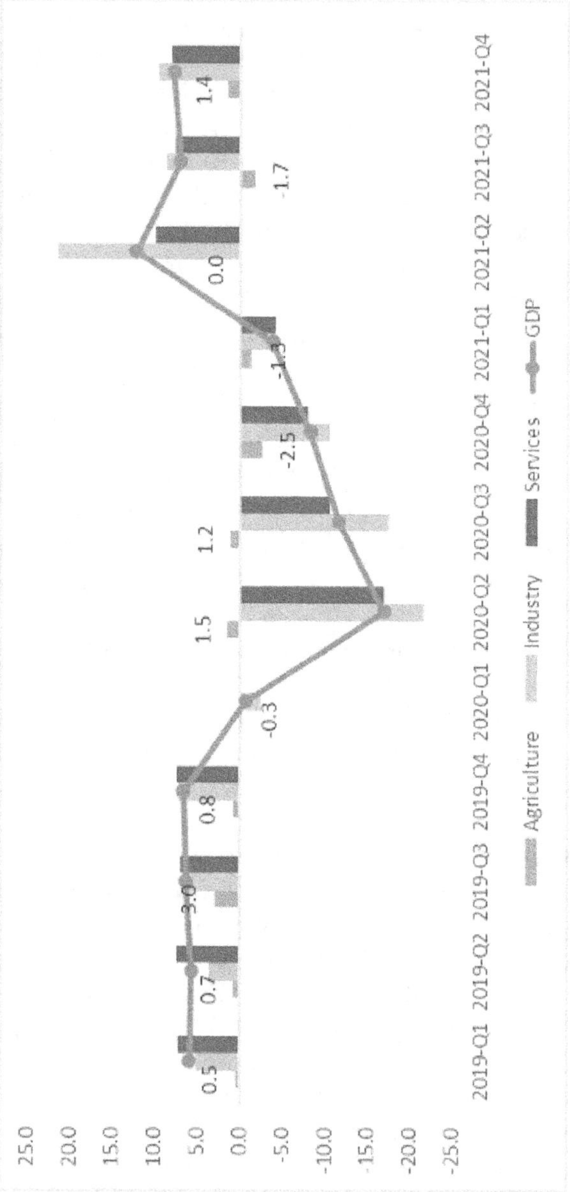

Source: PSA Openstat.

national debt burden to 61 per cent of GDP by end-2021, up from 40 per cent as of end-2019, has severely compressed the government's fiscal room for manoeuvring through the various global crisis now buffeting the economy, namely the commodity price shocks, the supply chain squeeze, contractionary monetary policies in the developed world, and the ongoing war in Ukraine.

THE PHILIPPINE RICE INDUSTRY

Rice Market in the Commonwealth and Early Republic

The Philippines as a political entity was founded as a Spanish colony in the sixteenth century. Upon gaining independence in 1898, the fledgling republic was annexed by the United States in the early twentieth century with its victory in the Philippine-American war. Throughout this period, the rice industry remained largely a free market under both the Spanish and American colonial governments, excepting the levy of import duty to raise revenues.

An independence movement led to a Commonwealth government established in 1935, which remained under the supervision of the United States, but with most government functions carried out by elected Filipino officials. Since joining the Commonwealth, maintaining a stable price for rice had become imperative for Filipino policymakers. In 1935–36, bad harvests followed by rising prices led to widespread unrest. The government attempted to reduce the import tariff; the Bureau of Commerce also undertook the importation of rice for the purpose of relief. However, both measures were opposed by rice landlords. The National Rice and Corn Corporation (NARIC) was founded to undertake rice importation, as well as trading of domestic rice, to regulate both the farmgate price of *palay* (the local term for paddy) and the selling price of milled rice (Chiba 2010). Yet, owing to limited facilities and funding, the NARIC purchased just 0.5 per cent of the rice harvest over the period 1936–41 (Doeppers 2016).

The NARIC had the twofold objective of providing a "just price" for farmers (consisting of production cost and a reasonable margin) and ensuring a steady supply for consumers at a reasonable price. Rice policy was supposed to strike this balance even as the Commonwealth maintained self-sufficiency in rice, a delicate task that was to vex policymakers in the subsequent decades. Continuing the mission of the NARIC in the 1950s and 1960s, the Rice and Corn Board (RICOB) regulated the rice and corn retail trade, and the Rice and Corn Administration (RCA) undertook the marketing and distribution of subsidized rice (Intal and Garcia 2008).

Transformation in the 1960s–70s

Following initial breakthroughs in China using semi-dwarf rice varieties, modern varieties (MVs) of rice were first introduced in tropical Asia in 1965 with the release of IR8 by the International Rice Research Institute (IRRI), based in the Philippines. The Philippine government began to distribute IR8 and succeeding generations widely; the spread of MVs was most rapid here compared with other countries. By the crop year 1979–80, MVs had reached 89 per cent adoption in irrigated rice land, and 77 per cent adoption in rainfed rice land (Herdt and Capule 1983).

The adoption of MVs was a "green revolution" in agriculture, a term first applied by W.S. Gaud, head of the United States Agency for International Development in 1968 (Patel 2013). For the Philippines, by 1980 *palay* harvest increased by 3.27 million tons over fifteen years, an increase of 76 per cent (Castillo 1975); 26 per cent of the increase was due purely to the adoption of MVs; 31 per cent was due to increased fertilizer use (MVs are much more responsive to fertilizer compared with traditional varieties); and 24 per cent due to increased irrigation (Herdt and Capule 1983).

The transformation of rice production and marketing was strongly driven by government policy under the authoritarian phase of the administration of Ferdinand Marcos (1972–86), who was first elected in 1965 and re-elected in 1969. On the production side, the government launched the Masagana 99 programme starting in 1973 to boost rice yield from 40 *cavans* (2.0 tons) to 99 *cavans* (4.95 tons). The "99" figure was chosen as the estimate of the production requirement (in *cavans*) for the country to end its dependence on rice imports and achieve self-sufficiency. Masagana 99 sought to increase yield by promoting a package of technologies (MVs and other modern inputs) through a subsidized credit scheme (Esguerra 1981). Accompanying the Masagana 99 in the 1970s was a massive government funding for expanding irrigation (Briones et al. 2021).

The government also promoted a land reform programme to defuse agrarian unrest, counter a dangerous communist insurgency, and cultivate an image of peace and order, thereby drawing in foreign capital (Kerkvliet 1974). Land reform was aggressively pursued in rice and corn lands, transferring ownership to former share tenants while fixing amortization rates at pr-MV levels, enabling the new landowners to capture the bulk of the gains arising from technological progress (Otsuka 1991).

On the marketing side, the National Grains Authority (NGA) was created under Presidential Decree (PD) No. 4 of 1972 to promote the integrated growth of the grains industry. The NGA absorbed the RICOB and the RCA, taking over rice market regulation and marketing. It controlled all rice importation, directly or by issuing import permits to private entities, subject to quantitative restrictions (QRs). Another task was to procure domestic paddy rice, based on a mandated support price, funded by the government. The support price was estimated at a level supposed to offer farmers a "reasonable" profit level.

In 1981, PD No. 1770 transformed the NGA into the National Food Authority (NFA). Under this law, the government established government retail stores (Kadiwa), which sold low-priced basic food and household items, including rice. Paddy procurement was implemented in conjunction with a buffer stocking scheme. The NFA targeted to have stocks equivalent to thirty days of national consumption every 1 July, ahead of the lean months between rice harvests. The scheme also aimed for at least half of that inventory year-round.

On the consumption side, the NFA provided milled rice as part of emergency response (i.e., disaster relief), as well as to sell subsidized rice. It was popularly known as "NFA rice" and was supposed to benefit poor households, although Jha and Mehta (2008) have shown that only one-quarter of the poor benefited from NFA rice, which means the programme had low coverage. Moreover, there was high leakage to the non-poor who made up 48 per cent of beneficiaries. In urban areas, the non-poor share of beneficiaries even reached 68 per cent. There was also an estimated 64 per cent discrepancy between the NFA's reported distribution and actual receipts as uncovered by a household consumption survey, implying large losses owing to pilferage and logistical inefficiency.

Paddy procurement by the NFA also did not significantly increase beyond the 1 per cent market share of its predecessor, NARIC (Intal and Garcia 2005). In contrast to other countries such as Thailand, patronage politics in the Philippines failed to support farmers with massive procurement programmes in the face of the government's inability to generate fiscal resources (Fang 2016).

The pursuit of a "reasonable return" to farming requires alternative means, such as market price support via agricultural protection. From the 1990s onward, the domestic price of rice has remained consistently above the world price. Intensifying agricultural protection has been attributed to the rise of advocacy groups consisting of farmer organizations, large land owners, and agribusiness firms engaging in livestock, poultry, seed production and input supply (David, Intal, and Balisacan 2007). The "peasant movement", which had been instrumental in installing the 1986 democratic regime, lobbied the new government intensely for agricultural protection and rice self-sufficiency and to expand the land reform programme to all agricultural sectors.

Although the domestic price of rice has been higher than the world price, the former has typically remained more stable than the latter (Briones 2017). Consumers seem able to tolerate high prices (relative to the border price) as long as marked volatility is avoided. This is accomplished in part by applying quantitative restrictions (QR) on rice imports to prevent the domestic price from falling to the world level while allowing enough imports to head off retail price spikes in the event of a domestic supply shortfall. Incidentally, this allowed the NFA patronage network to collect rent from the excess margin between domestic and world prices (Tolentino and de la Pena 2011). Kajisa and Akiyama (2005) show that price stabilization has been indeed a key consideration in rice pricing policy in Indonesia, the Philippines and Thailand. To a large extent, the unrealistic self-sufficiency goal has also been justified by price stability as a means to avoid vulnerability to external price shocks.

Tolentino and de la Pena (2011) argue that the NFA import monopoly imposed high opportunity costs on a majority of consumers and farmers. However, beneficiaries of reform are numerous, spread nationwide, and disorganized. In contrast, beneficiaries of the NFA policy are concentrated and well organized.

Accession to the World Trade Organization

After much domestic political controversy, the Philippines acceded to the World Trade Organization (WTO) in 1995, supposedly to abolish all QRs for agricultural imports. Yet the government negotiated a special clause exempting rice. Only the Philippines, South Korea, Japan and Israel invoked this clause under the WTO Agreement on Agriculture (AoA)—the first three countries for rice, and Israel for cheese and sheep meat (WTO 2022). This was not because WTO ended all QR policies in agriculture; countries such as Indonesia and Malaysia kept their rice QRs on a *de facto* basis as did the Philippines for sugar and fish. What special treatment did for the Philippines, South Korea, Japan and Israel was to convert *de facto* into *de jure* QRs, at least temporarily, thereby forestalling legal challenges against persistent protection of highly political commodities.

For the Philippines, although special treatment was to lapse in 2005, by then the government had managed to negotiate an extension to 2012. Subsequently it obtained a waiver for the QR in rice, up to 2017. In exchange, the government had to commit various concessions to other WTO members, namely an increase in minimum access volume of rice at a relatively lower tariff (35 per cent), as well as lower tariffs on several non-rice products, such as livestock, poultry, meat, peas, potatoes, and oil seeds (Tolentino and de la Pena 2020).

Two major crises during the WTO period provoked much handwringing over the reliability of NFA under the status quo of special treatment. The first occurred immediately upon joining the WTO when the NFA's import programme fell short owing to an overestimation of harvests and an underestimation of demand in early 1995. Rice prices increased by 28 per cent during the lean season (June–August) and long queues formed at NFA rice outlets (where rice was up to 43 per cent cheaper), but limited stocks had to be rationed. Subsequently NFA tended to err on the side of caution in the face of potential deficits. For example, as the El Niño event of 1997–98 unfolded, NFA embarked on a massive import programme, bringing in 2.17 million tons in 1998 (versus just 0.26 million tons in 1995). Notwithstanding severe harvest reductions, and the sizeable markups in the costs of the imports due to kickbacks, price increases were largely avoided (Davidson 2016).

The second crisis occurred in 2008. Even as world prices were soaring, the NFA managed to procure 1.3 million tons of rice in the first four months of the year, mostly by government-to-government contracts with Vietnam—a mad scramble referred to as "panic-buying" (Headey 2011). The NFA-imported stocks were unloaded at a great loss under its subsidized selling price. Such a precautionary stance for import in anticipation of rice shortages further bloated the burgeoning NFA debt. By 2013, the NFA had gained the dubious status of the most heavily indebted government corporation (DBM 2022).[2]

Rice Industry Liberalization

It took a unique set of circumstances to turn the tide in favour of reforming the NFA. First, in July 2017, the QR waiver from the WTO ended. A push for a third extension would have meant more and greater concessions to trade partners, to which the government was loath to commit. Second, internal conflict between the NFA Council and NFA management (amidst mutual accusations of corruption and incompetence) in the 2017–18 period led to delays in importing rice, leaving the NFA helpless in fending off a round of retail price increases in late 2018 (Figure 3.3).[3] Third, the executive branch, together with the country's central bank, convinced Congress to back the market reform, as they sought to stave off the inflation bursts driven by the country's main staple (Tolentino and de la Pena 2020).

Adding to the controversy were accusations of smuggling, which tarred both the NFA and the Bureau of Customs with accusations of complicity.[4] However, it was the QR regime that created the structural incentives for the illegal entry of cheap imports.

The upshot of these developments was the enactment, in 2018, of Republic Act (RA) 11203 by Congress, later signed into law in 2019. The full title of RA 11203 is "An Act Liberalizing the Importation, Exportation, and Trading of Rice, Lifting for the Purpose the Quantitative Import Restriction on Rice, and for Other Purposes", henceforth the Rice Liberalization Act (RLA). The RLA revoked the regulatory function of the NFA and limited its mandate to local paddy procurement and rice buffer stock management for emergency purposes. Other key provisions of the law include the following (Briones 2019):

- Tariffs are set in tiers: 35 per cent for imports from the Association of Southeast Asian Nations (ASEAN); 40 per cent for non-ASEAN countries (imports below 350,000 tons); and at least 180 per cent for non-ASEAN countries (imports above 350,000).
- The remaining legal non-tariff barrier for rice importation is sanitary and phytosanitary standards (SPS). SPS clearances are to be issued by the Department of Agriculture's Bureau of Plant Industry. The

FIGURE 3.3
Monthly Rice Retail Prices, WMR and RMR, Philippines, 2017–18

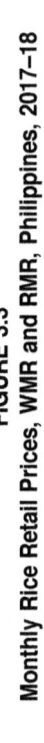

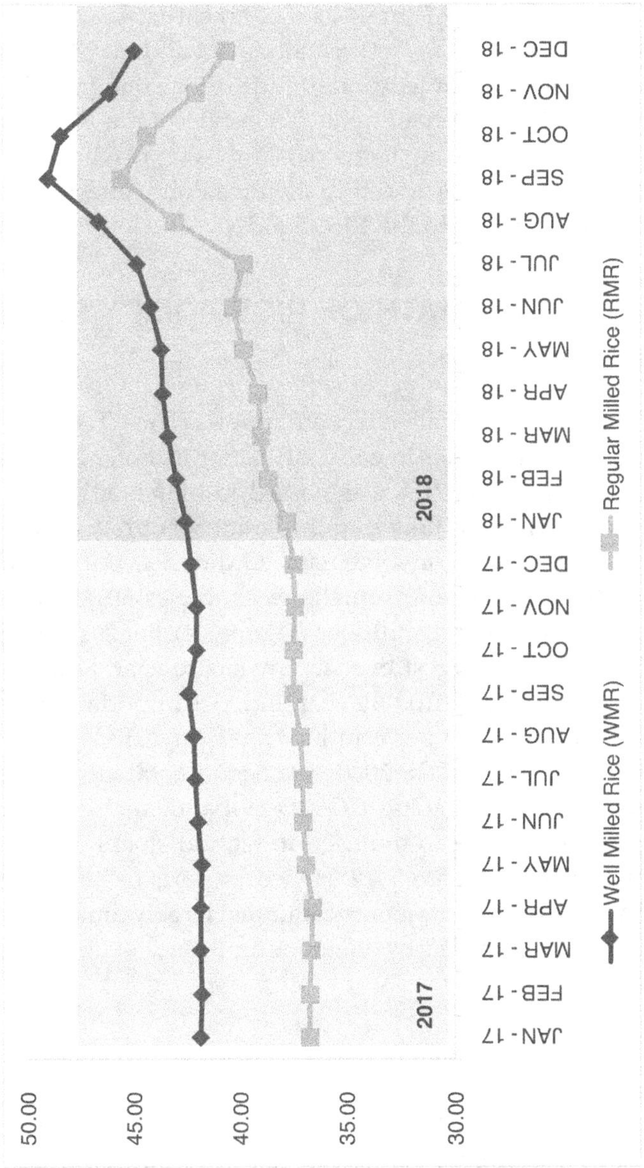

Source of basic data: PSA Openstat.

law forbids assigning quantity restrictions on the amount of rice to be covered by SPS clearance.
- The special safeguard provisions of an earlier law (namely RA 8800, the Special Safeguards Act) remain intact and may be invoked by the DA as additional but temporary tariff protection for rice.
- At least PhP10 billion annually is allocated for a Rice Fund. The law also provides that annual customs duties on rice imports in excess of PhP10 billion will be added to the Rice Fund, effectively earmarking rice customs duties to the Rice Fund.

THE AFTERMATH OF RICE POLICY REFORM

Imports

The RLA had an immediate effect on imports. The NFA had already been importing large quantities in early 2019 after its botched the 2018 import programme. When the RLA was passed in March 2019, large quantities of imports continued to flow into the country entirely as a private sector initiative, without NFA involvement. Ordinarily, imports ranged from 300,000 to 400,000 tons, but sometimes as low as 50,000 tons depending on market (and weather) conditions (Figure 3.4). For 2019, imports totalled 3.1 million tons, the largest ever in any single year. (The previous peak was 2.8 million tons in 2010.) By year-end, rice importation was estimated at 2.75 million tons, a 56 per cent increase over 2018 levels.

Significant arrivals in 2020 reached a total of 2.2 million tons, notwithstanding the ongoing COVID-19 pandemic. Peak imports were achieved in 2019 owing to the need to rebuild stocks after the abnormal inventory depletion in late 2018. Hence, imports began to slow down in 2020. Nonetheless, rice shipments continued largely uninterrupted, despite the export limits imposed by Vietnam on its rice exports from March to April 2020.

Prices

The deluge of imports had a noticeable impact on the domestic price (Figure 3.5). The export price of rice remained stable, as seen in the unit landed cost of imports (except in October 2020). Monthly prices of the two main types of milled rice in the country, well-milled (WMR) and regular

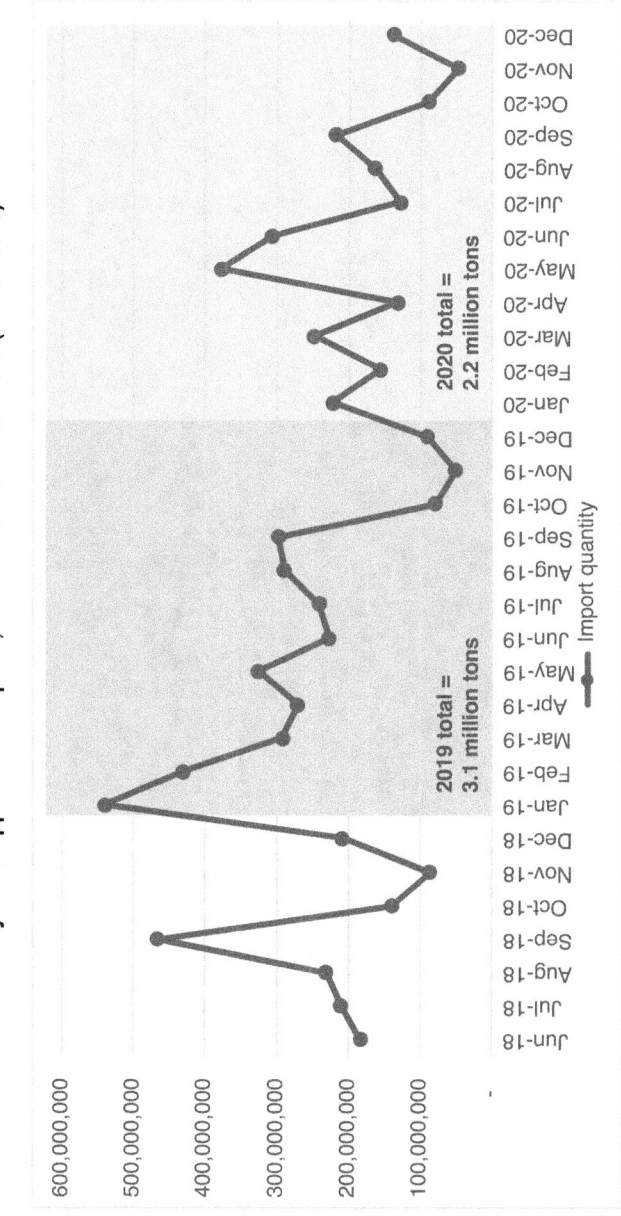

FIGURE 3.4
Quantity of Philippine Rice Imports, June 2018–December 2020 (million tons)

Source: Trademap.org.

Impact of COVID-19 on the Philippine Rice Sector

FIGURE 3.5
Unit Landed Value of Rice Imports and Wholesale Prices of Regular and Well-Milled Rice, June 2018–December 2020 (PhP)

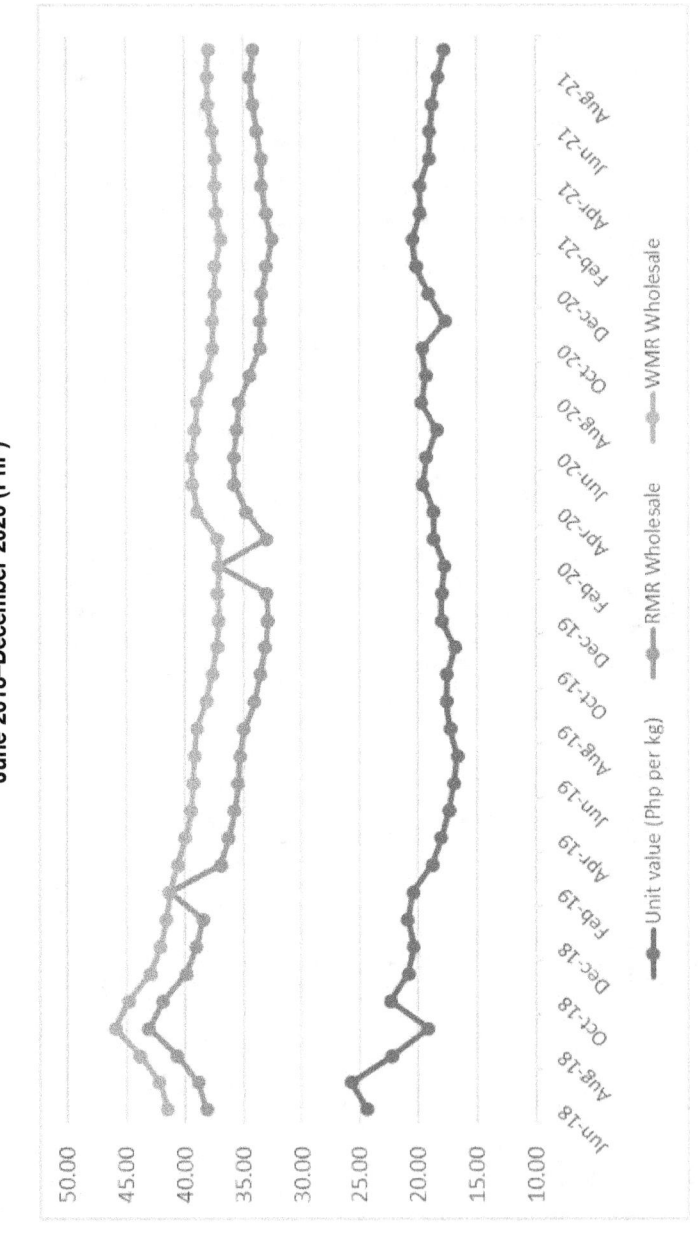

Source: Trademap (2022); PSA Openstat.

milled rice (RMR), show RMR slightly cheaper than WMR, both on a downward trajectory since late 2018.

Although the domestic price of RMR reacted somewhat to the COVID-19 crisis, retail prices mostly stabilized throughout 2020 and 2021, notwithstanding the spike in the landed cost of imports in October. The local rice market was held stable by stocks kept by marketing agents and millers. The overall trajectory was still downward, towards convergence with the prevailing international price.

Figure 3.6 shows additional details on the consumption side as of 2015. Rice accounted for a remarkably sizeable share of total expenditure for poor households, exceeding one-fifth compared to the average household share of one-eighth. The figure also indicates that the most important type of rice for the average Filipino consumer was RMR at 67 per cent of all household expenditure on rice. Among poor households, dependency on RMR was even greater at 72 per cent. The share of subsidized rice distributed by the NFA was 13 per cent; and for the average household, the NFA rice share was even lower at 6.7 per cent. The disappearance of NFA rice since 2019 has not led to a deleterious effect on poor households, as this was more than compensated by the more affordable price of the main rice consumed, RMR.

The decline in the market price of rice was further evident in the real opportunity cost in the purchasing power of a consumer for every kilogram (kg) of rice. The real cost to the consumer corrects the effect of inflation on the retail price. Based on a fixed value of the peso (2012 prices), 1 kg of RMR cost consumers PhP33.32 in 2017; by 2020 it was PhP29.95, or a 10 per cent decline in the real cost (Table 3.1). Similarly the real cost of WMR declined by 10 per cent.

Production

There was fear that intensified competition from imports would lead to a complete collapse of the domestic rice industry. On the contrary, from 2018 to 2019, paddy rice production increased at a rate of 1.2 per cent (Figure 3.7) and yields at a faster rate of 2.86 per cent. Although liberalization caused a contraction in the harvest area, yields grew when the more marginal areas, especially in rainfed zones, were taken out of cultivation, and already productive areas supported by modern irrigation continued to supply rice to the country (World Bank 2020).

FIGURE 3.6
Shares of Rice Expenditure, by Type of Household, 2015 (%)

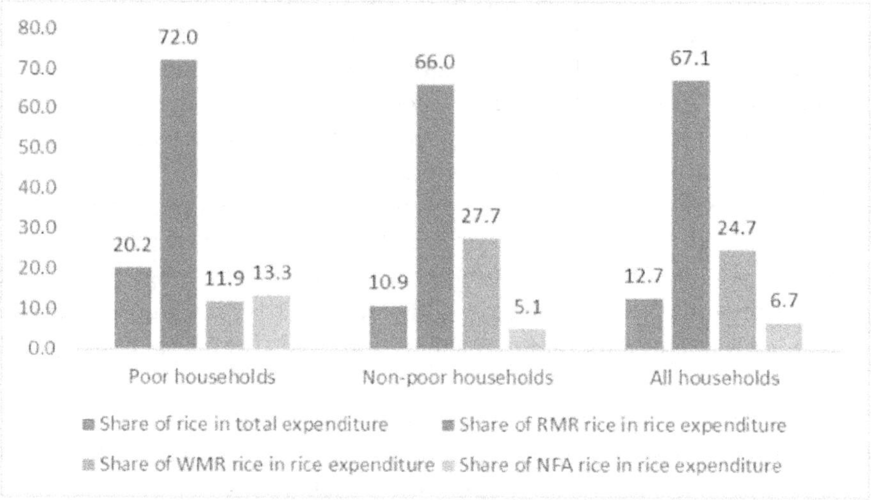

Household	Share of rice in total expenditure	Share of RMR rice in rice expenditure	Share of WMR rice in rice expenditure	Share of NFA rice in rice expenditure
Poor households	20.2	72.0	11.9	13.3
Non-poor households	10.9	66.0	27.7	5.1
All households	12.7	67.1	24.7	6.7

Source: PSA PUF of FIES 2018.

TABLE 3.1
Real Cost of Rice to the Consumer, 2017–20 (2012 = 100) (PhP per kg)

	2017	2018	2019	2020
WMR	37.79	38.35	35.55	33.80
RMR	33.32	34.74	31.52	29.95

Source of basic data: PSA Openstat.

Despite positive output trends, there is no denial of the economic losses suffered by farmers, as a counterpart to the welfare gains received by consumers. Initially, in some areas the drop in paddy price was quite dramatic. By August 2019, relative to average monthly prices in 2018, the average price nationwide was down by 20 per cent; in the Central Luzon "rice bowl", it fell 29 per cent, and 22 per cent in Cagayan Valley, another key rice-growing region. However, markets adjusted, and the differential outcomes by region tended to even out. The coefficient of variation of monthly paddy prices (a measure of the dispersion of prices across regions) started at 9.5 per cent in January, rising to its peak of 11.3 per cent in August,

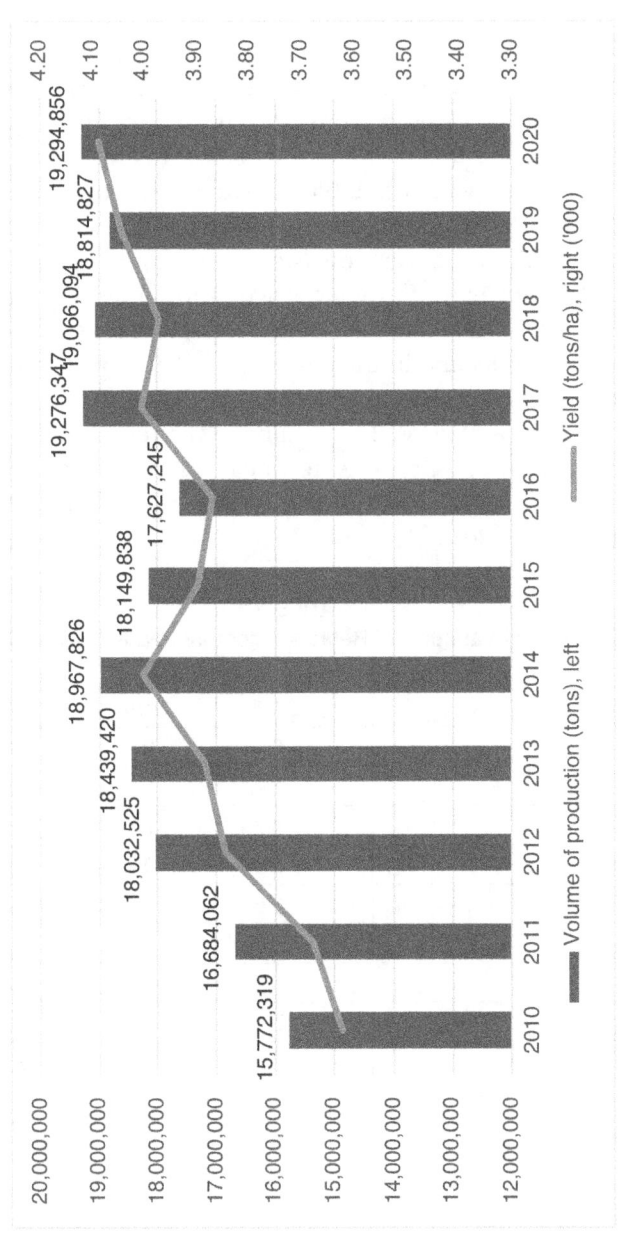

**FIGURE 3.7
Paddy Rice Output and Yield, 2010–20**

Source: PSA Openstat.

before declining to 8.4 per cent by December (Table 3.2). The full-year average coefficient of variation was 9.4 per cent in 2019, compared with 6.2 per cent in 2018; in contrast, the full-year average was approaching the 2018 level in 2020 at 7.4 per cent, and again in 2021 at 7.2 per cent.

Overall, paddy prices nationwide converged fairly quickly, hence the changing economic conditions of rice farmers can be gleaned from looking at national averages. Table 3.3 shows that the farmgate price of paddy rice rose to its highest levels in nominal terms in 2014 and 2018, the latter at PhP20.10 per kg, consistent with a retail price of PhP45 per kg. Since 2018, however, farmgate prices slid alongside the retail price, bringing the farmer back to 2013 paddy prices. However, there has been no commensurate decline in the cost of production per kg of paddy rice. Net returns per hectare (ha), from its peak of PhP32,976, fell by 35 per cent to PhP21,430 per ha in 2020. The decline in net returns was even sharper in real terms (in 2012 pesos)—the decline from the 2018 peak of PhP28,113 was 38 per cent down to PhP17,380, just slightly higher than real returns per ha way back in 2010.

TABLE 3.2
Coefficient of Variation of Regional Monthly Paddy Prices, 2018–21

	2018	*2019*	*2020*	*2021*
January	6.9	9.5	6.6	7.7
February	5.7	6.0	6.3	8.7
March	4.7	7.3	4.8	7.7
April	6.8	9.7	7.7	7.0
May	5.5	10.2	8.1	5.0
June	6.5	10.7	7.7	6.1
July	6.7	11.3	8.7	9.1
August	7.3	11.3	9.1	7.0
September	6.8	9.3	8.6	6.3
October	4.6	9.2	7.0	6.3
November	5.3	9.4	7.8	6.9
December	7.3	8.4	6.0	8.1
Average	6.2	9.4	7.4	7.2

TABLE 3.3
Cost and Returns per ha for the Average Rice Farmer, 2010–20 (in PhP)

	2010	2015	2016	2017	2018	2019	2020
Net returns	15,830	20,951	24,719	28,699	32,976	22,242	21,430
Cost per kg	10.5	12.0	11.0	11.1	11.8	11.5	11.5
Farmgate price per kg	14.9	17.3	17.4	18.2	20.1	17.0	16.8
Real returns (2012 = 100)	17,095	19,580	22,804	25,739	28,113	18,504	17,380

Source: PSA Openstat.

IMPLICATION OF THE REFORM

The RLA has had a great effect on the welfare of consumers. It helped to avoid a price spike even when Vietnam temporarily suspended exports in March and April 2020 due to shortage fears induced by the COVID-19 pandemic. Unlike the NFA, the private sector performed well in stabilizing the price of rice, without burdening government finances. The adverse economic impact of the COVID-19 crisis might have been much worse had there been no reform and the NFA still been in charge of imports. Another rice price crisis would have precipitated, especially as government funds were being reprioritized on a large scale towards the pandemic response.

This favourable assessment of the impact of reform should be balanced with the undeniable harm inflicted on another population segment, namely the rice farmer. Briones (2019) weighs benefits against cost and concludes that society as a whole was better off as a result of the reform. A later study shows that, with poverty measured purely in income terms (and not including the gain in purchasing power of consumers), it did increase slightly owing to the reduced income of paddy farmers.[5] However, the value of the Rice Fund was more than enough on an annual basis to sufficiently compensate rice farmers and eliminate the poverty effect (Briones 2020).[6] Nonetheless, owing in part to provisions of the RLA and bureaucratic inertia, farmers did not feel compensated for lower paddy prices. Hence, farmer organizations have pushed for the repeal of the law. As rice consumers are the chief beneficiaries of the RLA and also outnumber rice farmers, one may expect a much stronger counter-lobby in favour of preserving the law. There is, however, a curious asymmetry of political action, as lobbying has been entirely one-sided in favour of repeal.

One reason for the asymmetry is the lack of information. In an online survey conducted by the Philippine Institute of Development Studies with the support of the FAO, respondents were asked whether they believed the price of rice on January 2020 was above or below the price of rice in January 2019. The bulk of the respondents (76.3 per cent) thought that the price had increased over the interval (Table 3.4). More than a quarter (26.1 per cent) believed it was much higher than before. Only a small minority (11.9 per cent) presumed that prices had fallen. The share of those who believed the price was higher was high among those in Central Luzon (82 per cent), while Metro Luzon (NCR together with peripheral regions) had the lowest percentage of those holding this belief (73 per cent). This contradicts official statistics which show a decline from 2019 to 2020 (Table 3.1). The simplest explanation is that consumers are ignorant about the facts of the rice market—one may surmise that there is a psychological bias towards expecting rice price inflation over time.

Politicians tend to pander to popular opinion, however misinformed it is. The same survey elicited respondents' opinions of politicians promoting a policy of open importation. Options were in terms of the degree of agreement/disagreement with such a policy, ranging from strongly agree to strongly disagree. Table 3.5 shows that a majority (55 per cent)

TABLE 3.4
Distribution of Respondents' Estimate of Monthly Retail Price Change, January 2019–January 2020 (%)

	Total Sample	Central Luzon	Metro Luzon	Rest of the Philippines
Much higher	26.1	34.9	24.4	21.0
Moderately higher	26.9	25.0	26.7	28.5
Slightly higher	23.3	21.7	21.6	26.0
Same	11.7	10.5	13.6	11.0
Slightly lower	8.1	5.3	7.4	11.0
Moderately lower	3.4	2.6	5.7	2.0
Much lower	0.4	0.0	0.6	0.5

Source: Authors' data.

TABLE 3.5
Distribution of Respondents by Agreement/Disagreement with
Open Importation Policy (%)

	Full Sample	Central Luzon	Metro Luzon	Rest of the Philippines
Strongly agree	5.34	5.73	6.11	4.37
Agree	11.23	18.47	10	6.8
Neither agree nor disagree	28.18	32.48	23.33	29.13
Disagree	31.49	29.94	29.44	34.47
Strongly disagree	23.76	13.38	31.11	25.24

Source: Authors' data.

expressed disagreement with the policy, with the proportion of those disagreeing being highest in Metro Luzon (62 per cent). Remarkably, in Central Luzon, the largest rice-growing area of the country, less than half of the respondents expressed disagreement. Moreover, only 24 per cent expressed strong disagreement with the open import platform, with the proportion dropping to 13 per cent in Central Luzon. It is Metro Luzon, a heavily urbanized non-rice growing area, which has the largest proportion of respondents strongly disagreeing with the open import platform. Note further that a significant minority (28 per cent) expressed indifference to the policy; the proportion indifferent being largest in Central Luzon at 32 per cent, followed by the rest of the Philippines at 29 per cent.

CONCLUSION

The market reform in the rice industry was fortuitously timed, providing a reliable cushion for Filipino households enduring severe economic hardship under COVID-19 crisis conditions. Had the pre-reform policy regime been in place during the pandemic, another rice price crisis would have likely worsened the plight of the Filipino consumer already reeling from the economic crunch of the COVID-19 pandemic. However, the reform inflicted significant losses on paddy rice farmers, mainly due to competition from cheap rice imports rather than by any lasting effect of the pandemic. As a result, a powerful farmer lobby has been mobilized for the repeal of the RLA.

There is a very real prospect of the RLA being reviewed, amended or completely repealed, considering the populist pronouncements from candidates of the May 2022 elections. For instance, the presidential front runner, Ferdinand Marcos, Jr., the eventual winner, included an amendment of the RLA as part of his platform towards reverting the NFA to its regulatory and commercial function. Rice prices will be kept low for consumers, but paddy prices high for farmers—guaranteeing a worsening fiscal deficit just when fiscal space is constrained by the pandemic response. Unfortunately, owing to a lack of information or perhaps strong cultural attachment, consumers are politically predisposed towards rice self-sufficiency and against rice imports. Such proposals are puzzling only if one views political decisions as purely a result of rationalistic cost-benefit calculation. Very few political decisions are reached in this way; the reality is considerably messier with various interest groups in constant tension and opposition. From this perspective, uncertainty over the shelf life of contentious policies is inevitable.

Notwithstanding these risks, there is some basis for optimism. Sustaining reform does not lie in mobilizing consumers to seek its retention. Rather, the key is for the same confluence of factors that led to the reform in 2018–19 to hold firm. First, the anti-corruption message, effective in originally defusing advocacy for NFA intervention, should be kept fresh in the public consciousness. Second, the WTO must strongly resist the reversal of the QR, thereby lending support to the domestic constituency for maintaining WTO compliance. This role of the international community in the political economy of reform has been pointed out elsewhere (e.g. Anderson, Rausser, and Swinnen 2013). Third, the new government's economic team consisting of the Economic Cluster of the Cabinet (appointees of the President and approved by Congress), together with the monetary authority (holdovers from the current administration), must commit unwaveringly to fiscal sustainability and macroeconomic stability. Such commitment will hopefully persuade them to secure the support of the new President, to steer the country away from the fiscal maelstrom of an interventionist NFA.

Notes

1. Inter-agency Task Force for the Management of Emerging Infectious Disease Resolution No. 14, Series of 2020, Department of Health, Philippines.

2. Excepting the Board of Liquidators of the Bangko Sentral, the country's monetary authority.
3. The NFA Council is equivalent to a Board of Directors, while NFA management, led by the Administrator, is analogous to a corporate CEO. Council members are representatives of various government agencies, including economic planning, finance, and the monetary authority. The Council is chaired by the mother agency, at the time the Office of the Cabinet Secretary.
4. https://interaksyon.philstar.com/breaking-news/2018/02/28/121316/senators-grill-nfa-overdwindling-stock-panic-gaps-in-buying-practices-rice-smuggling/ (accessed 20 November 2021).
5. The analysis, however, could not distinguish between farmers using modern irrigation and rainfed systems.
6. Implementation of compensation, however, is another matter.

References

Anderson, Kym, Gordon Rausser, and Johan Swinnen. 2013. "Political Economy of Public Policies: Insights from Distortions to Agricultural and Food Markets". *Journal of Economic Literature* 51, no. 2:423–77.

Briones, Roehlano. 2017. "Food (In)security and the Price of Rice Self-Sufficiency". In *Unintended Consequences: The Folly of Uncritical Thinking*, edited by Vincente B. Paqueo, Arniceto C. Orbeta Jr., and Gilberto M. Llanto, pp. 91–102. Quezon City: Philippine Institute for Development Studies.

———. 2018. "Options for Reform of the National Food Authority". Policy Notes no. 2018-09. Quezon City: Philippine Institute for Development Studies.

———. 2019. "Welfare Impacts of Rice Tariffication". Discussion Paper Series no. 2019-16. Quezon City: PIDS.

———. 2020. "Did the Opening Up of Rice Importation in the Philippines Worsen Income Poverty and Inequality? A General Equilibrium with Microsimulation Approach". Discussion Paper Series no. 2020-43. Quezon City: Philippine Institute for Development Studies.

———, et al. 2021. *Revitalizing Philippine Irrigation: A Systems and Governance Assessment for the 21st Century*. Quezon City: Philippine Institute for Development Studies.

Castillo, Gelia T. 1975. *All in a Grain of Rice*. Los Baños, Laguna, Philippines: Southeast Asian Regional Centre for Graduate Study and Research in Agriculture.

Chiba, Yoshihiro. 2010. "The 1919 and 1935 Rice Crises in the Philippines: The Rice Market and Starvation in American Colonial Times". *Philippine Studies* 58, no. 4: 523–56.

David, Christina, Ponciano Intal, and Arsenio M. Balisacan. 2007. "Distortions to Agricultural Incentives in the Philippines". In *Distortions to Agricultural Incentives in Asia*, edited by Kym Anderson and Will Martin, pp. 223–54. Washington, DC: World Bank.

Davidson, Jamie S. 2016. "Why the Philippines Chooses to Import Rice". *Critical Asian Studies* 48, no. 1: 100–22.

Dawe, David C. 2006. "The Philippines Imports Rice Because It Is an Island Nation". In *Why Does the Philippines Import Rice? Meeting the Challenge of Trade Liberalization*, edited by David C. Dawe, Piedad F. Moya, and Cheryll B. Casiwan, pp. 3–8. Laguna, Philippines: International Rice Research Institute and Philippine Rice Research Institute.

DBM (Department of Budget Management). 2022. "National Government Expenditures". Budget of Expenditures and Sources of Financing FY 2022. https://www.dbm.gov.ph/index.php/budget-documents/2022/budget-of-expenditures-and-sources-of-financing-fy-2022 (accessed 30 April 2022).

Department of Health, Philippines. 2020. Inter-agency Task Force for the Management of Emerging Infectious Disease Resolution no. 14, Series of 2020. https://doh.gov.ph/sites/default/files/health-update/IATF-RESO-14.pdf (accessed 6 February 2022).

Doeppers, Daniel F. 2016. *Feeding Manila in Peace and War, 1850–1945*. Madison, WI: University of Wisconsin Press.

Esguerra, Emmanuel. F. 1981. "An Assessment of the Masagana 99 Credit Subsidy as an Equity Measure". *Philippine Review of Economics* 18, nos. 3 and 4: 168–91.

FAO. 2021. "Rapid Assessment of the Impact of COVID-19 on Food Supply Chains in the Philippines". Manila. https://doi.org/10.4060/cb2622en (accessed 19 November 2021).

———. 2022. "Crops and Livestock Products". FAOSTAT. https://www.fao.org/faostat/en/#data/TCL (accessed 20 January 2022).

Fang, Arnold H. 2016. "Linkage between Rural Voters and Politicians: Effects on Rice Policies in Philippines and Thailand". *Asia and the Pacific Policy Studies* 3, no. 3: 505–17.

Hapal, Karl. 2021. "The Philippines' COVID-19 Response: Securitising the Pandemic and Disciplining the Pasaway". *Journal of Current Southeast Asian Affairs* 40, no. 2: 224–44.

Headey, Derek D. 2011. "Rethinking the Global Food Crisis: The Role of Trade Shocks". *Food Policy* 36, no. 2: 136–46.

Herdt, Robert W., and C. Capule. 1983. *Adoption, Spread, and Production Impact of Modern Rice Varieties in Asia*. Los Baños, Laguna, Philippines: International Rice Research Institute.

Intal, Ponciano S., and Marissa C. Garcia, 2008. "Rice and Philippine Politics". PIDS Discussion Paper Series 2008-01. Makati City: Philippine Institute for Development Studies.

Jha, Shikha, and Anoju Mehta. 2008. *Effectiveness of Public Spending: The Case of Rice Subsidies in the Philippines.* Manila: Asian Development Bank.

Kajisa, Kei, and Takamasa Akiyama. 2005. "The Evolution of Rice Price Policies over Four Decades: Thailand, Indonesia and the Philippines". *Oxford Development Studies* 33, no. 2: 305–29.

Kerkvliet, Benedict J. 1974. "Land Reform in the Philippines since the Marcos Coup". *Pacific Affairs* 47, no. 3: 286–304.

Otsuka, Keijiro. 1991. "Determinants and Consequences of Land Reform Implementation in the Philippines". *Journal of Development Economics* 35, no. 2: 339–55.

Patel, R. 2013. "The Long Green Revolution". *Journal of Peasant Studies* 40, no. 1, p. 5.

PSA (Philippine Statistics Authority). 2022. *Statistical Tables on 2018 Family Income and Expenditure Survey.* https://psa.gov.ph/content/statistical-tables-2018-family-income-and-expenditure-survey

Tolentino, V. Bruce J., and Beulah Maria de la Pena. 2011. "Stymied Reforms in Rice Marketing in the Philippines". *Built on Dreams, Grounded on Reality*. Makati City: Asia Foundation.

———, and Beulah Maria de la Pena. 2020. "Deregulation and Tariffication at Last: The Saga of Rice Sector Reform in the Philippines". BSP Working Paper Series no. 2020–06. Manila: Bangko Sentral ng Pilipinas.

World Bank. 2020. *Transforming Philippine Agriculture During COVID-19 and Beyond.* Washington, DC: World Bank.

WTO (World Trade Organization). 2022. *Agriculture Explanation: Market Access.* https://www.wto.org/english/tratop_e/agric_e/ag_intro02_access_e.htm (accessed 30 April 2022).

4

The Indonesian Rice Economy during the COVID-19 Pandemic

Bustanul Arifin

INTRODUCTION

The COVID-19 pandemic caused an economic recession in Indonesia where growth contracted for four consecutive quarters. In 2020, the contraction was recorded at 2.07 per cent. Meanwhile, as of early 2022, the pandemic had infected an estimated 6 million people or more. More than 150,000 or 2.7 per cent of those infected have died. This death rate is slightly higher than the global average of 2.2 per cent. The pandemic caused by the severe acute respiratory syndrome coronavirus 2 (SARS-CoV-2) has crippled the Indonesian and global economies, reducing business interactions among residents due to the rapid infectiousness of the virus. The subsequent variant Delta hit Indonesia harder, spreading more quickly and deadlier.

In 2021, the Indonesian economy grew at 3.69 per cent (year-on-year), which was below the official forecast of 4.62 per cent. The agricultural sector, however, grew by 1.84 per cent, in part cushioning the COVID-19 recession. As a result, by September 2021, the country's poverty rate dipped to 9.71 per cent, or down by 26.50 million people. The majority of the poor live in rural areas, numbering 14.64 million or 12.53 per cent of the total population. They include farmers, smallholders, landless farmers and farm labourers who are disproportionately vulnerable to exogenous, economic shocks such as the COVID-19 pandemic. The pandemic also increased the unemployment rate to 7.07 per cent of total labour in August 2020, up from 5.23 per cent a year earlier. More specifically, the unemployment rate was 2.56 million or 14.28 per cent among the working-age population in 2020, based on workers who stopped working due to the pandemic since February 2020. Fortunately, total unemployment decreased to 6.49 per cent in August 2021 as the economy began showing signs of recovery.

Moreover, the pandemic has caused a "ruralization phenomenon" in the Indonesian economy, similar to what happened during the Asian Financial Crisis in 1997 and 1998. A significant number of urban labourers returned to rural areas to work in the agricultural sector when the urban-based industry and service sectors collapsed. Before the pandemic, in August 2019, the agricultural labour force was 35.45 million or 27.53 per cent of the total 128.76 million labour force. By August 2020, agricultural labour increased to 38.78 million or 29.76 per cent. A year later, the "ruralization phenomenon" seemed to have run its course; agricultural labour fell again to 28.33 per cent. This rural labour spike, even if temporary, would be a burden to the agricultural sector where labour productivity is low. Therefore, changes in agricultural production and post-harvest technology, including agricultural digitalization, are desperately needed.

Rice has been and remains a staple food in Indonesia, although the level of rice consumption has fallen, especially among the middle class. However, with total population growth at 1.64 per cent per year, total rice consumption has been growing at 2.14 per cent each year. Among middle-income groups, carbohydrates have shifted to flour-based foodstuffs. Because wheat is not grown in Indonesia, the country has become one of the world's largest wheat importers. The downward trend in rice consumption among the middle class will continue especially as consumption of food outside the home, including that of fast food among millennial youth and urban denizens, grows.

During the pandemic, the Indonesian rice economy was affected significantly, although less than the broader economy. Early in the pandemic, farmers remained tending their fields, growing rice and other crops as the virus was then spreading in dense urban areas. By late 2020, however, logistics and food distribution systems had been disrupted and the pandemic began to impact farmers' livelihoods and rural areas.

This chapter examines the impact of the COVID-19 pandemic on the Indonesian rice economy, by exploring recent developments in the rice sector and policy responses for food and agriculture. A data series of rice production, productivity and sustainability issues are analysed to present the performance of the rice economy amid disparities across regions. Future policy changes regarding social assistance, strategies to improve production and productivity, technological change, digitalization of value chain options and human capital investment beyond the pandemic are also explored.

PRODUCTIVITY AND COMPETITIVENESS OF THE RICE ECONOMY

Before the COVID-19 pandemic, the productivity and competitiveness of the Indonesian rice economy faced serious challenges, including an extreme drought in 2019. Using the new area sample frame (KSA) method, the Central Statistics Agency (BPS) reported that from 2018 to 2019, the harvest area of rice fell by 6.14 per cent, from 11.38 million to 10.68 million hectares (BPS 2022a). Accordingly, rice production declined from 33.94 to 31.33 million tonnes or a 7.81 per cent decrease (Table 4.1).

TABLE 4.1
Productivity Performance of the Indonesian Rice Economy, 2018–21

	2018	2019	2020	2021	Change 2018–19	Change 2019–20	Change 2020–21
Consumption (million tonnes)	29.56	28.93	29.40	30.04	−2.03	1.52	2.18
Production —dry paddy (million tonnes)	59.19	54.60	54.65	54.41	−7.76	0.09	−0.43
Production—rice (million tonnes)	33.94	31.31	31.50	31.36	−7.81	0.64	−0.45
Harvested Area (million Ha.)	11.38	10.68	10.66	10.41	−6.14	−0.18	−2.34
Productivity (tonne/ha)	5.20	5.11	5.13	5.23	−1.72	0.27	1.96

Source: Calculated from BPS data, the latest is February 2022.

Another challenge has been the massive conversion of paddy fields to non-agricultural use, especially in productive rice areas such as the north coast of Java. Consequently, rice productivity also fell from 5.20 to 5.11 tonnes/ha. This is due to the low level of technological change both on-farm and off-farm or in post-harvest sectors.

Successful agricultural development contributes greatly to poverty alleviation by increasing income, labour productivity and the sector's competitiveness. The ratio of land to labour in Indonesia, however, is decreasing because labour continues to grow, while land is almost constant, if not declining. The decline in rice productivity may be due to the decline in Indonesia's agricultural production capacity. Efforts to increase land productivity must continue to be higher than the reduction of the land-to-labour ratio. Agricultural development requires a technological change to increase production as well as land and labour productivity.

During the peak of the pandemic, rice production and productivity improved slightly, although the harvested area decreased to 10.66 million hectares in 2020. Compared to 2019, rice production in 2020 increased to 31.49 million tonnes and productivity improved to 5.13 tonnes/ha, although still a decrease from 2018. In 2021, rice production decreased slightly from 2020, although rice productivity had increased marginally mostly due to increasing rice intensification and marginal technological changes in both on-farm and off-farm sectors. Rice production decreased to 31.36 million tonnes in 2021 or a 0.41 per cent decrease from 2020 to 2021, whereas productivity increased to 5.23 tonnes/ha in 2021 or a 1.96 per cent improvement. In 2021, the weather was more favourable than in 2019 and 2020 (see Table 4.1). Technological changes, particularly the use of improved seed varieties and certified seeds as well as a rice production intensification strategy, also contributed to improved productivity in 2021. It is worth noting that Indonesia's rice productivity of 5.23 tonnes/ha is above the productivity of Thailand (3.1 tonnes/ha), Myanmar (3.8 tonnes/ha), the Philippines (4 tonnes/ha) and Malaysia (4.1 tonnes/ha), although lower than Vietnam (5.8 tonnes/ha), Japan (6.6 tonnes/ha) and China (7.0 tonnes/ha) (FAO 2021a).

From 2020 to 2021, Indonesia's harvested rice area declined by 245,000 hectares or a 2.34 per cent decrease. The decline was a threat to the government's target of achieving food self-sufficiency, especially for rice. The country's rice field expansion programme (extensification) does not immediately result in higher production, since the development of a new food production centre is a complex process that requires time. This includes food estate developments in non-traditional rice growing areas of Central Kalimantan, North Sumatra and East Nusa Tenggara. Converting forests and shrubs into food production areas requires adequate intervention, assistance and funding. The combination of extensification and intensification should contribute to improved food production and land productivity, but risks abound.

The legal instrument for preventing rice field conversion has long been enacted. Law Number 41 of 2009 for the Protection of Sustainable Food Agricultural Land has been in effect for more than a decade. There are also several government regulations related to rice field conversion. However, these legal instruments have been ineffective because they are related to the formulation of land use policies as well as spatial planning at the regional level which involves many agencies and conflicts of interest.

The legal approach requires bolstering with economic incentives, improvement of price policies, development of production technology, infrastructure improvement, governance and irrigation systems, and land use policies. For example, policy instruments for food availability and price stabilization need to be continued, accompanied by improvements in field implementation. Rice price stabilization has been quite good; it even dropped from Rp11,800 per kilogram (kg) in January 2021 to Rp11,750 a year later. Improvements in productivity and stock management appear to have been effective in containing price surges, including in cities or towns outside rice production centres. One impact of rice price stability has been the increase in consumption to 2.18 per cent per year.

An important wedge issue is the disparity between rice-producing provinces with higher productivity and rice-consuming provinces. The former includes provinces in Java, Bali, West Nusa Tenggara, Aceh, North Sumatra, West Sumatra, South Sumatra, Lampung and South Sulawesi. Their productivity is generally over five tonnes/ha, indicated by the lighter shades of grey in Figure 4.1. Other rice-producing provinces have acidic soils and swampy rice fields with lower productivity of three tonnes/ha or less. Some areas and certain districts in rice-deficit provinces enjoy high productivity, but are inadequate to serve as rice baskets for the regions. Strategies to boost production and productivity should ideally be based on local conditions, and cover both the agro-ecosystem and social-economic dimensions in policy intervention.

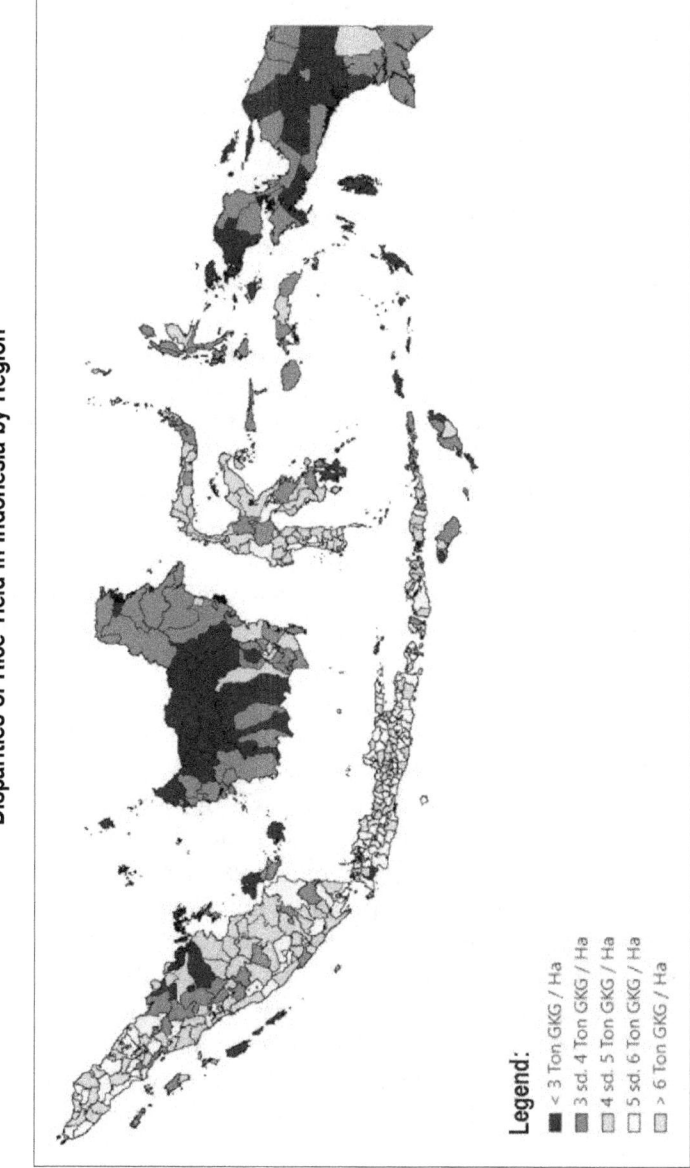

FIGURE 4.1
Disparities of Rice Yield in Indonesia by Region

Note: Calculated based on harvested area and rice production in 2021.

Local governments can offer tax relief for producers as an incentive to reduce the rate of paddy field conversion, which, in turn, would improve production and productivity. This should be complemented by farmers' empowerment, agricultural extension, technical assistance for farmers to adopt technological change, provision of high-yielding varieties, seed and fertilizers, access to information and capital and agricultural financing and farmers' connectedness with the market.

Both the central and local governments have legal and technical responsibilities in the improvement of the productive capacity of the agricultural sector. For example, rice production systems are highly vulnerable to disruptions in water availability, so the conservation of water resources is imperative. Changes in agricultural technology too can increase production capacity. The central and local governments need to improve the sustainability of agricultural systems, especially to maintain rice production and productivity. Investment in soil health matters is as crucial as improvements in irrigation management, environmental-friendly cropping patterns and crop-rotation systems, among others. Finally, the empowerment of farmer groups or organizations and other rural economic institutions will also prove beneficial.

Although rice productivity in Indonesia compares favourably to other rice-producing countries in the region, as we saw above, the competitiveness of the Indonesian rice economy fares less well. Based on a cost structure survey conducted by the BPS in 2018, the total production cost of rice was Rp13.56 million per hectare, with labour comprising the highest cost (48.79 per cent), followed by land rent (25.61 per cent) and cost of fertilizer (9.43 per cent) (BPS 2022b). Although BPS does not publish detailed cost structures for each region, the cost structures vary depending on the performance of the farming system in each region. These estimates are similar to those found in a previous comparative study among six Asian rice-producing countries (Bordey et al. 2016), which found that rice production in Indonesia costs Rp4,079 per kg. This is about 2.5 times higher than in Vietnam, and about double the costs in Thailand and India. More specifically, the labour cost of Rp1,115 per kg in Indonesia is nearly ten times that in Vietnam (Rp120 per kg) and about eight times higher than in Thailand (Rp172 per kg). Indonesia has been promoting agricultural mechanization, precision agriculture, smart farming and digitalization of agricultural value chains, all of which could contribute to reducing labour costs. Beyond labour costs, improvements in milling and processing technology could also help boost the competitiveness of Indonesian rice (Arifin 2020; Sawit 2021). Without these technological changes, Indonesian rice will lag in competitiveness in the international market.

The indicators of the coefficient of variation (CV) of medium and premium rice prices in Figure 4.2 shed light on price stability in the Indonesian rice economy. It shows the differences between the price of medium-quality Indonesian rice and the global price of 25 per cent broken rice in Thailand, Vietnam and India (panel A) and between premium Indonesian rice and the global rice prices for 5 per cent broken rice in Thailand and Vietnam (panel B).

In 2017, the CV of medium rice prices in the global market was 4.58 in Thailand, 5.74 in Vietnam and 3.69 in India, which were far higher than the CV of rice prices of 1.13 for medium quality I and 1.04 for medium quality II in the Indonesia market. The CV of global rice prices during the COVID-19 pandemic in 2020 and 2021 was far higher than those in domestic markets when Thailand and Vietnam reduced trade volumes on the global market. The same trend was seen in premium rice prices in the global market in 2020 and 2021; their CVs were 6.26 and 3.13 in Thailand and 10.50 and 10.41 in Vietnam, respectively. These are all far higher than the CV of rice prices in Indonesia, at 0.23 and 0.47 for rice of premium quality I and 0.28 and 0.63 for premium quality II rice.

The stability of Indonesian rice prices during the pandemic owed to more than successful government intervention. The private sector's increasing role in the national rice market also played a part. The association of rice millers and traders (PERPADI) has been quite active in mitigating the disruption of rice supply by encouraging specific arrangements such as contract farming between millers or traders and farmers or farmers' organizations. The performance of rice production during the main harvest season in March and April of 2020, as noted above, was also good, although less impressive than in 2018. Overall, rice production in the last two years showed a positive trend and seemed to have returned to normal or to production levels before the extreme drought in 2019, except for problems caused by paddy field conversion to other uses. Compared to other strategic foods such as maize and soybean, the logistics system for rice is relatively more advanced, as the flow of rice from production centres or rice-surplus regions to consumption centres or rice-deficit regions has not been significantly disrupted. The contract farming system between farmers and traders or millers, although not formally written, has

FIGURE 4.2
Coefficient Variation of Medium and Premium Rice Prices, 2017–21

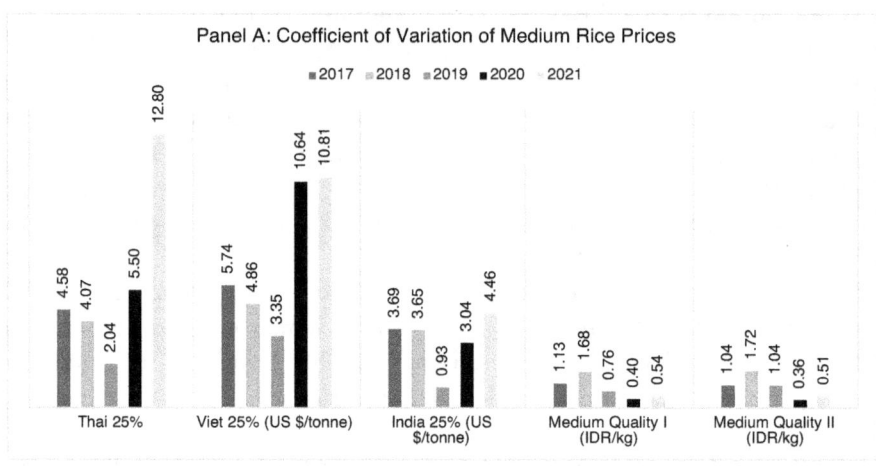

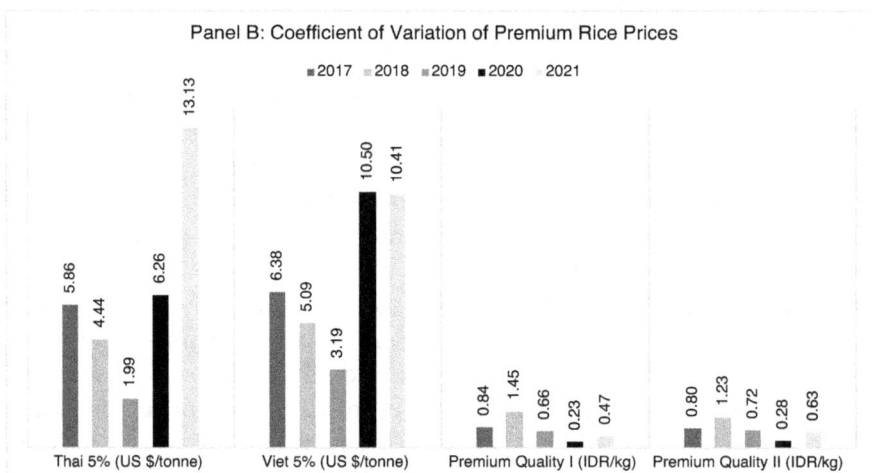

Source: Calculated from FAO for international prices; PIHPS (2022) for domestic prices.

contributed to the domestic and even inter-island rice trade in Indonesia. For example, the provincial capital of South Sulawesi, Makassar has become an important rice trade hub for eastern Indonesia, where rice from Java and other surplus regions are marketed throughout Sulawesi, the Maluku Islands and Papua New Guinea. Some amount of rice from

Sulawesi is also shipped to Surabaya and Jakarta based on the trading system arrangements between rice traders or private sectors in general.

Improving the competitiveness of Indonesian rice also requires the support of off-farm policies. Agricultural financing, increased market access, guaranteed buying of farmers' grains with adequate price incentives, guaranteed selling price for farmers and business certainty number among such policies. Similarly, the rice agribusiness system requires improvements in institutional arrangements, consolidation of farming system management and increases in the economies of scale of rice production. The application of mechanical technology in rice production, the use of tractors, combined harvesters and other post-harvest handling and management could potentially improve the efficiency of rice milling and processing. Improving rice productivity may reduce the unit costs of rice production in Indonesia and increase the competitiveness of the rice economy in general.

One important lesson from the disruption of the rice production system during the pandemic has been that the opportunity to produce higher-quality rice remains open, especially to meet the demand from the special market segment of the middle class with higher purchasing power. As the price fluctuation of rice in Indonesia is more stable than that in neighbouring countries, the future of the Indonesian rice economy should be veered towards improving the competitiveness of the rice industry and the efficiency of rice value chains.

VALUE-CHAIN RESILIENCE OF RICE AND OTHER STRATEGIC FOODS

The COVID-19 pandemic showed that the value-chain resilience of rice is as important as productivity and competitiveness. The price of rice and other strategic foods has fluctuated due to problems in food availability, supply issues and logistic systems.

The Indonesian government has acknowledged a looming food crisis as warned by the Food and Agriculture Organization (FAO) and other international agencies. In response, the government has allocated special funds for handling the pandemic while preparing a national economic recovery programme. The government has bolstered staple and strategic food stocks to ensure food access for those affected by COVID-19; it also has carried out comprehensive food policy reforms for the future.

Global food prices in 2020 did not experience a significant increase because global food stocks were good, crops were adequate, the weather was favourable and global oil prices were at record lows. Some global food commodities even experienced a surge in production, especially grain-based foods such as rice. Yet, international rice prices have crept up since April 2020, even reaching US$500 per tonne as the volume of rice trade declined (Figure 4.3). Major producers such as Thailand, Vietnam and Myanmar will prioritize domestic rice needs and the remainder for the global market. Despite high rice production, demand for Chinese rice remains very high due to the country's enormous population. India and Pakistan could serve as alternative sources of rice when traditional rice-producing countries are reluctant to export rice. Generally, rice prices in India and Pakistan are cheaper than those in Thailand and Vietnam, although Indonesia is not the main destination of rice exports from India and Pakistan. Their traditional market destinations include Africa and the Middle East, although the global rice market has witnessed an uptick in competitiveness of late.

When the problem of food access (demand side) is compounded by the problem of food availability (supply side), a food crisis is bound to occur. In addition, access to food among the lower-middle class has decreased dramatically due to their high unemployment rate. Food prices in real terms have become more expensive due to declining purchasing power, although nominal prices have not changed much. On the other hand, procuring food, especially import-based, has become problematic, because excessive dependence is a risk factor in itself. The government must avoid the two sources of food crisis transmission so that issues on the demand side do not occur simultaneously with those on the supply side. Failure or delay in anticipating this crisis will have devastating socio-economic and political impacts because the level of food sensitivity is very high.

Fortunately, there was no serious food crisis in Indonesia in 2021, except for a temporary shortage of cooking oil; by early 2022, this shortage was overcome with specific government interventions. In terms of value-chain resilience, rice is used as a barometer for food availability, although Indonesia has alternative carbohydrate sources such as cassava, sweet potatoes, canna, sago and others. The availability of local food is quite limited as the industrialization of carbohydrate-based ingredients into flour is yet to be available on a commercial scale. The anticipation of a rice price surge in 2022 is worrying, as the increase in global fertilizer prices

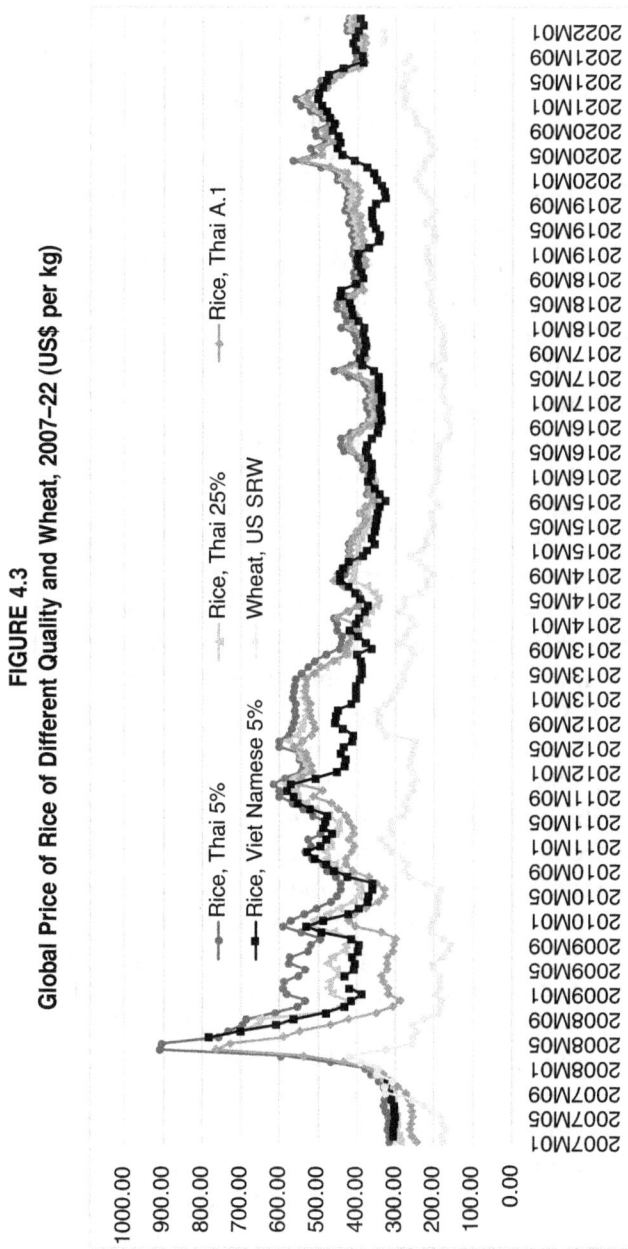

FIGURE 4.3
Global Price of Rice of Different Quality and Wheat, 2007–22 (US$ per kg)

Source: World Bank, Commodity Prospects, April 2022.

due to disruptions caused by Russia's invasion of Ukraine will push up the cost of rice production.

It is instructive to compare rice price dynamics with those of other strategic commodities in Indonesia. The retail price of imported sugar and beef has increased significantly since the end of 2021, especially during the Ramadan holiday season of 2022. A high import dependence on sugar (50 per cent) and beef (30 per cent) cause these commodity prices to fluctuate. Delays in the approval of import permits have worsened matters too, as have cattle supply problems in Australia. The price of horticulture products, such as shallots and red and hot chillies, has also fluctuated sharply, although this is not due to the pandemic; it is a regular feature of availability between rainy and dry seasons. Like Indonesia's rice economy, that of horticulture needs improvement too. Existing policies are overly focused on supply; those related to demand-driven or market-driven approaches are lacking. Improving the governance of contract farming between horticulture farmers and buyers, such as supermarket chain stores and hotels in big cities, could contribute to better price formation and the welfare of horticulture farmers (Firdaus et al. 2022).

A simple analysis of the coefficient of variation (CV), by dividing the standard deviation by the mean of the prices of staple and strategic foods in the domestic market shows some interesting results. Figure 4.4 shows that the smallest CV of prices before the pandemic in 2017 was found for cooking oil (0.72) and beef (0.79) and the highest was for hot chillies (47.32) and red chillies (19.41). At the time, their high prices became major contributors to the inflation rate and were widely discussed in public and within the government. To reduce the seasonal fluctuation of their prices, there have been some discussions and planned initiatives from the central and local governments as well as the private sector to develop cold storage and cold value chains. Price fluctuation of these strategic foods, however, remains high. After the 2020 peak of the pandemic in 2021, the smallest CV of prices was found for rice (0.51) and sugar (0.86), the highest for hot chillies (28.63), red chillies (20.49) and cooking oil (9.54). Overall, the CV for strategic food commodities dipped in 2021, compared to during the pandemic's peak in 2020 (Figure 4.5).

Generally, the modern rice industry involves large-scale private sector growth too, despite a lack of supporting, if not controversial, policies. Consider the case of PT IBU (Indo Beras Utama), which might hinder the growth of large-scale private sector involvement in the rice industry. In

FIGURE 4.4
Price Fluctuation of Staple and Strategic Foods, 2018–22

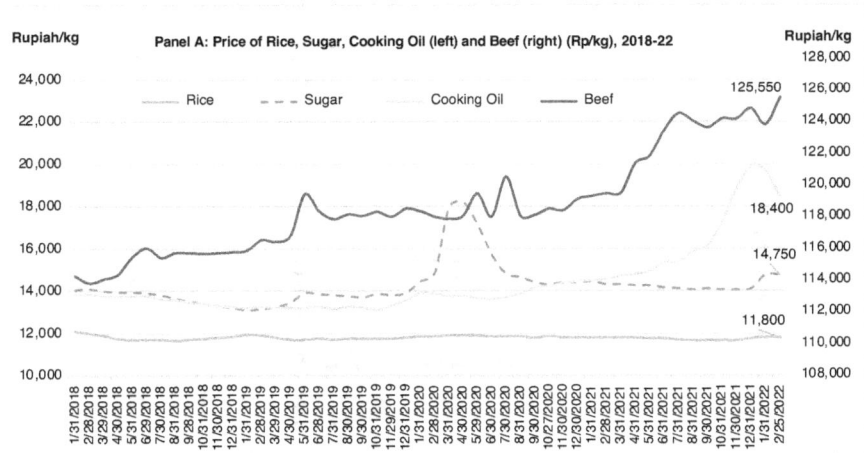
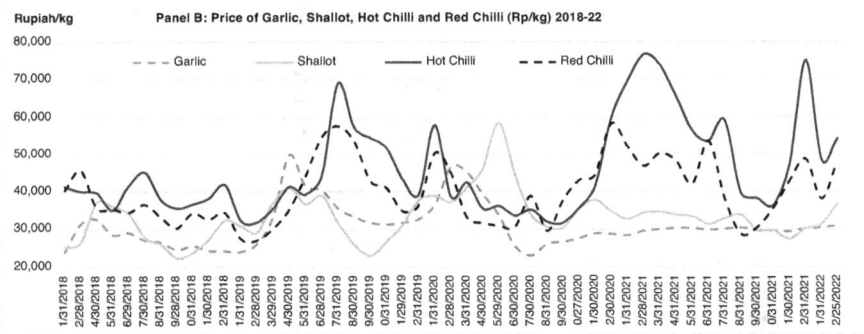

Source: PIHPS (Center of Price Information for Strategic Foods, Bank Indonesia, March 2022).

2017, PT IBU, a subsidiary of PT Tiga Pilar Sejahtera (TPS), was accused of selling subsidized rice (set by the government at Rp9,500 per kg) at premium grade prices (Rp13,700 and 20,400 per kg for two different brands). The company denied any wrongdoing, as medium-quality rice, it argued, could be processed into premium rice, using a simple rice-processing method (*Jakarta Post*, 25 August 2017). The scandal showed the lack of trust between the government and private actors, which will curtail the future participation of private capital in the sector.

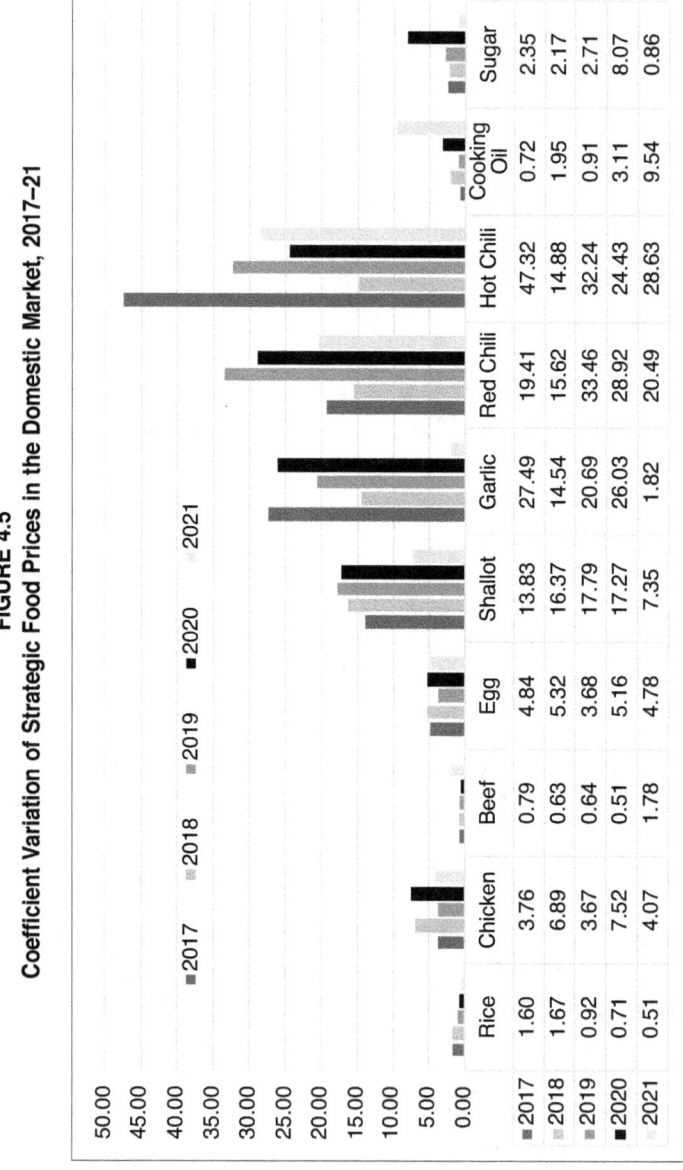

FIGURE 4.5
Coefficient Variation of Strategic Food Prices in the Domestic Market, 2017–21

Source: Calculated from PIHPS, 2017–21.

Prior to this, there had been moderate growth in private sector activity. The Wilmar Group, for instance, has invested in the integrated rice business in Indonesia. The group is among the world's largest rice millers, with more than 60 rice mills globally and an annual total supply of 7 million tonnes. In Indonesia, the company has established sales and distribution networks among traditional outlets, supermarkets, convenience stores and hypermarts. It also provides a wide range of premium rice products, including brown rice, milled rice, fragrant rice, enriched rice and broken rice, among others. A main challenge for private sector growth in Indonesia is how the government develops avenues for fair partnerships between private actors and smallholders. Developing contract farming between farmers and companies and maintaining efficient and transparent rice value chains are such avenues it employs.

PRICE STABILIZATION POLICY: THE CHANGING ROLES OF BULOG

Relationships among farmers, small-scale and large-scale traders and rice millers are generally quite strong as interactions have taken place for many years. A key factor in this relationship is Bulog, the government's rice agency. Bulog serves many functions: It procures paddy, processes or mills it, markets the rice to wholesale markets, interjects supplies in markets to tame price surges and stores rice in its warehouses located across the country. The storage capacity of the warehouses could accommodate as much as 4 million tonnes per year, although the average rice stock managed by Bulog is usually about half this amount. Bulog's role in managing rice stocks, however, has decreased substantially since 2017 when the government implemented a targeted rice subsidy for the poor (BPTN), run by the Ministry of Social Affairs. This contrasts with Bulog's former central role in all aspects of rice matters in Indonesia.

Under the centralistic governance of President Soeharto's New Order regime (1966–98), Bulog or the then National Logistics Agency was powerful. It served as the main guardian for food (rice) price stabilization. As a former general, President Soeharto used the term "logistic affairs" under the military doctrine that rice is the main logistic, especially under wartime conditions: "those who can control the logistics will win the war". The logistic institution was established as a vertical-line agency, from the central government down to provincial and district levels. During the

New Order, Bulog, headed by Generals Achmad Tirto Sudiro and Bustanil Arifin, was well-known for its tight, militaristic ability to carry out logistics management and price stabilization.

Then the government implemented a price stabilization policy for rice and other strategic foods through Bulog which played a central role in achieving price stabilization—keeping food prices stable at farm and consumer levels. Stabilization was effectively enforced from the central to regional government level before implementation troubles emerged in the 1990s. One major component of the policy was defending a floor price, keeping farm-gate prices above production costs. Bulog was tasked with procuring rice not absorbed by the market, especially during harvest season when farm-gate prices tend to fall. The procured rice was used to build a national buffer stock. The economic rationale was to protect against market failure, ensure profitability for farmers and procure enough rice for Bulog's market operations. A second component involved a ceiling price. It made rice affordable to low-income households, especially in urban areas. (Jakarta, the national capital, was considered the most sensitive area.) Whenever prices rose above the ceiling due to drought or other natural calamities, Bulog would conduct market operations and sell cheaper rice to targeted consumers (Arifin et al. 2019).

Maintaining this "price band", where fluctuations occur within an acceptable band of floor and ceiling prices, became harder as Indonesia's economic policy shifted toward greater openness in the mid-1980s and focused more on deregulating international trade, banking and finance. As a result, Bulog's centralized management system started losing its effectiveness. The rice trade, including distribution, became increasingly mismanaged, as did the corruption of government subsidies. President Soeharto was finally pushed out of power in 1998 amid the devastating Asian financial crisis. As the country democratized, it also adopted, in 2001, a significant political and economic decentralization policy, where local governments were allowed to formulate and implement their own food policy, including managing food stocks and stabilizing prices. The only powers that remained under the control of the central government were defence, finance, religion, justice, land and international affairs. As a result, there was significant uncertainty regarding food policies during the first two years of decentralization, when many local governments tried to control the warehouses and storage facilities of Bulog. After years of discussions involving some prominent economists and university-based experts, the government transformed the formal structure of Bulog into a state-owned enterprise (SOE) in the form of a quasi-public company in 2003. At the same time, the government also established the Food Security Council, which was chaired directly by the President, while the Agricultural Ministry oversaw day-to-day activities. Since then, staple food policies have been considered the responsibility of the central government. Unfortunately, democratic administrations in the post-Soeharto era have had difficulties in improving the governance of Bulog, where the problems of food procurement, stock management, distribution and price stabilization have remained unresolved.

Predicated on Government Regulation 13/2016 on Bulog and Presidential Regulation 48/2016 on Mandates for Bulog to Achieve National Food Security, Bulog has mandates to manage eleven strategic commodities from procurement and distribution to market operations and retail—rice, maize, soybean, sugar, cooking oil, wheat flour, shallot, chilli, beef, chicken and eggs. Accordingly, Bulog receives funding from the government to procure rice from Indonesian farmers, import rice, manage rice stocks and distribute rice in the form of market operations or food for the poor programmes. Under the food for the poor programme, for nearly two decades, Bulog had distributed 20-kg packs of rice (although the amount varied over time) to millions of poor families at Rp1,600 per kg, with local governments and village heads assisting in the distribution. Unfortunately, monitoring was poor. Not only did targeted families often receive less than the stipulated amount, but also those not qualified for the programme received portions too (Arifin et al. 2019). Under the current Joko "Jokowi" Widodo administration, the programme has morphed into a non-cash targeted rice subsidy (BPTN) managed by the Social Affairs Ministry.

Widodo's administration has been trying to increase the effectiveness of the food price policy and to improve the performance of Bulog as an SOE that implements state food policy. As seen from the regulations noted above, Bulog plays an integral role in maintaining food availability and price stabilization in the country. Previously, this programme was known as market operations. It was based on the supply and price monitoring of rice and other strategic foods at the district level. When food price rises and supply is limited, Bulog mobilizes its food stocks to local markets, selling at a government reference price. The programme is now known as KPSH (Ketersediaan Pasokan dan Stabilisasi Harga), with Bulog as the main implementer.

Figure 4.6 presents the retail price of rice from three different sources of data— BPS, the Center for Price Information of Strategic Foods (PIHPS) of Bank Indonesia and Jakarta Food Station. Data from PIHPS were initially intended to monitor the price of volatile foods as an important component of the inflation rate, together with core inflation and the administered price. Generally, BPS rice price data is relatively higher compared to the other two sources. BPS applies a weighting average of food data collected from field sample data from primarily major markets nationwide. PIHPS is also collected from traditional and modern markets in all thirty-four provinces, but some of the samples do not overlap with those of BPS. Finally, Food Station data is typically the lowest. It is collected from local stores, including rice stalls and kiosks across markets within a jurisdiction, although primarily around Jakarta. The data from Food Station should represent the wholesale level of rice data, which shall serve as the barometer for price stability in the country.

In implementing its public service obligation mandates such as KPSH, Bulog at times has to rely on funding from commercial banks as procedures for claiming expenses from the government, i.e., the Ministry of Finance, generally take a considerable amount of time. In terms of budget accounts, as of June 2020, Bulog experienced cash flow difficulties as the total amount receivable was large (Bulog 2020). The total outstanding balance of funds to be settled by the government to Bulog was Rp2.61 trillion (about US$180 million). It consisted of the KPSH budget of Rp369.80 billion in 2019 and Rp837.84 billion in 2020, total disaster funds of Rp47 billion for 2018 and 2019, and the sugar price stabilization budget in 2018 and 2019 of Rp1.35 trillion. Meanwhile, Bulog's domestic rice procurement has decreased significantly, as explained above.

Possible reasons for the declining role of Bulog in the KPSH programme include: (a) the low supply of rice in the market, (b) the aggressiveness of private traders in rice procurement, and (c) increasing rice stocking by households. The 2019 rice stock survey by BPS showed that during the major or rainy season harvest in March to April, more than 62 per cent of stocks were kept by households, 13 per cent by traders, 11 per cent by Bulog, 8 per cent by millers and 6 per cent by hotels-restaurants. During the secondary or dry season harvest in September to October, about 48 per

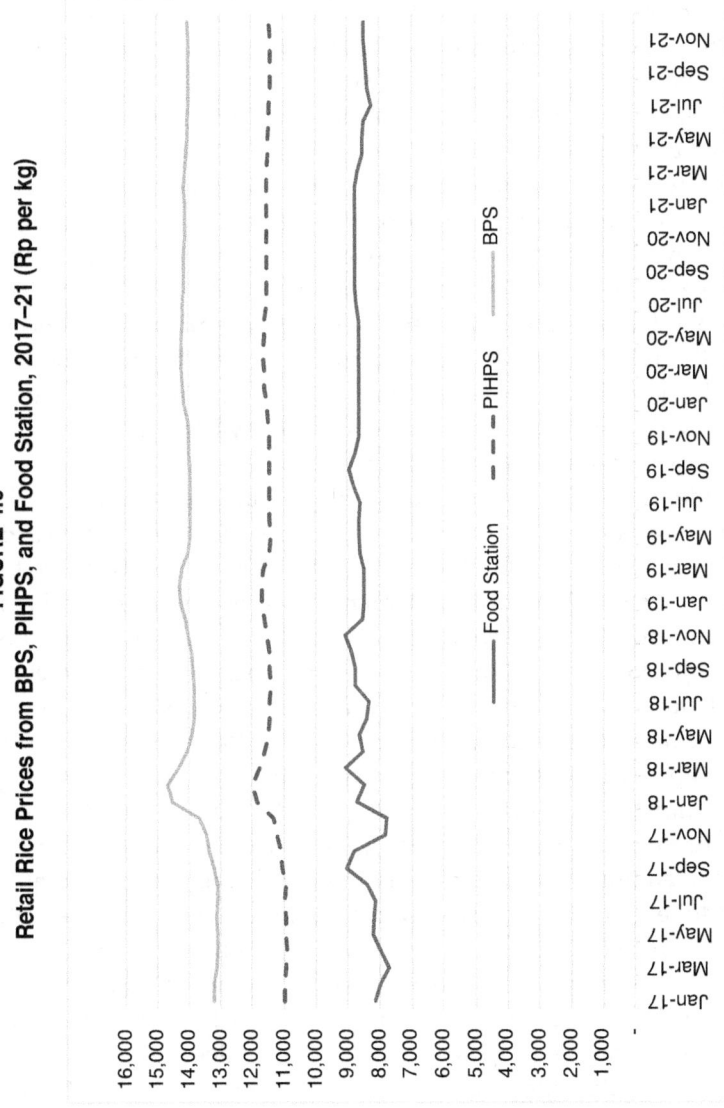

FIGURE 4.6
Retail Rice Prices from BPS, PIHPS, and Food Station, 2017–21 (Rp per kg)

cent was kept by households, 19 per cent by traders, 18 per cent by Bulog, 8 per cent by millers and 7 per cent by hotels-restaurants. In general, rice stocks are more secure during the rainy season, as the retail price declines slightly during this time too; it is more constant during the dry season harvest. Patterns of Bulog procurement (Figure 4.7) also imply that the agency has relatively secure rice stocks during dry season harvest, as mandated by KPSH. By the end of the year, Bulog's rice stocks generally dwindle considerably.

Figure 4.7 also demonstrates that domestic rice procurement by Bulog is a function of harvest season or the rice supply. Extreme drought in 2018 delayed the rice harvest for one month and in May 2019 there was another reduction in total rice production for the year. At the beginning of the pandemic in 2020, the peak of Bulog rice procurement occurred in May although the harvest season started in April. This might be associated with the government's announcement of the first lockdown, which constrained transportation and the logistics system. In 2021, the peak of Bulog procurement was in April as usual.

Under most of the New Order, Bulog's management of the food stock was a "remarkable success". Since then, I have elsewhere described its performance as "troubling" (Arifin 2008). The government continues to give mandates to Bulog for implementing rice stabilization and managing the government rice reserves (CBP). But Bulog does not have the monopoly power it did under Soeharto. Consider imports. The government assigns Bulog to import medium-quality rice, although in limited amounts. Imports of premium-quality and special rice, such as Basmati, glutinous rice and others can be purchased by the private sector, according to procedures set by the Ministries of Agriculture and of Trade. During the pandemic, when rice exporters experienced economic contractions and global prices were high, the amount of rice Indonesia imported was quite low (Table 4.2).

Indonesia only imported 356,000 tonnes of premium-quality rice in 2020, and 408,000 tonnes in 2021. The imports were conducted by private actors, mostly because of the strong domestic production. Imports conducted before the pandemic—for example, in 2018 when Bulog imported 2.25 million tonnes—triggered heated political debates about rent-seeking behaviour (Arifin 2021). By percentage, Indonesian imports have been quite modest at less than 5 per cent, even including the 2018 surge. Using the concept of self-sufficiency ratio developed by the FAO, Indonesia is categorized as a self-sufficient nation in rice production, a label in which

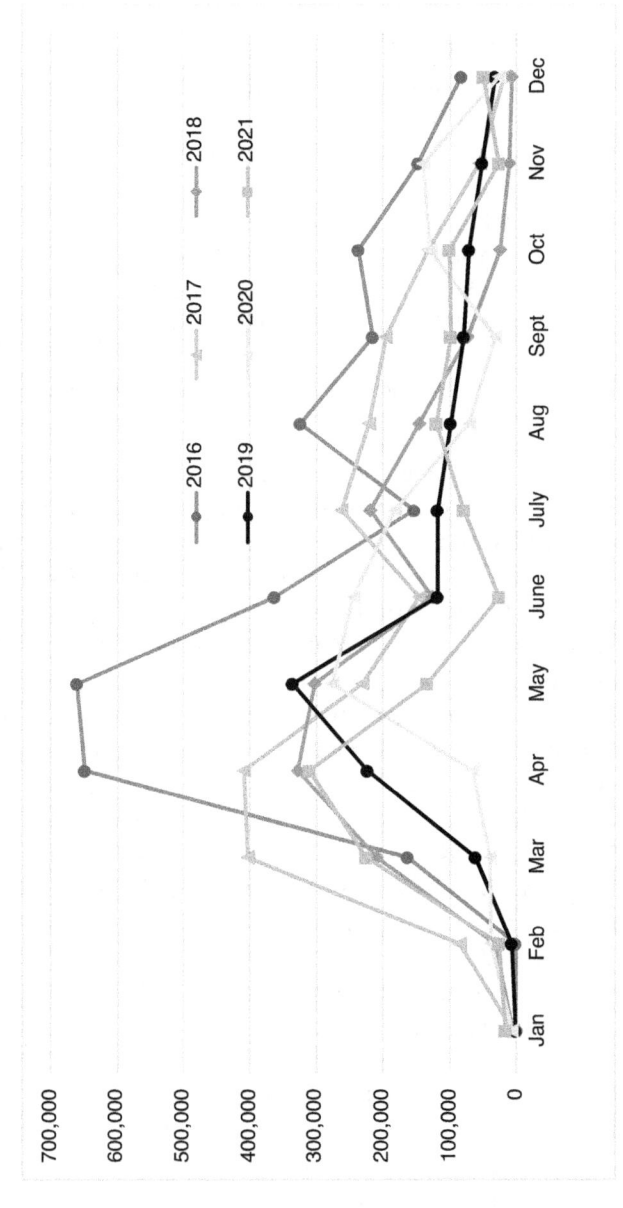

FIGURE 4.7
Domestic Procurement of Bulog, 2016–20 (in tonnes of rice equivalent)

Source: Bulog, January 2022.

TABLE 4.2
Total Rice Imports during the Jokowi Administration, 2014–21

Year	Volume (Tonnes)	US$	Rp billion
2014*	503,325	239,439,407	3,452,716
2015	861,601	351,602,090	5,070,102
2016	1,283,179	531,841,557	7,669,155
2017	311,525	143,206,447	2,065,037
2018	2,253,824	1,037,128,214	14,955,389
2019	444,509	184,254,091	2,656,944
2020	356,287	195,409,001	2,817,798
2021	407,727	183,801,804	2,650,422

Note: * Quarter 4 only.
Source: BPS (2022c) (Data collected from DG Customs and Excise, Ministry of Finance)

Indonesia takes pride (Davidson 2018). Some countries considered self-sufficient on a national scale may still have a proportion of their population facing hunger and suffering from malnutrition. These countries may also have high poverty levels that hinder adequate and nutritional food access in large segments of the population (FAO 2016).

Beyond imports, as we noted above, Bulog's management of the rice-for-the-poor programme (Raskin) was hampered by many difficulties. After a thorough policy review and field studies conducted by independent groups and experts, the government developed a more targeted non-cash rice subsidy system using Ration Cards (Kartu Sembako). Distributed to nearly 19 million families registered with Social-Welfare Integrated Data (DTKS), each card contained a value of Rp300,000 (about US$21) for beneficiaries to purchase rice and eggs locally. It could also be used to purchase higher quality rice from food stalls or *e-warong* not managed by Bulog (Arifin 2020).

When the government introduced the Non-Cash Food Subsidy Programme (Bantuan Pangan Non-Tunai [BPNT]), distributing rice from its warehouse to the distribution points across the country became trickier for Bulog. Consequently, the rice stocks deteriorated, and 20,000 tonnes rotted (*Jakarta Post*, 4 December 2019). Bulog blamed its troubles on "mafia" rice traders who manipulated rice meant for the poor (*Jakarta Post*, 3 October 2019). Many modern rice stalls and *e-warongs* involved in the BPNT programme receive rice from private suppliers, not Bulog.

In short, with the implementation of BPTN in 2018, the rice distribution system for the poor underwent considerable changes.

Bulog learnt important lessons from the BPNT experience, including the need to work harder to develop a modern rice industry by investing in high-tech milling facilities to compete with private companies. This includes supplying BPNT rice under fair and open competition. Instead of complaining about declining rice quality in its warehouses, Bulog should build a modern rice warehouse system that allows a first-in, first-out mechanism. Under this system, the rice that has been stored longest will be the first distributed to minimize stock deterioration. Rice distribution should be even easier now; since the pandemic, the government has involved Bulog in more social assistance programmes, including a cash social assistance scheme (BLT), the Family Hope Programme (PKH), and the Java-Bali Emergency Community Activity Restrictions (PPKM), among others.

Meanwhile, the disparity between domestic and global rice prices has been widening, mostly because the cost of production and distribution in Indonesia has increased considerably. Panel A in Figure 4.8 shows that the domestic price of rice (medium quality II) exceeded Rp11,500 per kg in January 2018, as a result of which the government imported 1.5 million tonnes. At the end of 2019, the domestic price fell below Rp11,500 per kg but rose again to nearly Rp11,500 per kg in December 2021. The trend for the price of premium rice was similar.

Unfortunately, domestic rice prices remained high throughout early 2022, creating significant food access problems, especially among the poor, while the average world price of rice was far lower at around Rp6,000 per kg. In terms of stability, Indonesia performed slightly better: Its domestic retail price of rice during the pandemic remained stable, while prices in Thailand, Vietnam and India fluctuated significantly (see panel A).

Moreover, domestic rice prices at the mill level, or at the Bulog level, in the last three years have been far above the government procurement price of Rp7,300 per kg (according to Inpres 5/2015) and Rp8,300 per kg (according to Ministry of Trade Regulation 24/2020). Theoretically, the maximum retail price policy is only for administrative purposes—as a signal for market operations and import decisions without the involvement of the public at large. Enforcing one will be difficult. Although the government does have the Task Force for Food (Satgas Pangan) at its disposal, the number of rice retailers and traditional markets is simply

FIGURE 4.8
Price of Medium Rice (Panel A) and Premium-Quality Rice (Panel B) at Global and Domestic Markets, 2017–22

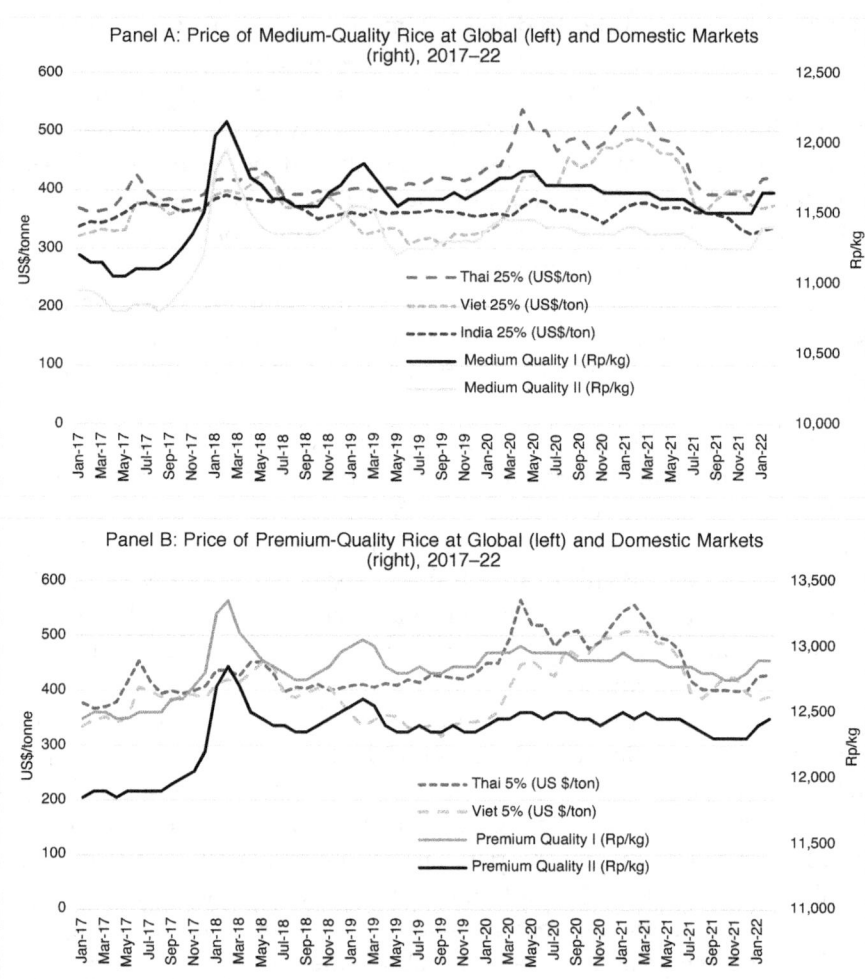

Source: Global Price is from FAO (2021b) and Domestic Price is from PIHPS (2022).

overwhelming. Food price stability is also related to the inefficiencies of food value chains in Indonesia. Rice and other strategic foods pass through the hands of traders, distributors, and retailers under conditions of asymmetric information and non-competitive market structures. High domestic rice prices are driven by restrictions on imports, increasing production costs including labour costs and land rental and high transportation and marketing costs. Importing additional cheaper rice from rice surplus countries should be a logical policy response to high-priced rice in Indonesia, but this is rarely explored.

Reform options for Bulog can be summarized as follows: First, in the short term, Bulog should continue procuring rice as part of KPSH mandates. The pandemic experience has shown that any efforts to strengthen domestic food stocks without Bulog's involvement are risky. Private companies and region-based food and logistic corporations should also be engaged in this task, including the task of anticipating the possibilities of a food crisis caused by the pandemic. Meanwhile, the government should continue to strengthen its social assistance programmes such as conditional cash transfers, staple food social assistance, BPNT and others to maintain purchasing power and food access for those most affected by the pandemic. These steps are especially imperative for ensuring adequate food and nutrition for children under five to reduce stunting and other incidences of chronic hunger.

Second, Bulog should improve the management of its rice distribution and marketing of rice stocks. This includes participating in social assistance programmes on a competitive basis driven by higher-quality rice value chains. Third, while implementing mandates on managing rice stocks and government rice reserves (CBP), Bulog should be also assigned to increase the capacity-building of locally owned, private food corporations in food distribution and value chains. At the same time, CBP management should be more flexible, in line with Government Regulation No. 71/2015 on Food and Nutrition Security which provides discretion for rice stock disposal. CBP management intends to address food shortages, food price fluctuations, natural disasters, social disasters and/or emergencies, as well as international cooperation and the provision of foreign food aid.

Fourth, provisions in the state budget for the CBP are based on budget availability, not on reserve requirements. The food security budget should be transferred from the central government to regional and local governments through special allocation funds that cover the provision of food services and nutritional improvement in urban and rural areas. CBP financing mechanisms could be implemented entirely by the government through the state budget, or partially implemented in partnership with the private sector. Implementing partial financing is certainly not easy, because the issue of governance has not been resolved entirely and few private actors in the rice business—and more broadly in Indonesia—are willing to be audited by the State Auditor. However, higher reliance on market mechanisms must involve the private sector for the future well-being of the country's rice economy.

CONCLUDING REMARKS: POLICY CHANGES FOR THE FUTURE

This chapter has explored the impact of the COVID-19 pandemic on Indonesia's rice economy by examining the productivity and competitiveness of rice, value chain resilience, price stability and the changing role of Bulog. It has found that rice productivity and competitiveness are associated with extreme weather, level of technological change, and policy strategies for maintaining the sustainability of the rice production system in Indonesia. During the (first) two years of the pandemic, domestic rice prices have shown relative stability compared to other strategic foods and compared to global market prices. The coefficient of variation of domestic rice prices has been well below that of global market prices, especially during the pandemic. The domestic performance of food availability has been quite modest, although the fluctuation of rice productivity has been alarming, especially in the absence of technological change in the on-farm and off-farm processing sectors. The Indonesian government has been working hard to implement reforms for Bulog, but this windy, bumpy road will take time to travel. The reforms' success will be crucial in bolstering the country's food security.

Improvements in rice productivity might provide momentum for developing intensification practices and adopting rice sustainability principles across Java and other producing centres. Technological innovation in the production system is potentially more beneficial and feasible than land expansion or expensive food estate development in Central Kalimantan and Papua. Compared to the logistic systems of other strategic foods, those for rice performs better as the flow of rice from production centres or rice-surplus regions to consumption centres or rice-deficit regions during the pandemic has not been markedly disrupted. Policies and reform programmes should address the improvement of food production systems, good agricultural practices at the farm level, technological change and innovation in production technology and post-harvest handling and management. This could also include changes in the management of food-agriculture technology, improvements in research and development and improvement in the innovation ecosystem for increasing total factor productivity. This will require greater cooperation among the quadruple helix of academia, businesses, government and civil society. Lessons from the pandemic show that Indonesia should also develop a more resilient agricultural system, climate-smart modern biotechnology, precision agriculture, digitization of value chains and more.

Assuming Bulog's rice procurement continues at current rates and households and traders continue to hold and manage rice stocks, Indonesia should be able to weather the threat of a possible food crisis. However, Bulog has experienced an institutional shock: It lost its mandate for distributing rice to poor households. Having incurred financial losses from this management change, it needs to be more active in improving its administration of rice distribution and marketing of rice stocks to prevent declines in the quality of its rice. This will generate the revenues it needs.

Finally, increasing farmers' income is not simply identical to increasing food production and food policies that emphasize the supply side alone. Food policies must include increasing the demand for food, which implies the need to boost income. Higher farmer earnings have been and will continue to be key to the reduction of rural poverty. Lower food prices could contribute to reducing inflation, which, in turn, will alleviate poverty in urban (and rural) areas too. Combining strategies for increasing food production and food demand may also promote food price stability. Therefore, policy changes that address human capital investment and institutional arrangements in the rice system in Indonesia can contribute considerably to developing coping mechanisms and evidence-based solutions beyond the pandemic.

References

Arifin, Bustanul. 2008. "From Remarkable Success to Troubling Present: The Case of Bulog in Indonesia". In *From Parastatals to Private Trade: Lessons from Asian Agriculture*, edited by Shahidur Rashid, Ashok Gulati, and Ralph Cummings Jr., pp. 137–64. Washington, DC: International Food Policy Research Institute (IFPRI) and Johns Hopkins University Press.
———. 2020. *Ekonomi Beras Kontemporer* [The Contemporary Rice Economy]. Jakarta: Gramedia.
———. 2021. *Pertanian Bantalan Resesi: Resiliensi Sektor Selama Pandemi COVID-19*

[Agriculture as a Cushion of Economic Recession: Sector's Resilience during COVID-19 Pandemic]. Jakarta: INDEF and PERHEPI.

———, Noer Achsani, Drajat Martianto, Linda K. Sari, and Ahmad H. Firdaus. 2019. "The Future of Indonesian Food Consumption". *Journal of the Indonesian Economy* 8, no. 1: 73–110.

Bordey, Flordeliza. H., Piedad. F. Moya, Jesusa C. Beltran, and David C. Dawe, eds. 2016. *Competitiveness of Philippine Rice in Asia*. Science City of Munoz (Philippines), Philippine Rice Research Institute, and Manila: International Rice Research Institute (IRRI).

Bulog. 2020. "Report to the House of Representatives (DPR)". 22 June 2020. Jakarta. (in author's possession) (in Indonesian).

Center for Price Information of Strategic Foods (PIHPS). 2022. *Informasi Harga Pangan Antar Daerah* [Inter-Regional Information on Food Prices]. Jakarta: PIHPS, Bank Indonesia. https://hargapangan.id (accessed 8 April 2022).

Central Agency of Statistics (BPS). 2022a. *Produksi Padi Tahun 2021 Turun 0,43 Persen: Angka Tetap* [Rice Production in 2021 Declines 0.43 percent: Fixed Number]. Jakarta: BPS. https://www.bps.go.id/pressrelease/2022/03/01/1909/produksi-padi-tahun-2021-turun-0-43-persen--angka-tetap-.html (accessed on 26 March 2022).

———. 2022b. *Statistik Indonesia* [Statistics of Indonesia]. Jakarta: BPS

———. 2022c. *Laporan Bulanan Data Sosial-Ekonomi, Edisi 141 Februari 2022* [Monthly Report of Social-Economic Data, Edition 141, February 2022]. Jakarta: BPS.

Davidson, Jamie S. 2018. "Then and Now: Campaigns to Achieve Rice Self-Sufficiency in Indonesia". *Bijdragen Tot de Taal-, Land- En Volkenkunde* 174, no. 2–3: 188–215.

Firdaus, Muhammad, Karen Tambayong, Andi Ikhwan, Soekam Parwadi, Siti Wahyuningrum, Henry Simarmata, Anita Suharyati, Freddy, Gea Andi Satria, and Ayu Tri Wahyuni. 2022. *Buku Pintar Kemitraan Closed-Loop Agribisnis Hortikultura* [Guidelines for Closed-Loop Partnership in Horticulture Agribusiness]. Jakarta: Deputy for Food and Agribusiness Coordination, Coordinating Ministry of Economic Affairs (CMEA).

Food and Agriculture Organization of the United Nations (FAO). 2016. *Food Self-Sufficiency and International Trade: A False Dichotomy?* Rome: FAO. https://www.fao.org/3/i5222e/i5222e.pdf (accessed 20 March 2022).

———. 2020. *Crops and Livestock Products*. Rome: FAO. http://www.fao.org/faostat/en/#data/TP (accessed 20 July 2020).

———. 2021a. FAOSTAT. Rome: FAO. https://www.fao.org/faostat/en/#data (accessed 15 April 2022).

———. 2021b. Food Price Monitoring and Analysis (FPMA) Tools. Rome: FAO. https://fpma.fao.org/giews/fpmat4/#/dashboard/home (accessed 15 April 2022).

Jakarta Post. 2017. "Minister Clarifies Rice Reports". 25 August 2017. https://

www.thejakartapost.com/news/2017/07/25/minister-clarifies-rice-reports.html (accessed 22 February 2022).

———. 2019a. "Bulog Accuses 'Mafia' of Manipulating Rice for the Poor". 3 October 2019. https://www.thejakartapost.com/news/2019/10/03/bulog-accuses-mafia-of-manipulating-rice-for-the-poor.html (accessed 22 February 2022).

———. 2019b. "Bulog Finds 20,000 Tons of Rotten Rice, Another 100,000 Tons in Poor Condition". 4 December 2019. https://www.thejakartapost.com/news/2019/12/04/bolog-finds-20000-tons-of-rotten-rice-another-100000-tons-in-poor-condition.html (accessed 22 February 2022).

Pusat Informasi Harga Pangan Strategis (PIHPS). 2022. "Informasi Harga Pangan Antar Daerah". Jakarta: PIHPS. https://hargapangan.id/tabel-harga/pasar-tradisional/daerah (accessed 15 April 2022).

Sawit, M. Husein. 2021. "Pasar Beras Dalam Negeri, Pengadaan dan Penyaluran Beras Bulog: Alternatif Pemerintah vs Skenario Baru" [Domestic Rice Market, Bulog's Rice Procurement and Distribution: Government Alternatives vs New Scenarios]. Paper presented at Focused Group Discussion (Virtual FGD) of PERHEPI and Coordinating Ministry of Economic Affairs, 7 March 2021.

World Bank. 2022. *Commodity Markets*. Washington, DC: World Bank. https://www.worldbank.org/en/research/commodity-markets. (accessed 4 April 2022).

5

From Controlling to Abandoning
State–Rice Sector Relations in Thailand

Thanapan Laiprakobsup and Manthana Noksawak

INTRODUCTION

This chapter examines how the Thai state formulates its rice policy, especially during the COVID-19 pandemic. It argues that if the Thai state sees rice farmers as political threats, it is likely to impose extractive policies such as taxes on rice farmers. Conversely, if the state considers rice farmers as political partners, it is likely to implement subsidy programmes. But if the state views farmers as neither, it is likely to abandon them altogether, as has happened under General Prayuth's administration during the COVID-19 pandemic. In short, the Thai state has shifted from interfering to abandoning the country's rice producers.

Depending on the regime in power, Thai rice policies can seem paradoxical. While the state imposes policies to control rice prices and tax farmers, it also guarantees farmgate prices to appeal to farmers. Although the COVID-19 pandemic has not rectified this paradox, the magnitude of assistance programmes and the significance of state policy has been reduced. For extractive reasons, the state seeks to control the rice sector to allocate resources from it to industrial and other agricultural sectors.

For electoral reasons, political leaders want to mobilize rice farmers via subsidy programmes because they are a huge voting bloc. Thai governments, especially those democratically elected from 2002 to 2014, implemented pledging schemes that procured paddy from farmers at high prices. From 2019 to the present, the government has implemented a price guarantee programme that set a floor price for paddy. Elected governments procure paddy and guarantee prices to solve the problem of falling prices. However, there has been considerable variation in the size of procurement programmes, which depends on the relationship between farmers and political leaders. Since the administrations led by Thai Rak Thai and its successor parties depended upon rice farmers' votes, procurement programmes were larger in scale than those of other governments. After the 2014 military coup led by General Prayuth Chan-o-Cha, the government abolished the pledging scheme and replaced it with a production assistance scheme which allocated less money to rice farmers. Rice farmers' problems such as falling prices, water shortages or indebtedness have not been solved. These problems have intensified as the COVID-19 pandemic unfolded. Prime Minister General Prayuth,[1] the former supreme commander of the Thai Royal Army, and his coalition government reduced the size of its production support programme, Rice Mega Farm, after negotiations with coalition partners. The Rice Mega Farm Programme, which was created by the Ministry of Agriculture and Agricultural Cooperatives in 2016, aims to reduce production costs. But it has failed in defending farmgate prices as a result of political fragmentation in the upper reaches of state administration. In general, because of the hierarchical relationship between the Thai state and rice farmers, how the former views the latter depends on the state's political aims.

This chapter is organized into four sections. The second section reviews the relationship between the state and the rice sector in Thailand by drawing on the concept of hierarchical capitalism. The third section surveys how rice production and prices in Thailand have changed over time. The fourth section explores the rice policy during the COVID-19 pandemic. We focus on the Rice Mega Farm and price guarantee programmes since they have been implemented to help rice farmers during the pandemic. We argue that since the programmes are hierarchically organized, rice farmers have not partaken in the policymaking process. Not only have the programmes failed to address the problem of falling rice prices, but their coverage has also shrunk. The final section concludes by suggesting that the politicization of rice policy impedes the effective address of farmers' long-term problems.

THE RELATIONSHIP BETWEEN THE THAI STATE AND RICE SECTOR IN HISTORY: HIERARCHICAL CAPITALISM PERSPECTIVE

One-way economic governance in developing countries can be described as hierarchical capitalism. Three main features characterize hierarchical capitalism. First, economic governance is controlled by the state, domestic big businesses and multinational corporations (MNCs) (Evans 1995; Schneider 2013). The latter two monopolize the resources and technological diffusion process in a country's supply chains. Second is the preference for exploiting resources and labour from the sector in question rather than upgrading and developing labour skills and industrial production. Therefore, labour relations and production development are dependent upon individual corporations; sectoral governance becomes atomized and segmented since major decisions are the purview of owners of capital. Relations and trust between businesses and labour are low. Third, the state controls policymaking, excluding labour and even domestic big businesses and MNCs. Policymaking is centralized under the state, which, in turn, directs sectoral development. Unfortunately, the state is often blind to the problems caused by its own policies. Worse, the state tends to abandon the sector once problems become intractable.

By applying this hierarchical capitalism framework to the Thai state's relationship with the rice sector, we argue that the Thai state controls the rice sector to extract resources and politically restrict rice farmers from participating in policymaking. From the 1950s to the 1980s, the state used export taxes (i.e., Rice Premium[2]) and a rice reserve requirement[3] scheme to intervene in the market. Behind the taxes and reserve requirement were bureaucratic agencies and representatives from rice business associations, not representatives from rice farmers' associations (Siamwalla and Setboonsarng 1991). By 1983, Thailand had transitioned to a semi-democratic regime; the army shared power with political parties in policymaking and exchange for parliamentary support for the prime minister, General Prem Tinsulanonda (Neher 1988).[4] General Prem introduced the rice-pledging scheme in 1984 as a result of political pressure from his coalition partners and economic advisors. The scheme continued under the elected governments of the 1990s. The size of its budget increased exponentially during the Thaksin administration (2004–8). To make rice farmers feel as if they could participate in rice policymaking, representatives from farmers' associations were invited into the subcommittee of the pledging scheme but were nevertheless excluded from the more influential and higher-ranking committee (Wangsachachoke 2019). The scheme was expanded under the Yingluck administration (2011–13) with procurement of all rice varieties without quantity limitations. It was criticized by the anti-Thaksin movement—Yingluck is Thaksin's sister—called the People's Democratic Reform Committee (PDRC), for corruption and budget mismanagement. In 2014 the National Council for Peace and Order (NCPO) led by General Prayuth overthrew the democratically elected Yingluck administration and abolished the rice-pledging scheme. General Prayuth replaced it with the Rice Mega programme that supports production.

Under Prime Minister General Prayuth, farmers' representatives were not invited into the Rice Mega and income guarantee programme committees. The Thai state typically centralizes policymaking with marginal participation of rice farmers. The central rice policymaking committee, presided over by the prime minister,[5] comprises mostly politicians and representatives from the prime minister's office and ministries of commerce and agriculture and cooperatives. Representatives of rice exporter and rice miller associations are minority committee members.

State control over rice policy is reflected in the policy of export taxation. From the 1950s to the 1980s, Thai governments imposed various kinds of taxes on rice exports. Government levies were high because these exports constituted a major source of revenues and transfers. From 1955 to 1965, for example, estimated revenues generated from these taxes accounted for more than 11 per cent of total government revenues (Siamwalla and Setboonsarng 1991; Falvey 2001; Warr 2001). From 1970 to 1986, the nominal rate of assistance (NRA)[6] was, on average, –24.76 per cent. During the same period, NRAs for cassava and maize were, on average, –11.35 and –3.18 per cent, respectively. Although the state has not taxed rice exports since 1986, it has consistently transferred revenues out of the sector. On average, the NRA of rice from 1986 to 2004 was –11.78 per cent compared to –5.72 per cent for maize. The state has, nonetheless, extracted fewer revenues from the rice sector since the late 1990s. Democratization and especially competitive elections have since empowered farmers, allowing them to pressure politicians to implement more subsidization programmes (Siamwalla and Setboonsarng 1991; Falvey 2001).

Nevertheless, governments have still sought to control domestic rice prices. A case in point is farmgate rice prices. Table 5.1 illustrates the difference between distorted and undistorted farmgate prices from 1970 to 2004.[7] Historically, authoritarian *and* democratic governments have distorted the paddy rice price. They intervened in the domestic rice market through their Rice Premium, Quota Restriction and rice reserve requirement programmes aimed at keeping domestic prices lower than global market prices (Laiprakobsup 2010), as the Thai economy had been in a downturn from the mid-1970s to early 1980s. Inflation was high amid global economic stagnation due to escalating oil prices. In addition, the domestic political situation was tense, with large-scale demonstrations, rocky transitions to authoritarian regimes and frequent clashes between the army and the Communist Party of Thailand in the country's north and northeast (Phongpaichit and Baker 2002). Rice farmers in corresponding provinces joined the communists in droves, and to restrict their economic resources for revolting, the government placed heavy controls on rice prices.

From 1982 to 1992, differences between distorted and undistorted prices narrowed, as Thai governments abandoned price controls and taxes and increasingly subsidized rice farmers via procurement programmes (Laiprakobsup 2013). The country's booming and industrializing economy was now less reliant on agriculture, while the rural insurgency subsided as

TABLE 5.1
Difference between Distorted and Undistorted Prices in Thailand, 1970–2004

Year	Undistorted[a]	Distorted[a]	Difference[b]
1970	76.4	56.9	19.5
1975	181.3	109.7	71.6
1980	208.4	157	51.4
1985	123.1	98.2	24.9
1990	148.7	128	20.7
1995	186	168.3	17.7
2000	116.7	101.4	15.3
2004	139	130.3	8.7

Notes: a. See Anderson and Valenzuela (2008).
b. Difference = Undistorted − Distorted (author's calculation).

did the Cold War (Doner 2009). In addition, the country had transitioned to an electoral regime in which rural politicians began to participate in the policy-making process in the cabinet. However, governments still controlled rice prices in favour of urban consumers.

Elected governments increasingly intervened in the rice market, especially during the 1997–98 Asian Financial Crisis. Subsequently, the gap between distorted and undistorted prices narrowed until it reached single digits after 2000. This was due mainly to the electoral success of the Thai Rak Thai (TRT) party led by Thaksin Shinawatra. The party's pro-rural policies included subsidizing farmers via a rice-pledging scheme and introducing a farmers' debt moratorium. The former sought to procure paddy from farmers at the price set by the TRT administration (2001–6). For the latter, the administration froze the farmers' debts with the Bank of Agriculture and Agricultural Cooperatives (BAAC) for three years.

The rice-pledging scheme was popular among farmers, a key electoral constituency for the TRT; as such, it became a permanent assistance programme with annual fiscal support from the state budget. Thaksin's government raised guaranteed rice prices close to market price and then above market price. This policy was continued by the TRT's successor party, Pralang Pracharat (People's Power),[8] after Thaksin was deposed by the army in 2006. The rice-pledging scheme became perilously politicized, championed by Thaksin's supporters (or the Red Shirt Movement) and vilified by his opponents (i.e., the PDRC or the Yellow Shirt Movement). The latter argued that the scheme was designed by the Pheu Thai government led by Yingluck Shinawatra to allocate procured rice to the party's business networks and to mobilize rice farmers for electoral support (Permani and Vanzetti 2016). The Yellow Shirts saw the corrupted scheme as wasting money on farmers for votes.

After the military overthrew the Yingluck administration, in 2014, the military-led NCPO abandoned the guaranteed paddy rice price programme since it was introduced by its political rival. Instead, it emphasized a rice production assistance programme that included the following:

- First, the administration helped farmers to pay part of their production costs (Laiprakobsup 2017). Government payment set the maximum level the farmers could receive each production year.
- Second, it paid farmers a lump sum to stockpile paddy, aimed at regulating (or lessening) the supply of paddy.

- Third, it tried to control the leasing fee for paddy fields by lowering it for farmers.
- Fourth, it supported farmers who cultivated organic rice to encourage food safety.
- Fifth, it assisted farmers to shift production from rice to other crops such as corn or beans.
- Sixth, it implemented the Rice Mega Programme to encourage rice farmers to establish new farmers' associations for production and marketing purposes.

However, implementation was ineffective. Many poor farmers were unable to register for the programmes due to difficulties with documentation. They also objected to the stockpiling directive because they preferred immediate cash payment for crops. Lastly, the transition to organic farming required a sizeable capital investment that farmers did not have or did not want to risk in an uncertain market.

In 2019, Thailand transitioned to an elected administration under an NCPO-written constitution. To continue its political control of the military and its networks, the NCPO passed a new constitution to stabilize the rule of General Prayuth, the former head of the NCPO. The NCPO inserted the 20-Year National Strategy Master Plan in the constitution to ensure that the incoming administration would implement it. The NCPO also determined that senators appointed by the NCPO were able to vote for a prime minister candidate. Moreover, the NCPO penned the organic law of the electoral system to disenfranchise the Pheu Thai party. Even though the latter won the most seats in parliament as a result of the 2019 general election (47 per cent), it was insufficient to establish a government on its own accord. The NCPO-backed Pralang Pracharat party supported General Prayuth's aspiration to be prime minister. The military offered cabinet posts and threatened lawsuits to convince popular politicians and candidates to join the party. Although Pralang Pracharat finished second in seat totals, through these methods, it was able to convince medium- and small-sized parties to partner in a coalition government. Invariably, General Prayuth was chosen as prime minister (McCargo 2019).

In sharing administrative power with the Democrat Party, one of its coalition parties, Prayuth's administration divided rice policies into two branches. The first was the Rice Mega Farm. The Department of Agricultural Extension (DOAE) launched a project called "Upgrading the Mega Farm with Modern Agriculture and Connecting the Market" to strengthen the NCPO's Mega Farm Programme. The second was the Income Guarantee Programme; it was administered by the ministers from the Democrat Party.

By April 2020, due to the COVID-19 pandemic, General Prayuth's administration shut down public agencies and businesses. It then established the Government's Lending Decree to Remedy and Restore the Economy and Society as Affected by the Coronavirus Disease Pandemic in the fiscal year 2021. The 500-billion-baht fund (approximately US$15.6 billion) was mainly aimed at compensating citizens, freelance workers, small business owners and workers in the social security system who lost their livelihood due to lockdown measures.[9]

THAILAND'S RICE SECTOR IN BRIEF

Rice productivity in Thailand has hardly changed. According to the Office of Agricultural Economics (2021), the average productivity of the first season in 2016 was 446 kilograms per *rai*.[10] In 2021 it was nearly identical at 440 kilograms. For the second season, it was 612 kilograms in 2016 and 603 in 2021. Although productivity depends upon factors such as climate or market demand, the state's rice policies also have had little positive effect on productivity.

In addition, paddy rice price is expected to decrease. According to the Thai Rice Mills Association, average prices have not increased since 2011. Table 5.2 presents the average price of jasmine rice, ordinary white rice and sticky rice, which are popular varieties in Thailand. The data indicates that average prices during Yingluck's administration (2011–14) were higher than those during Prayuth's term (2014–19).

RICE MEGA FARM PROGRAMME, INCOME GUARANTEE PROGRAMME AND STATE'S ABANDONMENT OF THE RICE SECTOR

One current significant programme, Rice Mega Farm,[11] was initially aimed at enhancing farmers' competitiveness in producing high-quality products that meet international market standards by increasing farm size (Wangsachachoke 2019). It seeks to promote farmers' integration in

TABLE 5.2
Total Amount of Subsidies Received by Each Department

Year/Rice Variety	Jasmine Rice	White Rice	Sticky Rice	Administration
2011	11,365	9,662	15,507	Abhijit (January to May) Yingluck (July onwards)
2012	13,094	10,650	13,502	Yingluck
2013	13,043	9,322	13,728	Yingluck
2014	9,534	7,999	12,787	Interim government under Pheu Thai (January to May) General Prayuth's NCPO (May)
2015	11,128	8,025	13,232	General Prayuth's NCPO
2016	9,946	7,994	14,073	General Prayuth's NCPO
2017	9,087	7,635	9,996	General Prayuth's NCPO
2018	11,117	NA	10,728	General Prayuth's NCPO
2019	9,514	7,932	14,857	General Prayuth's NCPO (January to May) General Prayuth's Pralang Pracharat (May onwards)
2020	9,181	9,244	15,021	General Prayuth's Pralang Pracharat

Source: The Thai Rice Mills Association (2021).

the agricultural supply chain by increasing their bargaining power and farming efficiency. The government provides high-quality inputs such as seeds, fertilizer, machinery and the latest technologies to increase farmers' profitability to develop products to meet market demand and produce certified and nutritious food (MOAC 2018).

The programme does not require a specific number of plots for each group, and plots of land must not be adjacent. The scheme covers many other agricultural government projects and their integration into supply chains for production and market access. Structurally, the programme consists of three parts. The first part involves the enhancement of farmers' capacity to produce higher-value rice using high technology. Components include the Agricultural Learning Center (ALC), Smart Farmer Project, Enhanced Quality of Agricultural Products Project, Organic Agriculture Development, New Theory Agriculture (Self-Sufficiency Economy Principle) and Promoting the Use of Agricultural Machinery. The second part involves improving farming production infrastructure by restructuring land, water and agricultural management. Components include Zoning by Agri-Map, Water Management Policy, Agricultural Bank and Land Allocation Policy. The final part involves increasing market accessibility through Comprehensive Rice Production and Marketing Plan and Farmers' Market.

After Prayuth's 2014 coup, the NCPO government assigned the project's implementation to the Department of Agricultural Extension (DOAE). The Rice Department spearheaded the project to assist production and cost efficiency, and to manage it, the NCPO cabinet established "The Board of Directors for the Operation of the Mega Farm Programme Extension System".[12] This Board collaborates with various departments within the MOAC, in addition to establishing management systems, procedures and operating principles, as well as regional or provincial connections through the Provincial Committee for Driving Significant Policies and Solving Problems in the Agricultural Sector at the provincial level, known as Chief of Operations (COO) (Office of Agricultural Economics, Evaluation Center, 2019).

The Implementation of the Rice Mega Farm Programme

According to MOAC Order No. 9/2018, the COO is designated as a committee that supervises, promotes and drives policy at the provincial level. In addition, the COO is responsible for monitoring farmers based on the area's needs. The director of the Provincial Agriculture Extension Office is the chairperson of the COO (Ministry of Agriculture and Cooperatives 2018).

The Administration Department and the Operations Department jointly manage the Rice Mega Farm Programme. The Provincial Agricultural and Cooperative Development Subcommittee (*Aor Por Kor*) is in charge of the former. The provincial governor, appointed by the Ministry of the Interior,[13] presides over the Provincial Committee for Driving Significant Policies and Solving Problems in the Agricultural Sector. The Provincial Agriculture and Cooperatives Subcommittee is responsible for researching and analysing policy from the government and the MOAC to comprehend the efficiency of operations at the provincial level. Furthermore it also guides the province's agricultural and cooperative development as well as oversees and implements policy in compliance with the national strategy (Office of the Permanent Secretary, Ministry of Agriculture and Cooperatives 2018).

In the local divisions, the Operation Team (OT) is the main organization in charge of implementing the central government's policies. It seeks collaboration from a variety of local network partners, and monitors and reports any arising issues to the COO. The director of the District Agricultural Extension Office is also head of the OT (Ministry of Agriculture and Cooperatives 2018).

A joint committee meeting is held regularly between the two networks, namely the Mega Farm Network Committee and the ALC Network Committee.

(1) At the district level, 882 districts, the participants in each district consisted of Representatives of the Mega Farm, the ALC and the District Agricultural Extension Officer.
(2) At the provincial level, 77 provinces, the meeting attendees in each province consisted of the chairperson of the district committee of the Mega Farm, the district committee of the ALC and the Provincial Agriculture Extension Officer.
(3) At the regional level, 6 regions, the meeting's participants consisted of the chairperson of the provincial committee of the Mega Farm, the provincial committee of the ALC and the Office of Agricultural Extension and Development Officer.
(4) At the national level, the meeting's participants consisted of the chairperson of the regional committee of Mega Farm, the regional committee of the ALC, the advisor of the ALC committee, the officer and the Director of the DOAE.

According to the Ministry of Agriculture and Cooperatives (2021), the project implementation procedure is divided into twelve steps, which are as follows:

(1) The Mega Farm Group registers as a communal enterprise (Juristic Person Type).
(2) The Mega Farm Group examines the project/operation plan and budget expenditure plan in detail.
(3) The district committee examines and approves the operating plan and budget expenditure, which it then submits to Provincial Committee.
(4) The Provincial Committee examines and approves the implementation plan and budget expenditure plan, then notifies the local organization in charge of the agricultural commodity of the Mega Farm.

(5) The organization at the local level in charge of agricultural goods presents the group's action plan and budget expenditure plan to obtain a budget allocation from the organization that oversees the agricultural commodities at the department level.
(6) The organization that administers the product at the central level allocates budgets based on operational plans and budget expenditure plans to agencies in charge of agricultural goods in the local area.
(7) The organization at the local level signs a memorandum of understanding (MOU) with the Mega Farm Group and then submits paperwork to the Bank for Agriculture and Agricultural Cooperatives (BAAC) and transfers the money to the group.
(8) The Mega Farm Group operates the farm according to the operating and budget expenditure plan.
(9) The organizations at the local level in charge of agricultural products of the Mega Farm monitor, advise and supervise operations in accordance with the action plan and the group budget expenditure plan.
(10) The Mega Farm Group prepares budget expenditure reports in accordance with the recommendations of the Cooperative Auditing Office (CAD).
(11) The CAD examines the project bank accounts and related paperwork.
(12) Summarize budget expenditures and evaluate the project.

The programme's formation and management are hierarchical and centralized to the central bureaucratic agencies. Figure 5.1 shows its implementation structure, noticeably the absence of private agencies and rice farmers in its procedures. Rice businesses and rice farmers had neither a role in the Rice Mega Farm policy formation nor any representation in its policymaking. The government has relied mainly upon agricultural agencies to formulate and manage policies. Meanwhile the District and Provincial Committees are the key agencies approving implementation plans and budgets without the participation of farmers who are supposedly the main target of the programme. Nor does there seem to be much participation from the local government administration.

The Allocation of Subsidies for Rice Policies

According to the 2021 budget for the MOAC, subsidies amounted to approximately 14 billion baht (see Table 5.3). Rice policy programmes are

FIGURE 5.1
Operation Procedure for Receiving and Disbursing Funds for the Project "Upgrading the Mega Farm with Modern Agriculture and Connecting the Market"

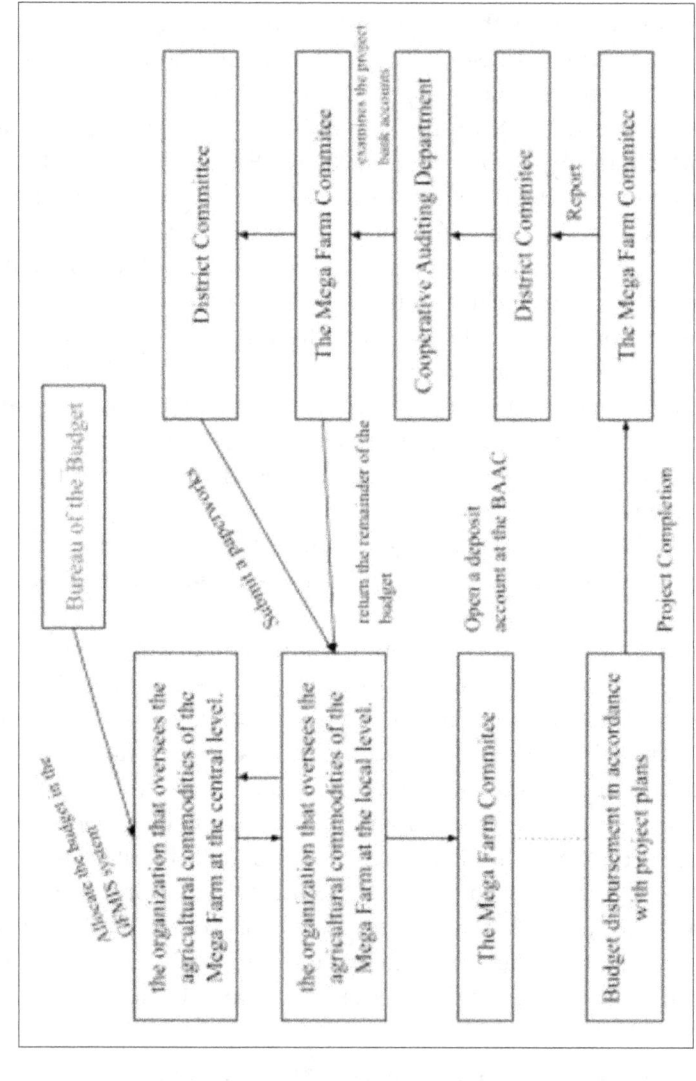

Source: Ministry of Agriculture and Cooperatives (2021).

administered by the Rice Department and DOAE. According to Table 5.3, the subsidy budget for these two agencies was about 12 billion baht or 90 per cent of the total agricultural subsidy programme budget in 2021. Seemingly the Pralang Pracharat administration had allocated far more budget subsidies to rice farmers than farmers of other commodities.

However, we have to be cautious when analysing the subsidy in the budget allocation. Not all the money is spent on rice farmers, as there are administrative costs involved such as programme management, government official allowances or wages for private agencies authorized to help farmers. The actual budget for farmers' subsidies is unknown since there has been no official report or evaluation of the programme's implementation.

In addition, a cabinet resolution in July 2021, authorizing the DOAE to make amendments to the project, led to a 40 per cent cut in its subsidies.[14] This budget reduction indicates an abandonment of the Rice Mega Programme. Due to the contraction of economic growth caused by the pandemic, the government has reallocated public resources from rice farmers to unemployed workers in business and industry, signifying its current priority.

TABLE 5.3
Summary of the Project's Data Comparing the Government's Goal to the Present Project Advancement on Rice, 2020

No.	Organizations	Total Number of Plots	Total Budget (baht)
1	Rice Department (RD)	2,637	7,267,450,300
2	The Queen Sirikit Department of Sericulture (QSDS)	26	70,525,300
3	Department of Livestock Development (DLD)	186	488,448,400
4	Department of Fisheries (DOF)	90	212,975,700
5	Rubber Authority of Thailand (RAOT)	299	753,673,100
6	Department of Agriculture Extension (DOAE)	2,012	5,085,047,200
	Total	5,250	13,878,120,000

Source: Ministry of Agriculture and Cooperatives (2021).

Implementation Problems of the Rice Mega Farm during COVID-19

Even before the pandemic and the budget cuts, the Rice Mega Programme under General Prayuth's administration had been facing difficulties. Notably, the number of participating rice farmers had been decreasing (see Figure 5.2), and producers did not see the programme as useful because of its many requirements and terms for programme participation.

As such, with the COVID-19 pandemic came a dramatic drop in participants (see Figure 5.2). From 2020 to 2021, for instance, the number of farms participating in the Rice Mega Farm Programme fell from 535 to 228—a 52 per cent decline. Many farmer groups withdrew from the project because they could not meet its bureaucratic criteria. Some groups, comprising 120 plots of land, were rejected by the Provincial Project Management Committee because their performance was below the committee's requirements.

According to the Mega Farm Operation Committee, as of June 2021, farmers of 72 plots of the Rice Mega Farm had requested to withdraw from the project, costing it 190 million baht. One reason was that the project required signing a contract with the private sector for the purchase of agricultural machinery. Any group wishing to do so had to be juridically

FIGURE 5.2
Number of Mega Farms Participating in the Programme, 2016–21

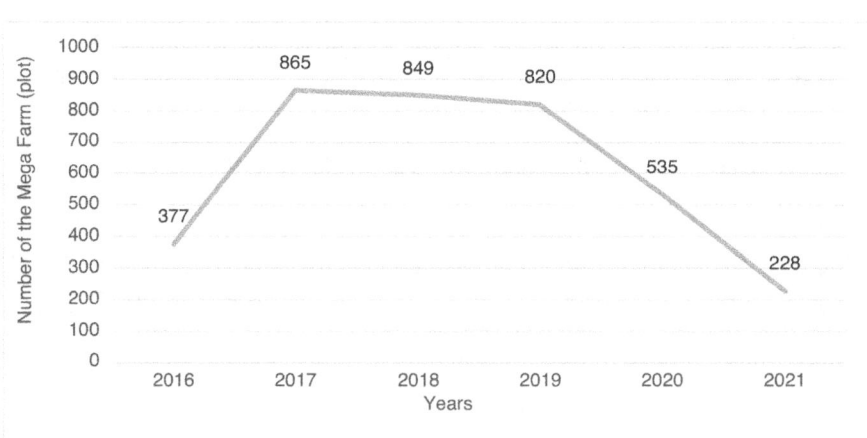

Source: Department of Agriculture Extension, n.d. https://co-farm.doae.go.th/graph/Dashboard1dsb.php

FIGURE 5.3
Summary of the Project's Data Comparing the Government's Goal to the Present Project Advancement on Rice, 2020

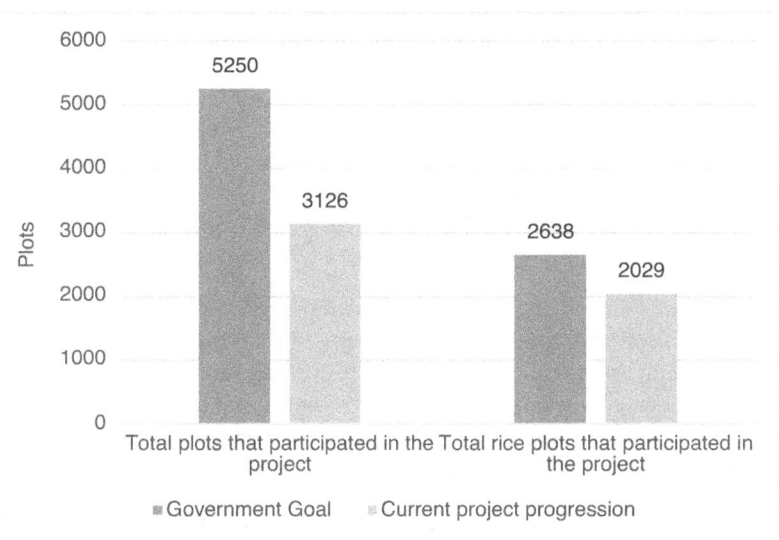

Note: Information updated as of 6 August 2021.
Source: MRG Online (2021).

legal as defined by the Civil and Commercial Code. There were also laws contradictory to the responsibilities of the project's committee in the operation and administration of agricultural cooperative–farmer groups. Additionally, Mega Farm committees may be distinct from cooperative committees or farmer organizations. Money obtained through project funding must be reinvested in the cooperative, not in the Mega Farm Group (MGR Online 2021).

According to a newspaper report, farmers have found the terms of participation in the programme rather confusing. At the start, farmer groups understood that they had to register as an agricultural cooperative–farmer group or community enterprise in order to participate. In December 2020, the DOAE altered this requirement; participants have to be juridical persons to be eligible for the contract signing for loans or machinery purchases. Furthermore farmers are concerned that they, like those under contract farming, would be under the control of large private capital groups such as rice millers, owners of commodity warehouses, fertilizer and agricultural machinery businesses and rice exporters (Prachachat 2021) that dominate Thailand's rice production and marketing industry. As a result, rice farmers depend upon these businesses, and farmers are unable to set the paddy price in the Rice Mega Farm Programme.[15]

Farmers have been confused by what is meant as a "limited partnership" only for the purpose of acquiring legal entity status to engage with a private dealer. The dealer is the intermediary connecting farmers to rice businesses, machinery and fertilizer merchants or capital. It is risky for growers to make an agreement or contract with private dealers who are unfamiliar with farmers. The following is a quote from a farmer not participating in the programme:

> Farmers are worried about obligations and the prospect of incurring debt through a limited partnership. Additionally, farmers are unable to manage bookkeeping and taxation. As a result, it's unsurprising that there are so few farmer groups interested in this programme, despite its good intention to assist farmers. There is an issue with the management strategy used by the DOAE in setting participation criteria (Prachachat 2021).

Additionally, private enterprises desiring to sign contracts with Mega Farm groups have been unable to sell agricultural inputs and equipment as expected because rice farmers do not purchase products and equipment in large quantities. As a result, in some places, the private sector has had to deploy representatives to contact farmers directly in order to urge them to join the project and register as a limited partnership (Prachachat 2021). The limited partnership indicates the government's hesitation to facilitate farmers' access to agricultural businesses. The government, if it so desires, could have played an intermediary role between farmers and agricultural businesses.

Smallholder farmers, landless farmers or farmers without sufficient agricultural machinery who are unable to cultivate have been vulnerable during the COVID-19 pandemic. One such farmer reports that earning additional income in non-agricultural sectors has become even more challenging:

> When I was unable to cultivate, I went fishing and sold vegetables like eggplants, lemons and banana leaves. Typically, the local vendors come to my house to pick up the produce and take them to the marketplace. However, salespeople couldn't come to my house during the COVID outbreak because they were afraid of being infected. As a result, we let all the vegetable rot (Farmer 2, interviewed on 29 September 2021).

Wealthier farmers, who own agricultural equipment, and who can harvest even in poor weather conditions, have also reported facing difficulties in selling their harvests due to the fall in paddy rice prices during the pandemic:

> There were very few farmers in the area capable of farming. To ensure that we had enough water for rice growing, we rented a well and have been using it ever since. I grew the RD 41 rice variety, which sold for a low price of around 6,000–7,000 baht per 1,000 kilograms. Furthermore I supplemented my income through gardening. We carried vegetables and bananas to the market in order to sell them ourselves (Farmer 3, interviewed on 29 September 2021).

Both farmers and officials found the concurrent drought more disastrous than the spread of COVID-19. A farmer reports, "To produce large quantities of paddy rice, water supply has to be consistent. When it comes to farming, irrigation is the most crucial component" (Farmer 1, interviewed on 29 September 2021). According to a Mega Farm manager:

> The Mega Farm is unable to continue operating because of the drought. We have not had any meetings or activities for the past two years. The Mega Farm Group and the farmer would have continued their cultivations/ activities if there had been enough water for the upcoming growing season. The most critical aspect is the irrigation system that should work efficiently" (interviewed on 29 September 2021).

Another farmer reports, "I believe that the difficulties we are experiencing now have nothing to do with COVID. The problem is lack of available water for farming" (Farmer 1, interviewed on 29 September 2021).

Drought is a natural problem for rice farmers, but the government has not planned adequately for water supply and management for the farmers in its Rice Mega Programme. To produce a large quantity of rice to meet market demand, programme farmers need a consistent water supply. They are solely dependent on rain for producing and harvesting rice; this should not have been the case. The government has failed to provide irrigation or water reservoirs to support production.

The problem of water supply also has caused conflict among consumers. The government has built industrial estates near rice paddy fields and has allocated them water supply, leaving farmers short of water (Manorom 2020). The Pralang Pracharat administration recently asked farmers not to grow rice from February to May because of water shortages.[16] The problem of water supply is thus related to the government's poor planning and policy bias against rice farmers.

Income Guarantee Programme

After the 2019 general elections, General Prayuth's administration implemented the Income Guarantee Programme to help rice farmers. The programme aims to guarantee a paddy price and pay a lump sum to farmers if they are unable to sell the harvest at the guaranteed price. The Ministry of Commerce is responsible for setting paddy prices, while the BAAC transfers money to rice farmers. The Democrat Party controls the Ministry of Commerce while Pralang Pracharat controls the BAAC. The programme's implementation thus depends upon the Pralang Pracharat-Democrat Party relationship. If it turns sour, implementation suffers.

The programme was formulated by the Rice Policy and Management Committee headed by the Prime Minister. To stabilize paddy prices when prices fall, the Commerce Ministry set the guaranteed price at the beginning of the harvest season. The higher the quality of paddy rice (for example, jasmine rice), the higher the guarantee. The formula for the guaranteed price is [(The value of wholesale price + Product)[17] × processing cost] − (milling cost + transportation cost).[18] For the 2021/22 harvest season, the government allocated about 89 billion baht (or US$2.8 billion) to this programme. This was much lower than prior allocations. For 2016/17, the NCPO administration budgeted approximately 190 billion baht (or US$5.75 billion) for its rice assistance programme (Voice TV Online 2018).

To receive the guaranteed price, farmers must register with the local DOAE and provide evidence that they cultivate paddy. If they had sold paddy to a private miller or warehouse owner below the set price, the administration would pay the difference. Each farmer had quotas for 25 tonnes, even if they harvested more than this figure. The money was paid via farmers' accounts in the BAAC.

The Income Guarantee Programme, however, could not effectively shore up the paddy rice price. Since its implementation in 2019, the paddy rice price has not increased (see Table 5.3). It was lower during Pralang Pracharat's administration than during Yingluck's government. The income guarantee programme has been ineffective in boosting prices.

The programme's implementation had been difficult before and during the COVID-19 pandemic. One problem involved public relations: The administration did not announce the calculation of the guaranteed price but posted it on an obscure website.[19] More importantly, the guaranteed price formula was unrealistic. The wholesale price of rice depends upon local market conditions, which often differ from that in the Bangkok market. Milling and transportation costs also vary among areas. In areas with many mills, transportation costs are more reasonable than in areas with few mills. During the pandemic, milling and transportation costs rose due to labour shortages. The committee failed to factor this into its price formulation.

Implementation problems also extended to politics. The Democrat Party was mainly responsible for the programme since the commerce and agriculture ministers hailed from this party. Meanwhile Pralang Pracharat controlled the finance ministry responsible for allocating the programme's budget. The two parties constantly clashed over the size of the programme's budget. The Democrat Party wanted more money for the Income Guarantee Programme since it did not want to face rice farmers' dissatisfaction and possible protests, especially during the pandemic. Pralang Pracharat preferred to keep this budget in check because it would squeeze budget allocation for other programmes, especially those for COVID-19 relief. Moreover, the budget expansion for the income guarantee programme would violate the Public Financial and Fiscal Discipline Act,[20] which limits public debt to 60 per cent of the country's gross domestic product. The Democrat Party threatened to leave the coalition if the Ministry of Finance and BAAC refused to expand the budget for the income guarantee programme. This worked, and the finance ministry decided to gradually allocate more money to rice farmers in November 2021.

DISCUSSION

The relationship between the Thai state and its rice sector has shifted from intervention with taxes and price controls to intervention with subsidy programmes. State intervention with taxes and price controls stemmed from policy bias against rice farmers in favour of consumers. The Thai political elite saw consumers (especially urban and middle-class groups) as politically powerful. Consumers and business owners desired low rice prices to maintain a low cost of living and wages; both expected the government to follow suit (Siamwalla and Setboonsarng 1991). Massive urban protests could prove destabilizing. Moreover, large numbers of Thai rice farmers joined the Thai Communist Party's insurgency from the 1950s to the 1980s. This provided the government with another reason to subsidize urban consumers at the expense of rice farmers.

When Thai politics transitioned to a more open system, and its economy grew so that it depended less on rice exports, the Thai state's policy shifted to the subsidization of the rice sector via price guarantees and production support. Rice farmers have become increasingly important for electoral politics since they comprise the major bloc of voters, and subsidization programmes appeal to them (Ricks and Laiprakobsup 2021). Since 2006 the various governments have continued to implement a price guarantee programme for the rice sector.

Unfortunately, rice farmers are constantly excluded from policymaking. All policymaking is centralized under political leaders, bureaucratic agencies, and rice businesses and industries. Representatives from rice farmer associations are not found in this group. Even during the democratization period (1992–2006), they only participated as members of a subcommittee, not in the main committee.

The implementation problems of rice policies reflect the state's abandonment of the rice sector since 2014. In the case of the Rice Mega Farm Programme, the falling participation of producers indicates that the Thai state has not seriously tried to promote or encourage them to join and stay with the programme in the long run. The government hardly explores reasons for farmers' exit or attempts to boost participation. During the COVID-19 pandemic, when the programme's budget allocation was cut, government officials should have assisted rice farmers in addressing rice production problems, providing technological assistance and access to markets. In the case of the Income Guarantee Programme, the government's price formula proved impractical. The pandemic worsened implementation problems, for the government failed to consider crucial factors such as labour or logistical shortages. Although the pandemic did not directly impact the Income Guarantee Programme, it led to tensions between the coalition parties in General Prayuth's administration due to different policy preferences.

The COVID-19 pandemic indirectly affected budget allocation for the implementation of rice programmes when the focus shifted to COVID-19 relief funding. The emphasis has shifted to the problem of urban unemployment. Although this is understandable, the government should pay more heed to the problems of the rice sector, and those of agriculture more broadly.

CONCLUSION

The chronic problems of rice farmers in Thailand reflect the hierarchical relationship between the state and the rice sector. Using a hierarchical capitalism framework, we argue that the Thai state has attempted to control the rice sector and its farmers for extractive *and* political reasons. Once political incumbents do not consider rice farmers as a political threat or contributor to their political stability, they are less likely to favour farmers' interests. From the 1950s to the 1980s, the Thai state heavily controlled rice farmers via taxation and price controls to extract revenue from them. It also sought to weaken them politically because they supported the communists. However, state policy began to shift to subsidization in order to gain the electoral support of rice farmers. As such elected politicians use subsidization programmes to mobilize farmers' votes, rather than control rice export taxes which is more likely of an authoritarian regime. Still, farmers have never been equal partners in rice policymaking regardless of whether the regime in power is democratic or authoritarian.

The COVID-19 pandemic has worsened the situation for rice farmers because the government has not paid due consideration to their problems. The proposal of General Prayuth's administration to empower rice farmers to negotiate with capital holders in the sector ideally should improve their leverage with crops aggregated on a large scale. The budget allocated, however, is too small compared to other programmes such as the Pandemic Relief Fund, and has been cut further due to the programme's low popularity. It is also administratively difficult for farmers to join the programme. The Income Guarantee Programme, aimed at shoring up paddy prices, has also proved ineffective. Paddy prices have fallen every season. The pandemic has hijacked the administration's attention and budget to COVID-19 relief funds. Although rice farmers deny the pandemic's direct impact on production and marketing, poor government implementation during the pandemic certainly has affected their livelihoods.

Notes

1. The government allows retired military officers to use their final title or rank. This is why the prime minister, who retired in 2014, is still known as General Prayuth.
2. See Warr (2001) for an explanation of the Rice Premium.
3. Ibid.
4. Under semi-democracy, the prime minister was a military leader, and not a member of parliament or a political party. Yet, there were general elections, and civilian politicians were invited to join the coalition government.
5. The name of the rice committee is changed with each administration. Currently, under General Prayuth it is the Committee for Rice Policy and Management.
6. The nominal rate of assistance measures the extent to which the government sets the domestic producer price above (or below) the border (i.e., export) price (Warr and Kohpaiboon 2009). A positive NRA percentage indicates that the government is likely to transfer revenues to the producers and implies that the government subsidizes the agricultural commodity sector in any given year.
7. Farmgate is the price of paddy for farmers to sell. There are distorted and undistorted farmgate prices. The former refers to the domestic paddy rice price which is distorted by government policy and the marketing process, while the latter refers to the global market price for selling paddy rice (see Anderson and Martin 2009).
8. Pralang Prachachon was established by some key leaders of the TRT in 2007 after the Constitutional Court charged the party with constitutional violations by some of its leaders and dissolved it (Forsyth 2010).
9. Bank of Thailand, n.d.
10. 1 *rai* is equal to 0.16 hectares.
11. The programme arose from "The Development Guidelines" (roadmap) formulated during the term of Pitipong Puengboon Na Ayudhya, who was the Minister of Agriculture and Cooperatives (MOAC) from 2013 to 2014. It was considered a significant project for agricultural production reformation (MOAC 2016).
12. Department of Agriculture Extension, Mega Farm Program Promotion, 2019, https://www.opsmoac.go.th/dwl-files-402891791956 (accessed 15 April 2022).
13. The provincial governor has the power to enforce only policies and programmes of the Ministry of the Interior, not of other ministries.
14. Department of Empowerment of Persons with Disabilities, "Cabinet Resolution Summary", 27 July 2021, https://dep.go.th/images/uploads/files/thaigov_27_Jul_2021.pdf; https://co-farm.doae.go.th/up/doc/gove2.pdf
15. Since the programme does not intervene in rice prices, the price of paddy rice depends on the market.

16. Thai PBS, "Warning Rice Farmers Not to Grow Rice for the Second Crop" (เตือนชาวนาห้ามปลูกข้าวนาปรังรอบ 2), 2020, https://news.thaipbs.or.th/content/302570 (accessed 15 April 2022).
17. The committee used the wholesale price of 5 per cent white rice in the Bangkok market as a reference.
18. The committee referred to the milling and transportation costs of the previous year.
19. For the calculation of the guaranteed price, see https://www.opsmoac.go.th/phetchaburi-regulation-files-412891791800
20. For more information, see Fiscal Policy Office, "Financial and Fiscal Discipline Act of 2018" (พระราชบัญญัติวินัยการเงินการคลังของรัฐ พ.ศ. 2561), 2018, https://www.fpo.go.th/main/The-law-in-charge-of-FPO/Law-of-Finance-and-Taxation/8519.aspx (accessed 15 April 2022).

References

Anderson, Kym, and Will Martin, eds. 2009. *Distortions to Agricultural Incentives in Asia*. Washington, DC: International Bank for Reconstruction and Development and World Bank.

———, and Ernesto Valenzuela. 2008. "Estimates of Global Distortions to Agricultural Incentives, 1955 to 2007". World Bank. www.worldbank.org/agdistortions (accessed 15 April 2022).

Bank of Thailand. n.d. "Measures for Assistance and Data of Financial Institutions during COVID-19" (มาตรการช่วยเหลือและข้อมูลสถาบันการเงินในสถานการณ์ COVID-19). https://www.bot.or.th/covid19/Pages/default.aspx (in Thai) (accessed 15 April 2022).

Doner, Richard F. 2009. *The Politics of Uneven Development: Thailand's Economic Growth in Comparative Perspective*. New York: Cambridge University Press.

Evans, Peter. 1995. *Embedded Autonomy: State and Industrial Transformation*. Princeton, NJ: Princeton University Press.

Falvey, Lindsay. 2001. *Thai Agriculture: Golden Cradle of Millennia*. Bangkok: Kasetsart University Press.

Forsyth, Tim. 2010. "Thailand's Red Shirt Protests: Popular Movement or Dangerous Street Theatre?". *Social Movement Studies: Journal of Social, Cultural and Political Protest* 9, no. 4: 461–67.

Laiprakobsup, Thanapan. 2010. "Political Regime, Business, Coordination, Unity of Rural Farmers, and Agricultural Politics in Developing Countries: A Case Study of Thailand". PhD dissertation. University of Houston, Texas.

———. 2013. "Tax Abandonment, Political Regime Type, and Rice Export Growth in Thailand". *International Journal of Civic, Political, and Community Studies* 10, no. 3: 39–50.

———. 2017. "Inequality in Rice Farmers' Access to a Government Assistance Program in Rural Thailand". *Asian Politics & Policy* 9, no. 3: 442–61.
Manorom, Kanokwan. 2020. "Thailand's Water Shortage and Inequality Crisis". East Asia Forum, 20 March 2020. https://www.eastasiaforum.org/2020/03/20/thailands-water-shortage-and-inequality-crisis/ (accessed 15 April 2022).
McCargo, Duncan. 2019. "Southeast Asia's Troubling Elections: Democratic Demolition in Thailand". *Journal of Democracy* 30, no. 4: 119–33.
MGR Online. 2021. "Thousands of the Mega Farm 'Withdraw' from the 13 billion baht COVID Financing Scheme after the Ministry of Agriculture Reimburses the Ministry of Finance for 4.3 billion" (in Thai). https://mgronline.com/politics/detail/9640000077161 (accessed 15 April 2022).
Ministry of Agriculture and Cooperatives. 2016. "Manual for the Operation of the Mega Farm Agricultural Extension Systems" (in Thai). http://www.oic.go.th/FILEWEB/CABINFOCENTER2/DRAWER068/GENERAL/DATA0000/00000407.PDF (accessed 15 April 2022).
———. 2018. *Document of the Ministry of Agriculture and Cooperatives No. 9/2018 (January 4, 2018) on the Appointment of the Chief of Operation Committee and Operation Team*. Bangkok: Ministry of Agriculture and Cooperatives.
———. 2021. *Handbook of the Upgrading the Mega Farm with Modern Agriculture and Connecting the Market Project* (in Thai). https://co-farm.doae.go.th/up/doc/handbook.pdf (accessed 15 April 2022).
Neher, Clark D. 1988. "Thailand in 1987: Semi-successful Semi-democracy". *Asian Survey* 28, no. 2: 192–201.
Office of Agricultural Economics, Evaluation Center. 2019. *Evaluation Report on the Mega Farm Program Extension System in 2016–2018 (Assessment Document No. 510)*. Bangkok: Office of Agricultural Economics.
Office of the Permanent Secretary, Ministry of Agriculture and Cooperatives, Office of Planning and Special Projects. 2018. *Manual for the Operation of the Provincial Agricultural and Cooperative Development Subcommittee (Aor Por Kor)*. Bangkok: Ministry of Agriculture and Cooperatives.
Permani, Risti, and David Vanzetti. 2016. "Rice Mountain: Assessment of the Thai Rice Pledging Program". *Agricultural Economics*, 47, no. 3: 273–84.
Phongpaichit, Pasuk, and Chris Baker. 2002. *Thailand: Economy and Politics*. 2nd ed. New York: Oxford University Press.
Prachachat. 2021. *The Mega Farm May Not Be Successful, Because the Farmers Are Unwilling to Establish the Partnership Limited* (in Thai). 26 March 2021. https://www.prachachat.net/economy/news-635329 (accessed 15 April 2022).
Ricks, Jacob, and Thanpan Laiprakobsup. 2021. "Becoming Citizens: Policy Feedback and the Transformation of the Thai Rice Farmer". *Journal of Rural Studies* 81: 139–47.

Schneider, Ben R. 2013. *Hierarchical Capitalism in Latin America*. New York: Cambridge University Press.
Siamwalla, Amar, and Suthad Setboonsarng. 1991. "Thailand". In *The Political Economy of Agricultural Pricing Policy: Volume 2, Asia*. 2nd ed., edited by Anne O. Krueger, Maurice Schiff, and Alberto Valds, pp. 236–80. Baltimore, MD: World Bank and Johns Hopkins University.
Voice TV Online. 2018. "4 Years of NCPO: Subsidizing Grassroots More Than 600 Billion Baht but Inequality Increased?" (4 ปี คสช. อัดฉีดงบซื้อใจรากหญ้ากว่า 6 แสนล้าน ไฉนความเหลื่อมล้ำไม่ลดลง?). https://voicetv.co.th/read/SykLEcYCz (accessed 15 April 2022).
Wangsachachoke, W. 2019. "Research Report on Agricultural Economic Development and Political Regime between 2014 and 2018: A Case Study of the Mega Farm Program in Eastern Thailand". N.p.
Warr, Peter G. 2001. "Welfare Effects of an Export Tax: Thailand's Rice Premium". *American Journal of Agricultural Economics* 83, no. 4: 903–20.
———, and A. Kohpaiboon. 2009. "Thailand". In *Distortions to Agricultural Incentives in Asia*, edited by Kym Anderson and Will Martin, pp. 255–80. Washington, DC: International Bank for Reconstruction and Development and World Bank.

6

Impact of COVID-19 on Singapore's Rice Supplies and Future Food Security Challenges

Jose Ma. Luis Montesclaros and Paul S. Teng

Singapore imports more than 90 per cent of its daily food consumption. Imports are one of the four key "taps" on the supply side for meeting demand. The other three include domestic production, reserves and growing food overseas and re-importing it into the country. Within the island city-state, rice plays a crucial role, since it is a staple in the Singaporean diet. According to the country's 2010 National Nutrition Survey, rice and rice alternatives (e.g., wheat) composed the largest share of consumption requirements (44 per cent), followed by meat and meat alternatives (30 per cent), fruits (12 per cent), vegetables (12 per cent) and wholegrains (2 per cent) (HPB 2010).[1] Despite rice's importance, Singapore relies purely on international sources to meet rice consumption requirements. This is because rice is a land-extensive commodity, requiring vast expanses of land that the city-state lacks.

The COVID-19 outbreak was declared a pandemic by the World Health Organization in March 2020,[2] and it has been a significant disruptor to global health, with more than 450 million cases recorded as of March 2022. It has also disrupted the global economy, causing economic contractions that have not been seen since the Great Depression of the 1930s.[3] This chapter presents policy insights for Singapore's food security in the face of COVID-19, learning from its experience in its rice sector. It is divided into three sections. The first section describes the policy context for food security in Singapore prior to COVID-19, describing the evolution of Singapore's approaches, including the investments in domestic production after the Global Food Price Crisis of 2007–8; the development of its Food Security Roadmap in 2013; the restructuring of its food authority, the Agri-Veterinary Authority and its transformation into the Singapore Food Authority announced in 2018; and the launching in 2019 of the "30-by-30" target of 30 per cent food self-sufficiency by 2030. This section highlights that across these transitions, Singapore has forgone attempts to boost domestic production and stayed the course of import reliance *for rice*, by focusing on diversifying foreign sources for rice, as well as other commodities.

The second section discusses the impact of the COVID-19 pandemic on Singapore's food security, with a focus on its impacts on rice supplies and rice prices. We show that while Singapore has been resilient in drawing sufficient quantities of rice from alternative sources, this comes at the cost of higher prices. The third section concludes with policy implications. It argues that the challenges faced in the rice sector, wherein Singapore is completely reliant on imports, are reflective of the challenges Singapore is likely to face in the case of the other food items which Singapore cannot produce, and which augur poorly for future food security in the city-state. This applies in particular to the 70 per cent portion of food supplies which Singapore still envisions it would need to import by 2030, assuming the success of Singapore's new "30-by-30" goal.

POLICY CONTEXT: SINGAPORE'S FOOD SECURITY POLICIES BEFORE COVID-19

The U-Turn Towards Food Security

Singapore's extreme dependence on food imports has been partly a result of deliberate state policies to structurally transform the national economy. As the country achieved First World economic status by the late twentieth century, its farming lands were significantly reduced to just 1.8 per cent of the total land area (728 square kilometres). The 2007–8 Global Food Price Crisis (GFPC) put Singapore, however, on high alert for the vulnerabilities posed by its model of high import reliance, resulting from volatilities in the international trade system. In particular, when droughts in India led to the fear that it would not have sufficient stockpiles to meet its consumption requirements, it restricted its exports. This triggered an upward spiral in grain prices within the international trading system—global prices for grains (which include rice, wheat and maize) doubled, and in some cases nearly tripled (Dawe and Slayton 2010).

Disruptions to the global rice sector during the 2007–8 GFPC presented clear evidence of the risks that Singapore faced with respect to rice and other imported commodities. For example, meat products (pork, chicken or beef) were also entirely sourced from imports. While the country was producing some leafy vegetables, eggs and fish, the majority were still purchased from abroad. In short, the crisis exposed the country's vulnerability and posed a credible risk to its food security, defined by the Food and Agriculture Organization of the United Nations (UN FAO) as a "situation that exists when all people, at all times, have physical, social and economic access to sufficient, safe and nutritious food that meets their dietary needs and food preferences for an active and healthy life".[4]

Therefore, the Singapore government felt compelled to boost investment in its domestic food sector. In December 2009, it developed a "Food Fund" with an initial funding of S$5 million to strengthen strategies for diversifying sources and raising local farm production (AVA 2010, p. 20). This fund received further tranches of S$19.37 million in August 2011 and S$10 million in October 2013. The government also established an Inter-Ministry Committee on Food Security (IMCFS) in 2012, helmed by the Ministry of National Development (MND), with active participation by the Agri-Food and Veterinary Authority of Singapore (AVA), which was under the MND at that time. The importance placed by the state on food security was reflected in the broad membership of the IMCFS which comprised the Economic Development Board, International Enterprises Singapore, Internal Security Division, Ministry of Foreign Affairs, Ministry of Home Affairs, Ministry of Health, National Environment Agency (NEA), National Security Coordination Secretariat, Agency for Science, Technology and Research (A*STAR), the Standards, Productivity and Innovation Board and even the Singapore Police Force (Ludher and Paramasilvam 2018).

The Food Security Roadmap

Correspondingly, Singapore launched a Food Security Roadmap at AVA's inaugural Food Industry Convention in October 2013.[5] A concrete initiative in the roadmap was to set target levels for increasing domestic production. Goals included achieving self-sufficiency of 30 per cent of hen shell eggs, 10 per cent of leafy vegetables and 15 per cent of fish (Ludher and Paramasilvam 2018), modestly up from 2010 levels of 22 per cent (hen shell eggs), 7 per cent (leafy vegetables) and 4 per cent (fish) (AVA 2011, p. 56). As these target levels required improvements in productivity, the state further established an Agricultural Productivity Fund of S$63 million in August 2014 for farm modernization (SFA 2021, p. 22). At this time, AVA's Annual Report (AVA 2015, p. 110) reported 3 hen farms (48 hectares), 54 vegetable farms (114 hectares), 9 farms for land-based food fish and shrimp production (34 hectares) and 117 farms for sea-based food fish, crustaceans and molluscs (103 hectares).[6]

Despite the policy push and financial support to boost Singapore's self-sufficiency in vegetables, eggs and fish, results have been mixed. By 2018, only one of the three targets set in the FS Roadmap had been met. While it exceeded its targets for leafy vegetables (13 per cent self-sufficiency achievement relative to 10 per cent), it fell short for hen shell eggs (24 per cent to 30 per cent) and fish (9 per cent versus 15 per cent) (AVA 2019). The reasons for the underperformance are unclear, although what is certain is that AVA was eventually reorganized. While one author described the AVA as "ceas(ing) to exist" (Wong 2018), it is more accurate to say that it was transformed into the Singapore Food Authority (SFA) as a means to rationalize its operations, so that it could better focus on food security. In the transformation, the AVA was divested of its animal- and plant-related functions, such as animal welfare and management, plant health control and laboratory functions, which were transferred to the National Parks Board. The SFA was also given new functions, including the management of the food safety lab (transferred from the Health Sciences Authority) and food hygiene and food-related laboratory functions (transferred from the NEA). Under this reorganization, the SFA was likewise transferred from the MND to the Ministry of Sustainability and the Environment (MSE).

The "30-by-30" Target

March 2019 marked the next transition in Singapore's food security policy, when the catchphrase "30-by-30" target was coined. This was an evolution away from the "90-10" model of imports-to-production and towards a 70-30 model, with a timeline to achieve this new goal by 2030. It was first announced by the then Minister of MSE during his 2019 budget speech, in which he premised the new target on the realization that "climate change brings new existential threats" that also impact Singapore's source countries for food.[7] Thus Singapore cannot afford to be complacent about its food supply from its current sources since the landscape for food cultivation is rapidly changing.

While this new target signalled that the city-state would pay more attention to boosting its self-production capacity to guard against uncertainties in source countries, it is uncertain how the 30 per cent target was precisely calculated. An earlier media report in Channel NewsAsia (which has since been removed) noted the inclusion of animal proteins like meats, alongside staples, for instance (Teng and Montesclaros 2019). This showed a lack of clarity on what the 30 per cent target's achievement would look like when it was first announced. In November 2019, the SFA's CEO gave a talk on "What Singapore's '30 by 30' Food Security Goal Means for Businesses",[8] where he shared that the "30 per cent" focuses on Singapore's "nutritional needs".[9] The use of the term "nutritional needs" as the basis for self-sufficiency has since been mentioned in the SFA Annual Report 2019/20 (SFA 2020, p. 4). Using "nutritional self-sufficiency" implies pivoting from the previous approach of measuring self-sufficiency per commodity in total tonnage of self-production and towards a nutrition-focused approach. The CEO further detailed this, by noting that it will comprise "20 per cent veg + fruits" and "10 per cent proteins" (with the image including meats, fish and eggs) (p. 4).

The new 30-by-30 target conveyed the message that Singapore would be taking bold steps to expand its domestic production capacities, as 30 per cent is ambitious, considering it entails tripling production from 10 per cent to 30 per cent. It was also accompanied by a significant fund allocation of S$144 million to the Singapore Food Story Programme in 2019 (SFA 2020, p. 22). This was more than double the previous funding of S$63 million under the Agricultural Productivity Grant in 2014. This funding was tailored towards scaling up "sustainable urban food production", i.e., ramping up local production of eggs, vegetables and fish (including the "30 × 30 express grant call"), alongside objectives of "advanced biotech-based protein production" and "food safety science and innovation" (p. 22).

The Singapore government has also evolved a multipronged approach to food security, in which it has attempted to address the supply-demand situation for certain food items and also seize the opportunity to turn food security concerns into a potential new sector for technology development for export (Teng et al. 2019). With the two policy goals of improving the resilience of food security and promoting a new agrifood technology sector, the government has taken further steps to finance as well as develop its agrifood ecosystem or "urban food cluster" (Montesclaros and Teng 2018a). Regarding financing, the government has leveraged both public and private equity, by channelling them to support start-up enterprises to grow more food or invent new technologies. Hence venture capital companies and accelerators have become part of the Singapore agrifood ecosystem, as exemplified by AgFunder, Yield Lab, and the GROW Accelerator. These ventures support technology companies in their early stages, helping them scale up their operations to be significant contributors to food security in Singapore and in the region. Within ecosystem development, the government has sought to develop the infrastructure, including a physical ecosystem in the island's north and western parts where a food hub comprising production, processing and packaging activities will all be integrated into a contiguous area called the Lim Chu Kang Agrifood Production Hub. This hub will house an innovation facility known as the Agrifood Innovation Park (Teng 2020a). Further initiatives include developing human capital to support the growth in the agrifood sector. Two polytechnics currently offer diplomas in agriculture/ and or aquaculture, while two of Singapore's universities, the National University of Singapore and the Nanyang Technological University, have both announced new training programmes in food technology and in urban controlled environment agriculture or indoor farming.

Amid these developments, the city-state faces looming challenges as far as the governance of its food security is concerned. For instance, the shift in the measurement of self-sufficiency introduced in the new 30-by-30 target, from one based on tonnage to one based on nutrition, has blurred Singapore's targeted self-production levels by making them more ambiguous. In this regard, SFA has not published any reference statistics on the baseline nutritional self-sufficiency of Singapore, in stark contrast to its annual reporting of food self-sufficiency in total tonnage. Additionally, it is questionable whether the allocation of "20 per cent veg + fruits" and "10 per cent proteins", which were indicated in the SFA CEO's speech, would equate in essence to the bold "30 per cent self-sufficiency" originally envisioned in the MSE Minister's 2019 speech. In the absence of publicly available information on what the baseline level of nutrition self-sufficiency is for fruits and vegetables, it is hard to determine whether these are challenging targets to reach at all, or whether they have already been achieved or even exceeded. This also leaves the city-state in the dark as far as what the target additional levels of domestic production its farms should aspire to achieve, apart from the general notion that it is important to boost productivity levels. According to SFA Annual Report 2020/21, it would appear that some progress has been made. Self-sufficiency in eggs rose from 24 per cent in 2014 to 28 per cent in 2020, although this was mitigated by a fall in self-sufficiency in fish, from 9 per cent to 8 per cent. Self-sufficiency in leafy vegetables remained constant at 13 per cent (SFA 2021, p. 16).

IMPACT OF THE COVID-19 PANDEMIC ON SINGAPORE'S RICE SUPPLIES AND PRICES: THE CASE OF VIETNAM'S RICE EXPORT RESTRICTION

When the COVID-19 virus spread globally, Singapore was among the first countries to feel its impact, owing to its close trade and tourist relations with China and its status as a trading hub. However, the spotlight on Singapore soon dissipated as people in countries across the world caught the virus.[10]

In response to the emerging pandemic then, Singapore implemented policies to provide fiscal support to citizens through four budgets, namely, the Unity budget (which was part of the 2020 Budget announced in parliament) and the Resilience, Solidarity and Fortitude supplementary budgets. While the names of these budgets can be seen as providing a boost in morale amid the crisis, they were also substantial in terms of ensuring food security, given the disruptions brought about by the pandemic to the livelihoods and incomes of individual Singaporeans. These included monthly wage subsidies to companies which were passed on to employees, as well as tax rebates and discounts on utilities and other expenses (Montesclaros 2021, pp. 23–41).

In line with this volume's focus, we zoom in on the impact of the pandemic's disruption on the country's rice supplies. While the previous section notes that Singapore has given much attention to increasing its food self-sufficiency, this has been limited to eggs, vegetables and fish. The remainder of commodities, including rice and meats (chicken, pork and beef) are still intended to be purely import-dependent. Even for those commodities which Singapore intends to produce at home, the objective is still to achieve a "70-30" model of imports to production, indicating that 70 per cent of the country's food consumption requirements are still to be drawn from imports. As such, insights drawn from this analysis on Singapore's rice supplies can also apply to the other commodities for which Singapore continues to be import-dependent, whether wholly (meats) or partially (eggs, fish, vegetables).

Singapore's Rice Market

Traditionally, key sources for Singapore's rice imports have been Vietnam, India and Thailand. They account for approximately 90 per cent of rice imports since 2011 (Figure 6.1). There are two key reasons for the preference for these three rice exporters. The first is affordability; Vietnam and India have had among the lowest import prices across Singapore's source countries (Figure 6.2). Their prices have been low, at US$545 and US$575 per tonne respectively. In the first quarter of 2020, Singapore's import prices for rice from Cambodia and Pakistan were 54 per cent higher. The price of rice from Taiwan was practically double of that from Vietnam and triple of that from China.

The second reason lies in quality. Thailand has been ranked as having the best quality rice in the world in 2016,[11] 2017,[12] 2020[13] and 2021,[14] based on blind taste tests organized by the annual Rice Trader World Rice Conferences. While Myanmar's rice is considered cheap, its quality is considered suspect. Vietnam's rice ranked second-best in 2020,[15] while India's basmati rice is unique in its own regard, famous for its traits such as having "slender grains, pleasant, exquisite aroma, fine cooking quality, sweet taste, soft texture" (Bhattacharjee, Singhal, and Kulkarni 2002, p. 1).

The Resilience of Singapore's Rice Supplies Amid Vietnam's COVID-Induced Export Disruption

In late March 2020, however, Vietnam announced the suspension of new rice export contracts for a month.[16] During the time of Vietnam's lockdown, it was nearing the harvest season for the country's seasonal winter-spring rice, and the planting season for its summer-autumn rice, both of which are in April to June (GRiSP 2014, p. 127). Owing to fears of poor harvests from lockdown restrictions and instabilities in global supply chains,

FIGURE 6.1
Contribution of Singapore's Key Sources of Rice to Total Rice Supplies (percentage share, in tonnage)

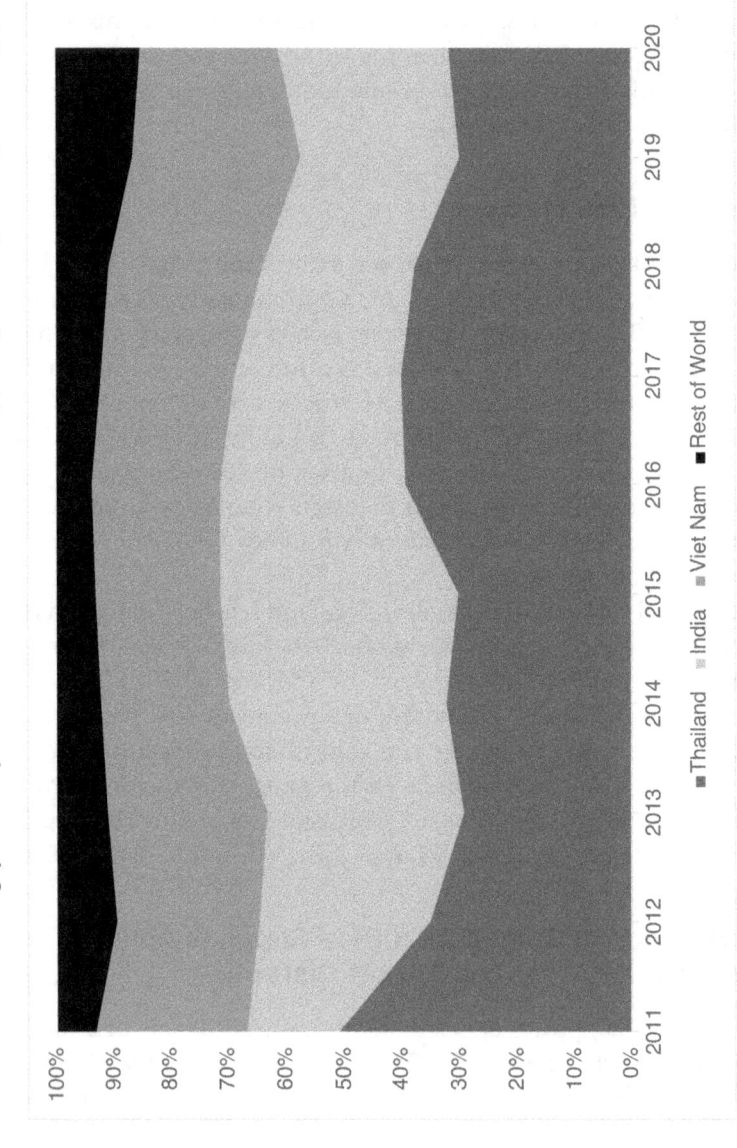

Source: International Trade Centre, "List of Supplying Markets for a Product Imported by Singapore, Product: Rice", www.trademap.org/ (accessed 16 January 2022).

FIGURE 6.2
Comparative Import Prices by Singapore from Key Sources (Vietnam, India, Thailand) and from Alternative Sources (Prior to Vietnam Import Ban), in US$ per tonne

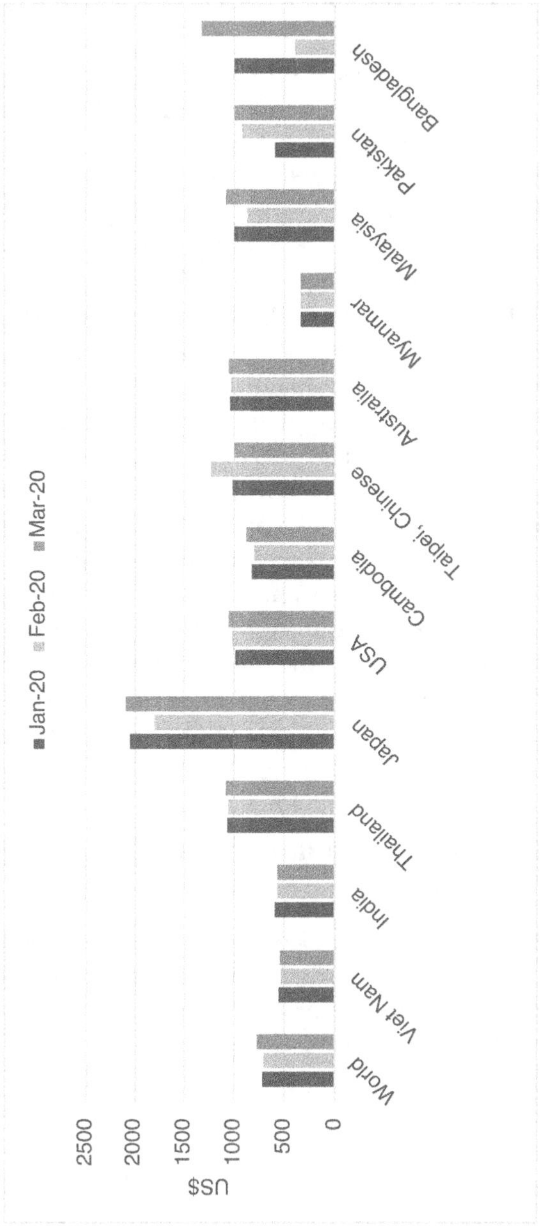

Source: International Trade Centre, "List of Supplying Markets, Product: Rice".

Vietnam imposed a rice export ban to secure its own domestic consumption requirements. It endeavoured to stockpile over 270,000 tonnes of rice for food security purposes, triggering the export restrictions.[17]

As a result, Singapore's rice imports from Vietnam subsequently fell from more than 10,000 tonnes to less than 1,000 tonnes by end of April 2020[18] (Figure 6.3). In percentage terms, they plunged from about a third of Singapore's total rice imports to just 2 per cent. Even when Vietnam lifted its ban a month later,[19] Vietnam rice imports did not immediately return to the previous level. Rather, it gradually increased to 18 per cent of Singapore's rice imports by the end of May 2020, and 22 per cent at the end of June. It eventually normalized to the pre-pandemic level in July.

Fortunately, Vietnam's ban did not lead to a reduction in the quantity of rice imports by Singapore. Singapore's total rice imports from all sources increased from 35,000 tonnes at the end of March to more than 62,000 tonnes at the end of May (Figure 6.4). The ability to procure supply from other rice suppliers is a key benefit of the city-state's diversified network of rice import countries. To make up for the close to 10,000 missing tonnes from Vietnam, private traders were able to quickly source an additional 3,700 tonnes from Cambodia and Pakistan in April 2020, 2,400 tonnes from Thailand, and 15,000 tonnes from India; the additional imports from India were more than double the normal imports from the country. Given that the volume of rice Singapore needs was small relative to the overall volume of rice available in the marketplace, sourcing extra supplies was not very challenging.

Price Vulnerability of Singapore Rice Imports during Vietnam Export Ban

As a result of the Vietnam rice export ban, Singapore's import prices increased considerably. Average import prices increased from US$708 per tonne at the end of February 2020 (prior to the March ban) to US$815 per tonne by the end of April 2020—a non-negligible 15 per cent increase (Figure 6.4).

This increase was a result of diversification when Singapore was forced to import from higher-priced alternative sources (Figure 6.5). We enumerate the key price changes below that resulted from this diversification, highlighting the countries from which Singapore imported significantly, with more than 2,000 tonnes of additional rice imports.

FIGURE 6.3
Singapore's Rice Import Quantities, for Three Major Sources

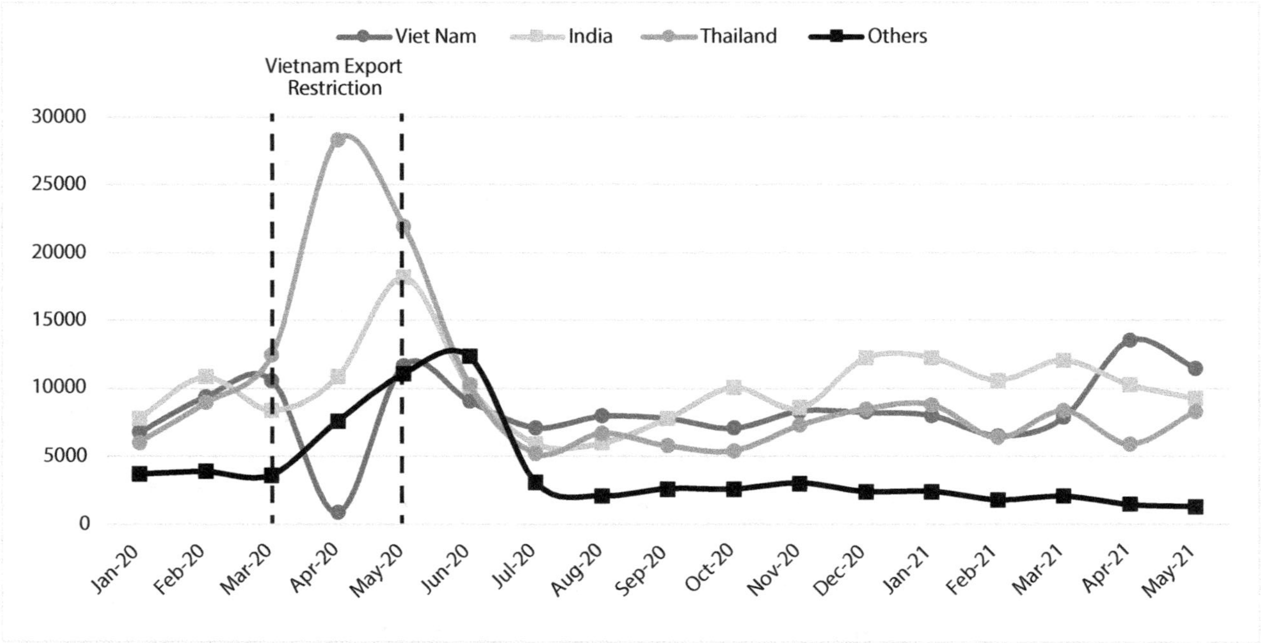

Source: International Trade Centre, "List of Supplying Markets, Product: Rice".

Impact of COVID-19 on Singapore's Rice Supplies

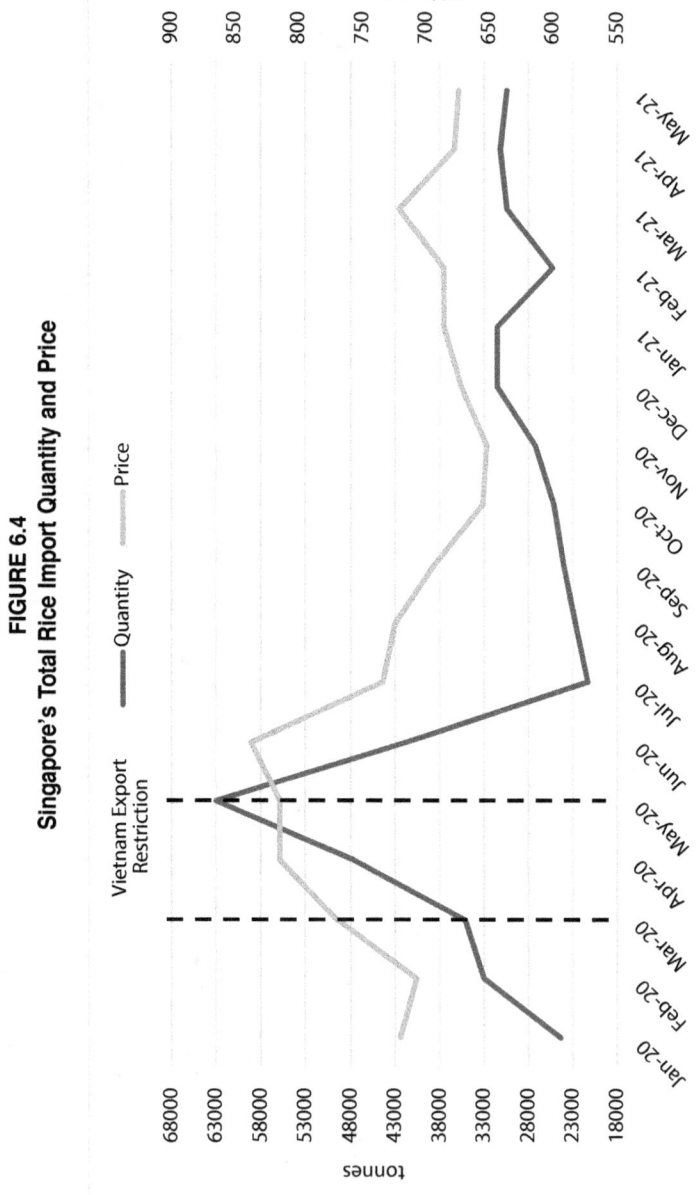

FIGURE 6.4
Singapore's Total Rice Import Quantity and Price

Source: International Trade Centre, "List of Supplying Markets, Product: Rice".

FIGURE 6.5
Singapore Rice Import Diversification after Vietnamese Rice Export Restrictions, in tonnes of Rice per Source Country

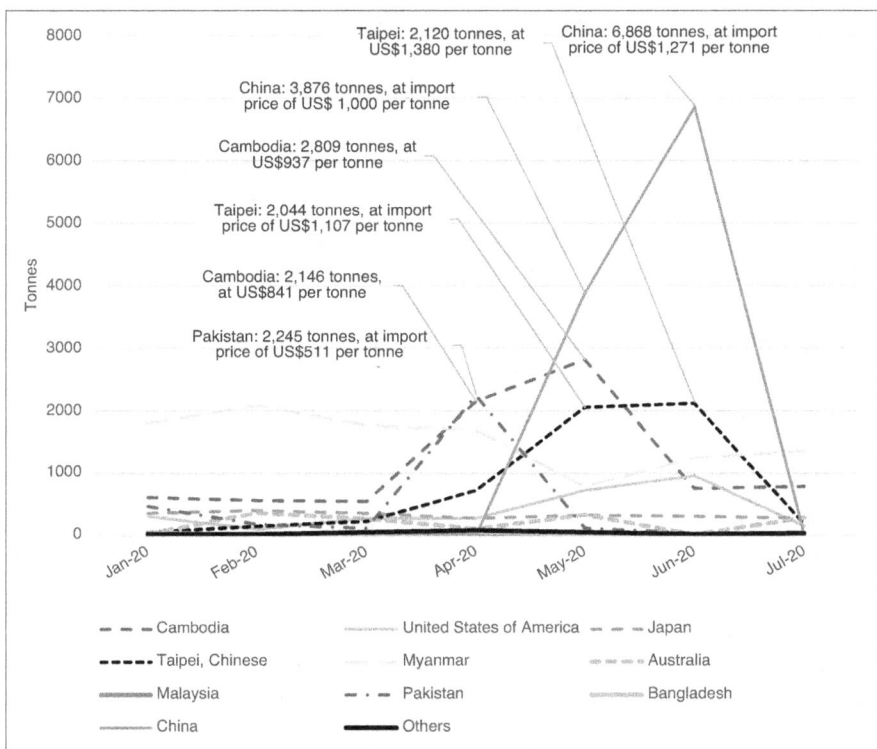

Source: International Trade Centre, "List of Supplying Markets, Product: Rice".

1. Whereas Singapore used to import rice from Vietnam at an average price of US$544 per tonne in the first quarter of 2020, the city-state had to practically quadruple its imports from Cambodia, from 540 tonnes in March 2020 to more than 2,245 tonnes in April 2020, at a much higher price of US$841 per tonne. This is close to 50 per cent higher than the import price from Vietnam prior to the disruption.
2. By May 2020, Singapore imported a larger quantity of 2,809 tonnes at an even higher price of US$937 per tonne. In the same month, it also imported 3,876 tonnes of rice from China at US$1,000 per tonne, and 2,120 tonnes from Taiwan at US$1,107 per tonne, both more than double the initial import prices from Vietnam.

3. Prices continued to increase in June 2020, reaching a peak of US$1,271 per tonne for 6,868 tonnes of rice from China, and US$1,380 per tonne for 2,120 tonnes of rice from Taiwan; the latter was 2.5 times the pre-pandemic prices for rice imported from Vietnam.

Thus, even if there are available alternative rice sources from which to draw additional rice supplies, they do not necessarily shield Singapore from higher import prices. Taking the diversification of imports into account, in fact, Singapore's import prices increased further to US$8.37 per kilogramme (kg) in June 2020, representing an 18 per cent increase in Singapore's import prices from before Vietnam's export ban.

Nonetheless, Singapore's capable traders were still able to secure rice at lower prices from Thailand and India during the rush to replace supplies from Vietnam. Traders were able to secure lower prices at US$5.03–US$5.17 per kg from India and US$9.62– US$10.34 from Thailand; these were below the usual US$5.75 and US$10.92 per kg respectively, prior to the pandemic (see Figure 6.6).

Elevated import prices were partially transmitted to domestic retail prices. To track domestic retail price movements, we leverage the database on average retail prices of selected consumer items of the Singapore Department of Statistics. It tracks the price of 5 kg of premium Thai rice (no other retail rice categories are tracked, apart from the price of chicken rice meal and the economic rice meal).[20] The database shows an increase in the retail price of a 5-kg pack of premium Thai rice from S$13.68 to S$14.08 in April 2020, and S$14.10 in May 2020, with gradual reductions to S$14.00 in June 2020 and to S$13.90 in July 2020 (see Figure 6.7). These price movements were below the 15 per cent rise in rice import prices.

While there seems to be a weak link between rice import prices and retail prices, premium Thai rice does not represent all rice available in Singapore. It is a premium that differs from the relatively cheaper Vietnam rice that went "missing" due to the pandemic. Thus, because the prices of the lower-priced rice market subsegment are not reported, it is hard to evaluate price movements with precision. The possibility remains that traders who used to import from Vietnam and were forced to find alternatives at higher prices had passed to consumers a share of the price increase.

FIGURE 6.6
Singapore's Rice Import Prices from Three Major Sources (US$ per tonne)

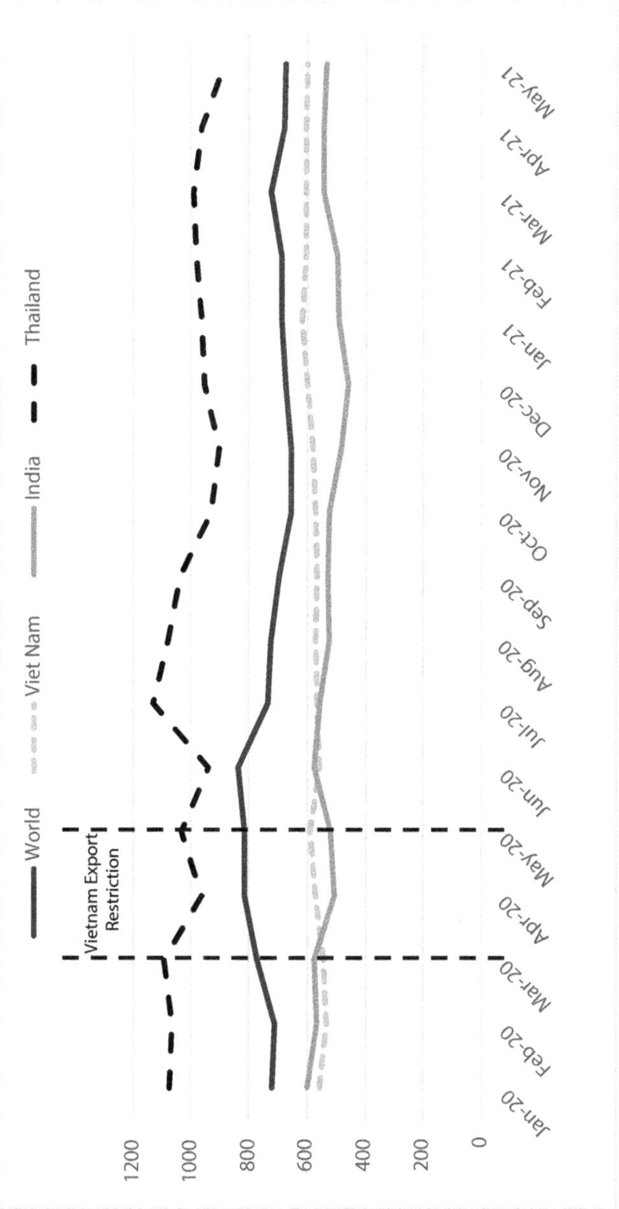

[Line chart showing rice import prices from World, Viet Nam, India, and Thailand from Jan-20 to May-21, with dashed lines marking the Vietnam Export Restriction period around Mar-20 to May-20. Y-axis ranges from 0 to 1200 US$/tonne.]

Source: International Trade Centre, "List of Supplying Markets, Product: Rice".

Impact of COVID-19 on Singapore's Rice Supplies 177

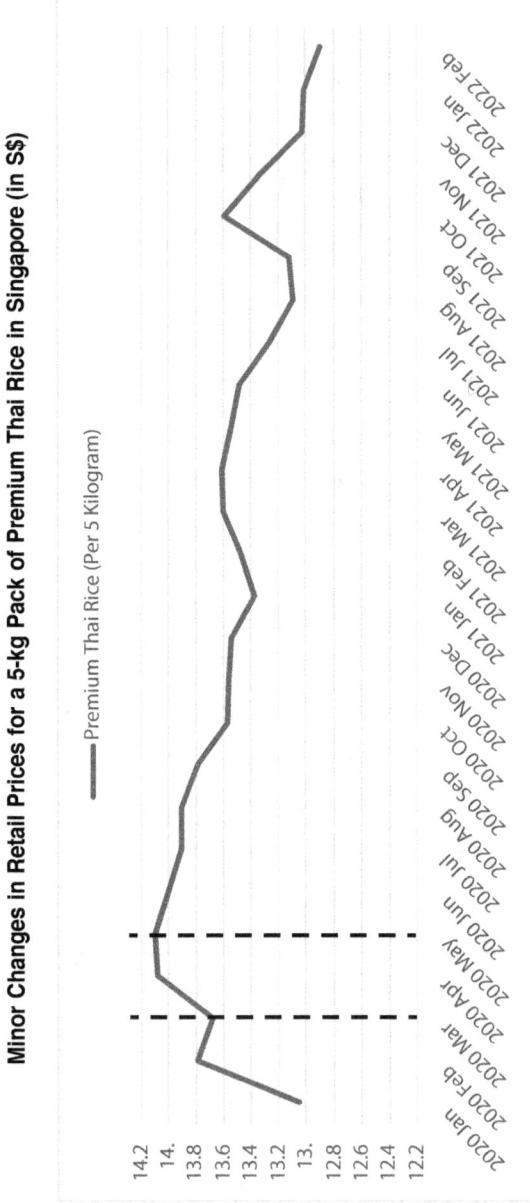

FIGURE 6.7
Minor Changes in Retail Prices for a 5-kg Pack of Premium Thai Rice in Singapore (in S$)

Source: Department of Statistics, Singapore, "Average Retail Prices of Selected Consumer Items".

IMPLICATIONS OF THE RICE SECTOR DISRUPTION ON SINGAPORE'S DIVERSIFICATION STRATEGY

If a key vulnerability of Singapore's diversification strategy is that it is not immune to price differentials between the main sources of rice and alternative sources, then this insight applies to other import-dependent sectors. As such, below we reflect on the relevance of Singapore's current approaches to food security, premised on the experience of the import-dependent rice sector during the COVID-19 pandemic before drawing policy implications for other sectors too.

The Inferiority of Alternative Sources Relative to Key Import Sources

From the rice sector's experience, a key lesson is that turning to alternative sources during disruptions can come at a hefty price. Alternative sources may inevitably provide higher prices or inferior quality relative to current sources, as otherwise, they would have been among Singapore's current sources in the first place.

This applies to other food items for which Singapore is purely import-dependent. For instance, the SFA Annual Report 2020/21 notes that Brazil and the United States are two key sources for pork, chicken and beef imports, while Australia is a primary source for pork and beef imports (SFA 2021, p. 16). The exact quantities are not readily available as the SFA would have its own categorizations of commodities, although aggregated data from International Trade Centre (ITC) statistics show that Singapore has relied on Australia, Brazil and the United States for two-thirds of its total meat imports since 2002. (China was initially a key source for Singapore's meat but it steadily declined to less than 1 per cent towards 2019.)[21] Therefore, should an export restriction occur among the top three countries, Singapore's prices are likely to rise.

This also applies to the commodities that Singapore produces at a small share of what it consumes such as vegetables, fish and eggs. According to aggregated data in the ITC database, it shows that for edible vegetables as a whole (of which leafy vegetables are a subcomponent) Malaysia and China have contributed to more than 50 per cent of Singapore's import requirements; in fact, they contributed 61 per cent in 2020.[22] Similarly, ITC data for birds' shell eggs as a whole, which are likely to be more aggregated than SFA's data on hen eggs indicate that 74 per cent of egg imports in 2020 came from Malaysia, although this was a decline from 92 per cent in 2001.[23] The data show less import concentration in the case of seafood, including fish and crustaceans. The largest share came from Malaysia but only at 14 per cent, followed by Indonesia (12 per cent), Norway (10 per cent) and China (10 per cent).[24]

Ramping Up Accreditation of New Food Sources and Focus on Price Competitiveness

Across commodities, therefore, significant degrees of concentration exist. This reflects the concentration of lower-priced and/or high-quality producers among exporters as well, and the disparity in prices and quality among the key source countries and alternatives. Singapore should thus address this concentration.

This is more within the traders' control than that of the SFA, however. Nonetheless, the SFA plays a supportive role, by accrediting overseas establishments in terms of food safety and animal health standards before products are allowed to enter Singapore. In 2020, it accredited 122 new exporting establishments.[25] Nonetheless, experience from the rice import disruption shows that the current approach of diversification can be improved. This is likely to apply to other imports, given the high levels of concentration.

To ensure accessible food prices during disruptions, the onus lies jointly on SFA's information-gathering capabilities to identify further establishments that can provide goods at more affordable prices (or at least comparable to the current dominant sources, for each food item), as well as on Singapore's traders in pursuing these new establishments. In the case of rice, this would entail identifying producers in non-traditional exporting countries that are able to produce rice at prices that are comparable to those of Vietnam and India.

This approach is rather crucial at this juncture. While the COVID-19 pandemic presents a graphic case of disruption to food security, there have been others. In 2020, for instance, Asia reeled from a number of disruptions. China, which is the world's largest pork consumer was impacted by the African swine fever; corn crops in South, Southeast and East Asia were eaten away by fall armyworms; and Thailand, a top-three rice producer globally, was facing a generational drought.[26] These made for a "perfect storm" for the food and agricultural sector (Teng 2020b). Singapore's import-diversification scheme in identifying competitively priced alternative producers will thus be even more critical in the future.

Adopting a Networked Approach to Food Security through Knowledge Diffusion of Singapore's Food Technologies

Singapore is no "island" as far as food security is concerned, as it will continue to depend on the ability of source countries to boost productivity levels. In this regard, the city-state can benefit from adopting a "networked" approach to food security. This means serving as a knowledge base for sharing information on practices for improving agricultural productivity in other countries (Montesclaros and Teng 2018a). Such an initiative can potentially fast-track the rate of adoption of novel technologies within source countries. This builds on Singapore's comparative advantage in high-tech production, which allows it to develop technologies that can be launched in source countries through this networked approach.

By helping to boost productivity levels in source countries, Singapore also helps itself as higher productivity levels lower production costs of food items. This, in turn, broadens the pool of low-cost producers from which Singapore can import its rice (and other commodities) in the long term.

Doing so entails collaboration between Singapore institutions and companies and overseas entities. The former includes dedicated agencies, such as A*STAR's Singapore Institute of Food and Biotechnology Innovation, institutes of higher learning, such as universities and polytechnics and other research organizations like Temasek Life Sciences Laboratories (TLL), among others. For example, TLL has developed rice with improved climate resilience traits that demonstrates higher yields as well. This rice variety has great potential to be adopted elsewhere in Southeast Asia too.[27] Singapore should therefore explore collaborations through bilateral means, public-private partnerships, or even leverage multilateral institutions such as the Association of Southeast Asian Nations (ASEAN), in diffusing this knowledge.

The solutions developed can be calibrated against existing technologies in a manner that allows for easy and low-cost adoption of novel technologies within the producing countries and establishments overseas. This need not be limited to those currently producing and exporting food to Singapore. Rather, SFA's accreditation of new producers and exports may include countries participating in future international collaborations with Singapore-based entities, given that productivity improvements will allow overseas establishments to be more price competitive in international markets as well.

A further benefit of the networked approach is that in the long term it is uncertain whether current source countries can boost their productivity levels to continue exporting and meeting domestic consumption requirements. For example, we discussed earlier Vietnam's COVID-19-induced export ban stemming from worries about feeding its own people. India had done likewise in 2007–8. Undoubtedly, for a country as vulnerable as Singapore, the food security of its source countries is in its vital interests. By extension, helping to spread the adoption of new technologies will help to improve productivity levels in source countries in order to meet their future consumption requirements as well as those of Singapore.

A key long-term threat facing Singapore's source countries is climate change, which may act as a brake on agricultural productivity growth. Worryingly, temperatures in Southeast Asia have increased by 0.14°C to 0.20°C per decade from the 1960s to the present; correspondingly there have been more hot days and warm nights and fewer days of cooler weather (Hijioka et al. 2014). These changes have led to increased migration and the emergence of pests and diseases (UN FAO 2008), alongside other challenges in the form of heightened resistance of pests to pesticides (Elad and Pertot 2014, p. 103), declining soil nutrients (soil erosion) and the presence of weeds that rob food crops of essential nutrients (Settele et al. 2014). In 2020 Cambodia suffered damage to 65,000 hectares of its rice lands due to floods and droughts, which pushed average rice yields down by 1.5 per cent.[28] Similar declines in Thailand and Vietnam will hit Singapore hard.

Climate change presents a case for novel technologies that boost long-term productivity in food production in Singapore's source countries. Structural changes to the economies of these countries are just as important. Future income growth among ASEAN member states will likely increase agricultural demand, whether from increases in living standards, or from migration out of agriculture. For instance, should Vietnam and Thailand decide to similarly prioritize non-agricultural sectors, then this can create a significant strain on the food import market, especially since rice is internationally a "thinly traded commodity" concentrated in a few producers. This applies to other developing countries in the region that are pursuing industrialization and service sector development.

Therefore, the bolstering of food security across Southeast Asia amid structural economic transformation is something that Singapore should pay heed to. But there are complications. For instance, despite economic growth in Southeast Asia, undernourishment has worsened since 2014 (Figure 6.8).[29] This presents a potential "inflection point" for regional food security (Montesclaros 2019). As undernourishment is an outcome indicator for food security in line with the UN FAO's definition,[30] Singapore should be wary of the shifts in food self-sufficiency, which its source countries might implement in the future.

A further implication of structural transformation in ASEAN economies is the potential for an increase in international demand for lower-priced food categories of rice and other commodities that Singapore imports. For instance, Singapore imports rice from Vietnam and India (not a member of ASEAN) currently at half the price of Thai rice. In the long term, as Southeast Asia's economies develop, higher demand for lower-priced rice may lead to upward pressure on prices. Thus, it is in Singapore's interest to take special note of demographic and economic development trends within the region, in its future sourcing of food products and also in identifying the countries which prove to be competitors for these commodities.

Counting (On) Alternative Proteins within the 30-by-30 Targets

Singapore's experience over the past decade has revealed that the task of increasing the production of vegetables, eggs and fish is by no means straightforward or easy. This brings to the fore the importance of exploring novel alternative food products to supplement these locally produced commodities.

The city-state has been doing so prior to the pandemic. Since Singapore Food Story Programme was launched in 2019, particular attention has been paid to "Future food" or novel, alternative proteins such as plant-based proteins and cellular meat. We discussed earlier the first of its three themes, "sustainable urban food production". The second and third themes focus on the production and safety of novel food respectively (Teng 2020a).

This focus on alternative proteins appears to have been intentional, aimed at increasing the level of production of nutritious proteins within Singapore, especially in anticipation of disruptions to animal protein imports. In fact, the SFA became the world's first regulatory agency in

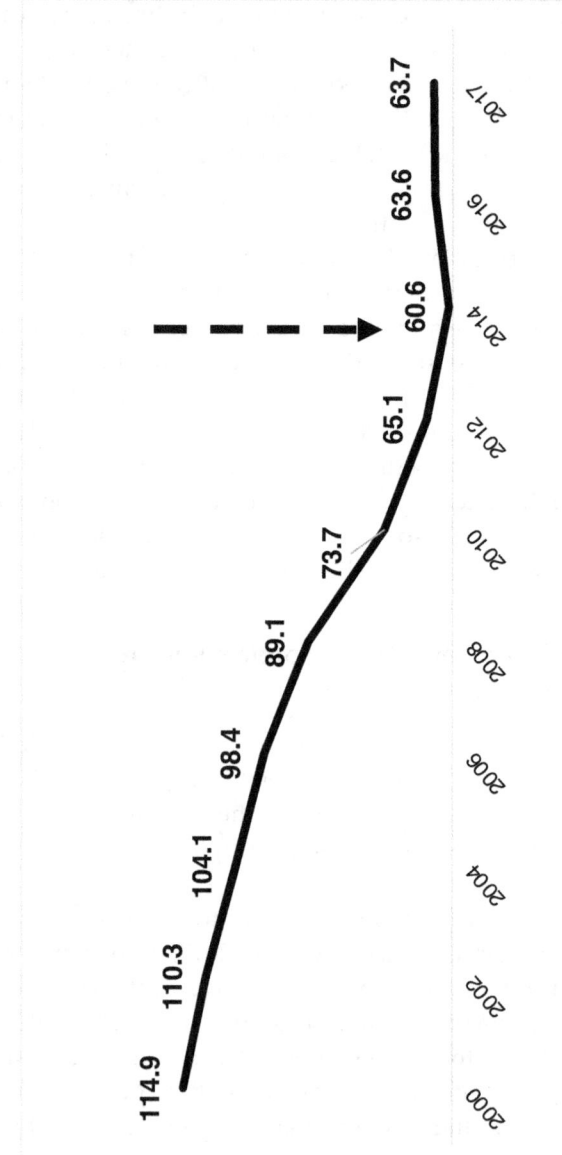

FIGURE 6.8
Number of People Undernourished (millions) in ASEAN

Source: UN FAO, "Suite of Food Security Indicators".

December 2020 to approve the safety of a novel chicken nugget produced from cells grown in an artificial medium.[31] As part of the Singapore Food Story, and to show the country as the leader in the booming alternative protein sector, a new centre called the Future Ready Food Safety Hub (FRESH) was set up as the world's first. FRESH researches the safety aspects of novel food, including alternative proteins.

SFA statistics, however, do not show the quantity of alternative protein production and its consumption. Although the initiative has been in place since 2019, yet there are no quantitative figures showing the extent of their contribution to local protein self-sufficiency. Perhaps the SFA considers only traditional farm-based commodities as part of the country's primary production since artificial proteins are manufactured rather than farmed per se.[32] Regardless, Singapore would benefit from including self-production targets for alternative proteins, similar to how it approaches its locally produced commodities.

CONCLUSION

Despite obvious space constraints and a related policy of turning away from local agriculture, the country has begun to slightly pivot back to this sector in the name of food security. This owes greatly to the scare of the 2007–8 Global Food Price Crisis that set off a chain of policy support and funding increases for developing food supply resiliency, notably the FS Roadmap and the 30-by-30 targets for food self-sufficiency.

Despite the greater attention given to the food sector in the face of the COVID-19 pandemic, this chapter emphasizes that the government needs to hone its import-diversification strategies. This especially pertains to the rice sector where adequate local production is not viable. Lessons learnt from Vietnam's export restrictions during the pandemic show that while Singapore has been able to source sufficient food supplies from elsewhere, these came at higher prices and lower quality. Moreover the rice imports which comprise 90 per cent of total rice consumption in Singapore are highly concentrated, coming from just three countries—Thailand, Vietnam and India.

The same applies to other import-dependent commodities, including meats, eggs and vegetables. Disruptions will occur and can be expected to have real consequences. Thus, Singapore needs to further tailor its current approach of import-diversification in ramping up the identification and accreditation of new establishments that can be price competitive. Success in this regard will be a reduction in the concentration of Singapore's imports in non-crisis settings or, in other words, before disruptions occur.

A further initiative in the long term is to develop a networked approach, with Singapore serving as a centre for knowledge diffusion within the region (through international collaborations or private-public partnerships) to boost productivity in alternative food sources. While the productivity of foreign sources is not within Singapore's immediate control, it can nonetheless help in raising productivity levels, as this should lower production costs and food export prices. This represents a more proactive approach to expanding the pool of alternative food exporters which are able to provide food items at more competitive prices and quality, and contribute to the de-concentration of Singapore's import markets. Beyond novel technologies, Singapore can share insights on developing conducive environments for agricultural innovation, based on its experience as a nascent urban food centre (Montesclaros and Teng 2018b). The different facets of this include parallel developments in education policies for agriculture, information and communications infrastructure and transport infrastructure, among others, as well as developing greater openness to novel biotechnologies.

At the level of ASEAN, there is a need to develop high-productivity regional food production baskets, which are a potential outcome of knowledge diffusion. This will require improving the sustainability of farming in terms of adapting to climate change, food safety practices of farmers as well as licensing and certification schemes of governments to enable green lanes for trade in agricultural products. Only through these can the region effectively "build back better" in the COVID and post-pandemic phases.

Notes

1. *Natural Nutrition Survey 2010* is the latest available survey by the Health Population Board, accessed on 22 March 2022. The other available surveys are found on the Health Population Board website, www.hpb.gov.sg/workplace/workplace-programmes/useful-information-for-organisations/national-reports-and-surveys (accessed 24 March 2022).
2. "WHO Director-General's Opening Remarks at the Media Briefing on COVID-19 – 11 March 2020". www.who.int/dg/speeches/detail/who-director-general-s-

opening-remarks-at-the-media-briefing-on-covid-19---11-march-2020 (accessed 17 January 2022).
3. Gita Gopinath, "The Great Lockdown: Worst Economic Downturn Since the Great Depression", *IMF Blog*, 14 April 2020.
4. UN FAO, IFAD, WFP, "The State of Food Insecurity in the World 2015", *The State of Food Insecurity in the World Series* (Rome, UN FAO, 2021), p. 53, www.fao.org/publications/sofi/2015/en/ (accessed 17 January 2022).
5. Agri-Food and Veterinary Authority of Singapore, "AVA's Food Security Roadmap for Singapore", 4 March 2013 (updated 27 February 2020), www.sfa.gov.sg/food-for-thought/article/detail/ava per cent27s-food-security-roadmap-for-singapore (accessed 30 March 2022).
6. The rest of the farms/areas recorded were for ornamental orchids (75 farms covering 247 hectares) and dog breeding/ boarding/training (29 areas covering 9.5 hectares) or for other food products (frogs, crocodiles, goats, mushrooms, beansprouts, aquatic plants, among others).
7. Speech by Mr Masagos Zulkifli, Minister for the Environment and Water Resources, the Committee of Supply Debate 2019, Ministry of Sustainability and the Environment, 7 March 2019, line 64.
8. "Ecosperity Conversations: What Singapore's '30 by 30' Food Security Goal Means for Businesses", www.ecosperity.sg/en/events/ecoconvo-30by30-food-security-goal-singapore-2019.html (accessed 31 March 2022).
9. Lim Kok Thai, "What Singapore's '30 by 30' Food Security Goal Means for Businesses", paper presented at Ecosperity Conversations, Singapore, 13 November 2019, Slide 6.
10. "WHO Director-General's Opening Remarks at the Media Briefing on COVID-19 – 11 March 2020".
11. Dora Whitaker, "Drum Roll–and the Winner of the World's Best Rice Is .... (Clue It Comes from Thailand)", *Lonely Planet*, 10 December 2016.
12. Phusadee Arunmas, "It's Official: Thai Rice is the World's Best", *Bangkok Post*, 8 November 2017.
13. "Thailand's Jasmine Rice Wins Championship for World's Best Rice Contest", *Xinhuanet*, 12 December 2020.
14. "Thailand Wins 6th Best Rice Title, While Market Achievement Award Goes to Mr. Rajiv Kumar (Executive Director of The Rice Exporters Association of India)", *Rice Trader*, 15 December 2021.
15. "Vietnamese Rice Ranked Second at World's Best Rice Contest 2020", *Nhan Dan*, 4 December 2020.
16. Sen Nguyen and Reuters, "Coronavirus: Vietnam Stockpiles Rice as Outbreak Spreads and Food Security Concerns Grow", *South China Morning Post*, 28 March 2020, www.scmp.com/week-asia/economics/article/3077272/coronavirus-vietnam-stockpiles-rice-outbreak-spreads-and-food (accessed 16 January 2021).

17. "Vietnam's Ban on Rice Exports still in Force, Govt may set Limit: Traders", *Business Times*, 30 March 2020.
18. International Trade Centre, "List of Supplying Markets for a Product Imported by Singapore, Product: Rice", bit.ly/3Fy78LR (accessed 16 January 2021).
19. UN Food and Agriculture Organization, "Viet Nam lifts Rice Export Restrictions", *Food Price and Monitoring Analysis*, 30 April 2020, www.fao.org/giews/food-prices/food-policies/detail/en/c/1273534/ (accessed 16 January 2021).
20. Department of Statistics, Singapore, "Average Retail Prices of Selected Consumer Items – SingStat Table Builder", tablebuilder.singstat.gov.sg/table/TS/M212891 (accessed 31 March 2022).
21. International Trade Centre, "List of Supplying Markets, Product: 02 Meat and Edible Meat Offal", www.trademap.org/ (accessed 31 March 2022).
22. International Trade Centre, "List of Supplying Markets, Product: 07 Edible Vegetables and Certain Roots and Tubers".www.trademap.org/ (accessed 31 March 2022).
23. International Trade Centre, "List of Supplying Markets, Product: 0407 Birds' Eggs, In Shell, Fresh, Preserved or Cookedwww.trademap.org/ (accessed 31 March 2022).
24. International Trade Centre, "List of Supplying Markets, Product: 03 Fish and Crustaceans, Molluscs and Other Aquatic Invertebrates". www.trademap.org/ (accessed 31 March 2022).
25. SFA 2021, p. 22.
26. European Commission's Directorate-General for European Civil Protection and Humanitarian Aid Operations, "Thailand - Drought (DG ECHO, government, media) (ECHO Daily Flash of 10 January 2020)", *ReliefWeb*. 10 January 2020. reliefweb.int/report/thailand/thailand-drought-dg-echo-government-media-echo-daily-flash-10-january-2020 (accessed 17 January 20222).
27. "Singapore's Temasek Rice Developed by TLL Scientists for Regional Food Security", http://www.tll.org.sg/wp-content/uploads/2016/08/TLL-Press-Release-Singapores-Temasek-Rice-Developed-by-TLL-Scientists-for-Regional-Food-Security.pdf (accessed 31 March 2022).
28. *ASEAN Early Warning Information no. 24*. ASEAN Plus Three Food Security Information System, http://www.aptfsis.org/uploads/normal/EWI per cent20Report per cent2024/EWI per cent20Report per cent2024 per cent20March per cent202020.pdf (accessed 16 September 2020).
29. Based on UN FAO, "Suite of Food Security Indicators" (Rome, UN FAO, 2018) http://www.fao.org/faostat/en/#data/FS (accessed 17 December 2018).
30. UN FAO, IFAD, WFP, "The State of Food Insecurity", p. 53.
31. Paul Teng, "Commentary: Is Lab-Grown Meat a New Frontier or a Passing Fad?", *Channel NewsAsia*, 5 December 2020. www.channelnewsasia.com/

news/commentary/lab-grown-chicken-eat-just-cell-cultured-meat-agriculture-food-13699840 (accessed 17 January 2022).
32. National Library Board (NLB) of Singapore, "Primary Production Department is Formed, 25th Jun 1959", eresources.nlb.gov.sg/history/events/14f36ce1-a54c-4bb3-8993-91c57fee7c50 (accessed 31 March 2022).

References

Agri-Food and Veterinary Authority of Singapore (AVA). 2010. *Annual Report 2009/10*. Singapore: Agri-Food & Veterinary Authority of Singapore.

———. 2011. *Annual Report 2010/11*. Singapore: Agri-Food & Veterinary Authority of Singapore.

———. 2015. *Annual Report 2014/15*. Singapore: Agri-Food & Veterinary Authority of Singapore.

———. 2019. *Annual Report 2018/19*. Singapore: Agri-Food & Veterinary Authority of Singapore.

Bhattacharjee, Paramita, Rekha S. Singhal, and Pushpa R. Kulkarni. 2002. "Basmati Rice: A Review". *International Journal of Food Science & Technology* 37, no. 1: 1–12.

Dawe, David, and Tom Slayton. 2010. "The World Rice Market Crisis of 2007–2008". In *The Rice Crisis: Markets, Policies and Food Security*, edited by David Dawe, pp. 39–52. London & Washington, DC: Earthscan.

Elad, Yigal, and Ilaria Pertot. 2014. "Climate Change Impacts on Plant Pathogens and Plant Diseases". *Journal of Crop Improvement* 28, no. 1: 99–139.

GRiSP (Global Rice Science Partnership). 2014. *The Rice Almanac*, 4th ed. Los Baños, Philippines): International Rice Research Institute.

Health Promotion Board (HPB). 2010. "Comparison of Mean Daily Intake of Healthy Diet Pyramid Food Groups (Weight in Grams) among Adult Singapore Residents, NNS 2004 and NNS 2010". *National Nutrition Survey 2010*. Singapore: Health Promotion Board.

Hijioka, Yasuaki, et al. 2014. "Asia". In *Climate Change 2014: Impacts, Adaptation, and Vulnerability. Part B: Regional Aspects. Contribution of Working Group II to the Fifth Assessment Report of the Intergovernmental Panel on Climate Change*, edited by Vicente R. Barros et al., pp. 1327–70. Cambridge, UK, and New York: Cambridge University Press. www.ipcc.ch/site/assets/uploads/2018/02/WGIIAR5-Chap24_FINAL.pdf (accessed 17 January 2022).

Ludher, Elyssa, and Thinesh Kumar Paramasilvam. 2018. *Food and the City: Overcoming Challenges for Food Security*. Singapore: Centre for Liveable Cities.

Montesclaros, Jose Ma. Luis. 2019. "Southeast Asia's Food Security: Inflection Point?". In *Non-Traditional Security Issues in ASEAN: Agendas for Action*, edited by Mely Caballero-Anthony and Lina Gong, pp. 67–93. Singapore: ISEAS – Yusof Ishak Institute.

———. 2021. "What Are the Economic Impacts of a Pandemic?". In *How to Prepare for the Next Pandemic: Behavioural Sciences Insights for Practitioners and Policymakers*, edited by Majeed Khader, Denise Dillon, Xingyu Ken Chen, Loo Seng Neo, and Jeffery Chin, pp. 23–41. Singapore: World Scientific.

———, and Paul P.S. Teng. 2018a. "Ensuring a Successful Singapore Urban Food Cluster". *NTS Insight*, no. IN18-02. Singapore: RSIS Centre for Non-Traditional Security (NTS) Studies.

———, and Paul S. Teng. 2018b. "Singapore's Nascent Urban Farming: Potential Future Regional Centre?". *RSIS Commentary*, 23 November 2018.

Settele, Josef, Robert Scholes, Richard A. Betts, Stuart Bunn, Paul Leadley, Daniel Nepstad, Jonathan T. Overpeck, and Miguel Angel Taboada, et al. 2014. "Terrestrial and Inland Water Systems". In *Climate Change 2014: Impacts, Adaptation, and Vulnerability, Part A: Global and Sectoral Aspects*, edited by Christopher B. Field, Vicente R. Barros, et al., pp. 271–359. Cambridge, UK and New York: Cambridge University Press.

Singapore Food Agency (SFA). 2020. *Annual Report 2019/20*. Singapore: Singapore Food Agency.

———. 2021. *Annual Report 2020/21*. Singapore: Singapore Food Agency.

Teng, Paul S. 2020a. "Assuring Food Security in Singapore, a Small Island State facing COVID-19". *Food Security* 12: 801–4. https://doi.org/10.1007/s12571-020-01077-0 (accessed 17 January 2022).

———. 2020b. "Swine Fever, Climate Change, Armyworm: A Perfect Storm for Asia's Food Prices". *South China Morning Post*, 10 January 2020. www.scmp.com/week-asia/health-environment/article/3045515/swine-fever-climate-change-armyworm-perfect-storm (accessed 17 January 2022).

———, and Jose Ma. Luis Montesclaros. 2019. "Singapore's '30 by 30' Strategy: Can Food Self-Production Be Achieved?". *RSIS Commentary*, 25 March 2019.

———, Jose Ma. Luis Montesclaros, Rob Hulme, and Andrew Powell. 2019. "The Evolving Singapore Agrifood Ecosystem". *NTS Insight*, no. IN19-03, August 2019.

Wong, Derek. 2018. "New Stat Board Singapore Food Agency to be formed in April 2019; AVA will Cease to Exist". *Straits Times*, 26 July 2018.

Index

A
Achmad Tirto Sudiro, 121
acidic soil, 109
African swine fever, 82, 179
Agency for Science, Technology and Research (A*STAR), 163, 180
AgFunder, 166
Agreement on Agriculture (AoA), 88
Agricultural Bank and Land Allocation Policy, 144
Agricultural Learning Center (ALC), 143
Agricultural Productivity Fund, 164
Agricultural Productivity Grant, 165
agrifood ecosystem, 166
Agrifood Innovation Park, 166
Agrifood Production Hub, 166
Agri-Veterinary Authority (AVA), 162–64
ALC Network Committee, 145
All Rice Price Index, 59
Area Farmers' Associations (AFAs), 40, 66
Asian Financial Crisis (AFC), 9, 17–19, 106, 121, 140
Asia, paddy production in, 28
association of rice millers and traders (PERPADI), 112
Association of Southeast Asian Nations (ASEAN), 22, 25, 89, 180–81, 185
authoritarianism, 9

B
Bank Indonesia, 123
Bank of Agriculture and Agricultural Cooperatives (BAAC), 140, 146, 153–54
Barisan Nasional (BN), 14
basmati rice, 125, 168
Bayanihan to Heal as One Act, 80
BERNAS (Padiberas Nasional Berhad), 4, 13–15, 36, 43–44, 47, 51, 54, 62–63, 65, 72
biodiesel, 51
biofuel, 9
BLT (cash social assistance scheme), 128
"Board of Directors for the Operation of the Mega Farm Programme Extension System, The", 144
BPNT (*Bantuan Pangan Non-Tunai*), 127–28, 130
BPS (Central Statistics Agency), 107, 111, 123
BPTN (targeted rice subsidy), 120, 122, 128
broken rice, 43, 71, 112, 120

brown rice, 120
Bulog (State Logistics Board), 4, 17–19
    changing roles of, 120–32
Bumiputera Rice Millers Schemes, 47
Bustanil Arifin, 121
Buyer of Last Resort, 47

C
capitalism, hierarchical, 136–37, 156
cash social assistance scheme (BLT), 128
cellular meat, 182
Center for Price Information of Strategic Foods (PIHPS), 123
centralized paddy seed distribution, 65–66
Central Statistics Agency (BPS), 107, 111, 123
cereal market, disruption in, 51
Channel NewsAsia, 165
chemical fertilizer, 5, 8
Civil and Commercial Code, 150
climate change, 69–70, 165, 181, 185
Coalition of Hope, *see* Pakatan Harapan
coefficient of variation (CV), 112–13, 117, 119
Cold War, 140
Commonwealth, 84
Communist Party of Thailand, 139, 155
Companies Act (Malaysia), 44
Comprehensive Rice Production and Marketing Plan, 144
Constitutional Court, 157
contract farming, 66, 112, 117, 120
corn, 51, 85–86, 141, 179
corruption, 4–7, 65, 89, 101, 121, 138, 140
cost of production (COP), 53
coup, 7, 136, 144

COVID-19 pandemic, 7–8, 23–27, 161, 185
    Indonesia, 18–19, 105–6, 107, 114, 131
    Malaysia, 13–14, 37, 55–63
    mitigating measures, 37
    Philippines, The 15, 17, 79–84, 91, 94, 98, 100
    public spending, 27
    rice production during, 55
    Singapore, 22, 162, 167, 178–79
    Southeast Asia, 10, 12
    Thailand, 20, 135–36, 142, 149, 151–53, 155–56
    virtual workshop on rice, 10–11

D
debt, 5, 61, 84, 89, 140, 151, 154
decentralization policy, 121
deforestation, 23
Delta variant, 105
Democrat Party, 141–42, 153–54
distorted price, 2, 139–40
    see also undistorted price
District Agricultural Extension Office, 145
Dominguez, Carlos "Sonny", 16
drought, 2, 8, 21, 107, 112, 121, 125, 152, 163, 179, 181
DTKS (Social-Welfare Integrated Data), 127
Duterte, Rodrigo, 15–17, 79

E
Economic Cluster of the Cabinet, 101
Economic Development Board, 163
Economic Transformation Plan, 66
Effective Protection Coefficient (EPC), 47
El Niño, 88

Index

enhanced community quarantine (ECQ), 79–80, 82
Enhanced Quality of Agricultural Products Project, 143
enriched rice, 120
Entry Point Projects (EPPs), 66–67
ethnic riot, 35
European Union, 69
e-warong, 127
export tax, 6, 137–38, 156

F

Family Hope Programme (PKH), 128
Farmers' Market, 144
farm mechanization, 54
farmgate price, 3, 6, 16, 84, 97–98, 135–36, 138–39, 157
fast food, 106
Federal Government Paddy Fertilizer Assistance Scheme, *see* SBPKP
fertilizer, 40, 53, 55–56, 65, 85, 111, 115, 143, 150–51
 chemical, 5, 8
 inorganic, 9, 13
Fertilizer, Pesticide and Weedicides for Hill Paddy Scheme, *see* SBRPB
flood, 2–3, 36, 82, 181
Food and Agriculture Organization (FAO), 55, 59, 80, 99, 114, 125, 163, 182
food crisis, 25, 114–15, 130, 132
"Food Fund", 163
Food Industry Convention, 163
food insecurity, 22, 37, 61–62
Food Lane Pass scheme, 82
food security, 3–4, 6, 8, 15, 20, 26, 34, 37, 130–31, 162, 164–67, 171, 178–79
 definition, 163
 measuring, 40

neoliberal approach, 24
"networked" approach, 180
rankings in, 22
Southeast Asia, in, 182
strategies, 54–55
Food Security Council, 122
Food Security Fund, 62
Food Security Policy, 51, 56
Food Security Roadmap, 162–64
Food Summit, 69
fragrant rice, 45, 66, 120
"Future food", 182
Future Ready Food Safety Hub (FRESH), 184

G

Gaud, W.S., 85
Global Food Price Crisis (GFPC), 162–63, 184
global food stocks, 115
"global pandemic", 24
global poverty, 71
global rice market, 115
global warming, 23
globalization, 36
glutinous rice, 45, 125
Government's Lending Decree to Remedy and Restore the Economy and Society as Affected by the Coronavirus Disease Pandemic, 142
Great Depression, 162
Green Revolution, 4, 9, 28, 35, 38, 40, 71, 85
GROW Accelerator, 166
Guaranteed Minimum Price (GMP), 41–42, 47, 54

H

Health Sciences Authority, 164
Herfindahl-Hirschman Index, 47

hierarchical capitalism, 136–37, 156
human capital, 23, 132, 166

I
Income Guarantee Programme, 142, 153–55
indirect tax, 40, 44
Indonesia
    COVID-19, 18–19, 105–6, 107, 114, 131
    food for the poor programme, 122
    government rice reserves (CBP), 130
    gross domestic product (GDP), 16, 19
    poverty in, 105, 127
    price stabilization policy, 120–31
    rice economy in, 107–14
    rice import, 1–4, 127
    value-chain resilience, 114–20
inflation, 16, 26, 41, 69, 89, 94, 99, 117, 123, 132, 139
inorganic fertilizer, 9, 13
Integrated Agricultural Development Authorities (IADAs), 67–68
Inter-Ministry Committee on Food Security (IMCFS), 163
International Enterprises Singapore, 163
International Fund for Agricultural Development, 69
International Monetary Fund (IMF), 17–18
International Rice Research Institute (IRRI), 85
International Trade Centre (ITC), 178
Internet of Things, 66
IR8, 85
irrigation, 9, 21, 28, 35, 85, 94, 102, 109, 111, 152
    infrastructure, 54, 67–68
    maintenance, 19

J
Jakarta Food Station, 123
Japanese occupation, 8
jasmine rice, 142–43, 153
Java-Bali Emergency Community Activity Restrictions (PPKM), 128
Joko "Jokowi" Widodo, 19–20, 122

K
Kartu Sembako (ration cards), 127
Kemudu Agricultural Development Area (KADA), 67
KPSH (*Ketersediaan Pasokan dan Stabilisasi Harga*), 123, 125, 130
Kuala Lumpur Share Exchange, 44

L
land reform, 85–86
land-to-labour ratio, 108
"limited partnership", 151
lockdown, 8, 19, 37, 59, 142, 168

M
"mafia" rice traders, 127
Mahathir Mohamad, 44
maize, 6, 9, 112, 122, 138, 163
Malaysia
    COVID-19, 13–14, 37, 55–63
    farm subsector, 41–43
    First Five-Year Plan, 38
    food security strategies, 54–55
    gross domestic product (GDP), 16, 19, 34, 60
    import subsector, 44–48
    income group, 61
    labour market, 61
    milling subsector, 43–44
    paddy and rice sector, policy interventions in, 38–48
    paddy community, 34–35

Index 195

pandemic policy response, 62–68
poverty, 61
retail subsector, 44
rice consumption, 60, 63
rice import, 1–4, 60, 63–64
Twelfth Malaysia Plan, 66
malnutrition, 15, 127
Marcos, Ferdinand, 85
Marcos Jr., Ferdinand, 17, 26, 101
"market manipulations", 38
Masagana 99 programme, 85
Mega Farm Group, 145–46, 150–52
Mega Farm Network Committee, 145
Mega Farm Operation Committee, 149
Megawati Sukarnoputri, 18
middle-class peasants, 7
milled rice, 11, 16, 55, 58, 78, 84, 86, 90–91, 93–94, 120
Ministry of Agriculture and Agro-based Industry (MoA), Malaysia, 35, 53
Ministry of Agriculture and Cooperatives (MOAC), Thailand, 136, 145, 157
Ministry of Agriculture and Food Industries (MAFI), Malaysia, 66, 72
Ministry of Agriculture, Indonesia, 122, 125
Ministry of Commerce, Thailand, 153
Ministry of Finance, Indonesia, 123
Ministry of Finance, Thailand, 154
Ministry of Foreign Affairs, Singapore, 163
Ministry of Health, Singapore, 163
Ministry of Home Affairs, Singapore, 163
Ministry of National Development (MND), Singapore, 163
Ministry of Social Affairs, Indonesia, 120, 122
Ministry of Sustainability and the Environment (MSE), Singapore, 164–66
Ministry of the Interior, Thailand, 144, 157
Ministry of Trade, Indonesia, 125, 128
monarchy, 7
money politics, 7
movement control orders (MCOs), 15, 37
Muda Agricultural Development Authority (MADA), 43, 67
Muhyiddin Yassin, 14, 28
multinational corporations (MNCs), 137
MySejahtera, 37

N

Nanyang Technological University, 166
National Alliance (Perikatan Nasional), 14
National Council for Peace and Order (NCPO), 138, 140–42, 144, 153
National Environment Agency (NEA), 163
National Farmers' Association (NAFAS), 40, 65, 68
National Food Authority (NFA), 4, 16–17, 86–89, 91, 94, 98, 101–2
National Front, see Barisan Nasional
National Grains Authority (NGA), 86
National Logistics Agency, see Bulog
National Nutrition Survey, 161
National Paddy and Rice Authority (NPRA), 36, 43–44, 47, 62, 71
National Paddy/Rice Stockpile, 47
National Parks Board, 164

National Rice and Corn Corporation (NARIC), 84–86
National Rice and Paddy Corporation, *see* BERNAS
National Security Coordination Secretariat, 163
National Strategy Master Plan, 141
National University of Singapore, 166
New Order, 18, 120–21, 125
New Theory Agriculture (Self-Sufficiency Economy Principle), 143
NFA rice, 86, 94
nominal rate of assistance (NRA), 138, 157
Non-Cash Food Subsidy Programme, *see* BPNT
nutritional needs, 165

O

oil
 cooking, 115, 117–18, 199, 122
 crisis, 9
 prices, 115, 139
Omicron variant, 55
Organic Agriculture Development, 143
Organization of the Exporting Petroleum Countries, 9

P

paddy farmers, poverty among, 35
paddy mortgage scheme, 6–7
Paddy Price Subsidy Scheme, *see* SSHP
Padiberas Nasional Berhad (BERNAS), 4, 13–15, 36, 43–44, 47, 51, 54, 62–63, 65, 72
Pakatan Harapan (PH), 14, 36
Pakatan Nasional (PN), 36

Palang Pracharath, 21
panic buying, 9, 51, 55, 88
path dependence policy, 37, 68, 70
patronage networks, 5, 14, 86–87
peasant movement, 87
People's Democratic Reform Committee (PDRC), 138, 140
People's Power, 140
Perikatan Nasional (National Alliance), 14
PERPADI (association of rice millers and traders), 112
pesticide, 40, 53, 181
Pheu Thai Party, 7, 20, 140–41
Philippine-American War, 78, 84
Philippine Institute of Development Studies, 99
Philippine Revolution, 78
Philippines, The
 COVID-19 in, 15, 17, 79–84, 91, 94, 98, 100
 Bureau of Commerce, 84
 Bureau of Customs, 89
 Department of Agriculture (DA), 82, 89, 91
 essential sectors, 79–80
 gross domestic product (GDP), 16, 19, 80–84
 local government unit (LGU), 80
 National Capital Region (NCR), 79, 99
 poverty in, 82
 Presidential Decree (PD), 86
 reform implication, 98–100
 rice import, 1–4, 78, 86, 91–93, 99–101
 rice industry in, 84–91
 rice policy reform, 91–98
 Spanish colony, as, 84
PIHPS (Center for Price Information of Strategic Foods), 123

Index

Pitipong Puengboon Na Ayudhya, 157
PKH (Family Hope Programme), 128
plant-based proteins, 182
political connection, 5
poverty, 2, 6, 8, 10, 16, 37
  absolute, 71
  alleviation, 9, 19, 108, 132
  global, 71
  Indonesia, in, 105, 127
  Malaysia, in, 61
  measured, 98
  paddy farmers, among, 35
  Philippines, in The, 82
  rural, 132
  urban, 11
PPKM (Java-Bali Emergency Community Activity Restrictions), 128
Pralang Pracharat, 140–41, 148, 152–54, 157
Prayuth Chan-o-cha, 20–21, 135–36, 138, 141–42, 144, 149, 153, 155, 157
Prem Tinsulanonda, 137
price band, 121
price distortion, *see* distorted price
price guarantee programme, 136
price vulnerability, 171
Producer Subsidy Equivalent (PSE), 47
production, and livelihood, 5–7
Promoting the Use of Agricultural Machinery, 143
pro-poor programmes, 3
Protection of Sustainable Food Agricultural Land law, 109
protectionism, 1, 5, 16, 25, 35–37, 40, 47, 53, 63, 68
Provincial Agriculture Extension Office, 144

Provincial Project Management Committee, 149
PT IBU (Indo Beras Utama), 117–18
PT Tiga Pilar Sejahtera (TPS), 118
Public Financial and Fiscal Discipline Act, 154
public-private partnerships (PPPs), 66, 68–69
purchasing power, 61, 63, 94, 98, 114–15, 130

Q

quantitative restrictions (QRs), 87–89, 101
Quota Restriction, 139

R

ration cards (*Kartu Sembako*), 127
recession, 18, 105
Red Shirt Movement, 140
rent-seeking, 10, 65
Republic Act, 80, 89, 91
rice
  harvest, 1, 3, 5, 8, 13, 24, 65, 84–86, 88, 94, 106–8, 110, 112, 114, 121–23, 125, 152–3, 168
  household expenditure, and, 12
  modern varieties (MVs), 85
  political commodity, as, 7, 20
  stockpile, 1, 14, 25, 47–48, 54, 63, 68, 71, 140, 163, 171
  subsidy, 5, 14–15, 17, 19–20, 22, 27, 35–36, 42–44, 47, 53–57, 66, 68–69, 85–86, 94, 118, 120, 122, 127, 136, 139–40, 143, 146, 148, 154–56
  trade, 3, 15, 17, 19, 22, 63–64, 113–14, 121, 127
  virtual workshop on, 10
Rice and Corn Administration (RCA), 85–86

Rice and Corn Board (RICOB), 85–86
"rice bowl", 79, 95
rice field conversion, 109, 111
Rice Fund, 17, 91, 98
rice imports, benefits of, 2–3
Rice Liberalization Act (RLA), 89, 91, 98, 100–101
Rice Mega Farm Programme, 21, 136, 138, 141–42, 148, 155
   implementation of, 144–47, 149–53
rice-pledging scheme, 137–38, 140
Rice Policy and Management Committee, 153, 157
Rice Premium, 137, 139
Rice Price Index, 59
rice products, 120
rice reserve requirement scheme, 137, 139
Rice Trader World Rice Conference, 168
rural inequality, 5–6
rural poverty, 132
"ruralization phenomenon", 18, 106
Russia, and invasion of Ukraine, 13, 28, 117

S
sanitary and phytosanitary standards (SPS), 89, 91
SARS-CoV-2, 105
Satgas Pangan (Task Force for Food), 128
SBPKP (*Skim Baja Padi Kerajaan Persekutuan*), 53, 65
SBRPB (*Skim Subsidi Baja dan Racun Padi Bukit/Huma*), 53
semi-democracy, 157
semi-dwarf rice, 85
Singapore
   30 by 30 policy, 23, 162, 164–66, 182

COVID-19 in, 22, 162, 167, 178–79
First World status, 162
food dependency, 22–23, 161
food security policies, 162–67, 180–82
gross domestic product (GDP), 16, 19
new food sources, accreditation of, 179–80
rice market, 168
sources of rice, 168–77
Unity budget, 167
Singapore Department of Statistics, 175
Singapore Food Authority (SFA), 162, 164, 166–67, 178–80, 182, 184
Singapore Food Story Programme, 165, 182, 184
Singapore Institute of Food and Biotechnology Innovation, 180
Singapore Police Force, 163
Smart Farmer Project, 143
smart farming, 111
Smart Paddy Field Programme (Smart SBB), 66–69
smuggling, 2, 89, 102
Social-Welfare Integrated Data (DTKS), 127
Soeharto, 18–19, 120–22, 125
soil erosion, 23, 181
Southeast Asia
   COVID-19, 10, 12
   food security in, 182
soya bean, 36, 112, 122
Special Purpose Vehicle (SPV), 66, 68
Special Safeguards Act, 91
SSHP (*Skim Subsidi Harga Padi*), 42, 47
SSL, 35, 40, 53, 60, 66, 68
Standard Operating Procedure (SOP), 37

Standards, Productivity and
  Innovation Board, 163
State Farmers' Associations, 40
State Logistics Board (Bulog), 4,
  17–19
  changing roles of, 120–32
state-owned enterprise (SOE), 122
state trading enterprise (STE), 35–36,
  38, 43–44, 47
sticky rice, 142–43
stimulus package, 15, 62
stockpile, rice, 1, 14, 25, 47–48, 54, 63,
  68, 71, 140, 163, 171
Super Special Tempatan (SST) rice,
  44, 71
Super Tempatan (ST) rice, 43–44, 71
supply chain, 8, 24–25, 47, 62, 65–67,
  84, 137, 143, 168
Susilo Bambang Yudhoyono, 18
swine fever, African, 82, 179
Syed Mokhtar Al-Bukhary, 14

T
Task Force for Food (*Satgas Pangan*),
  128
technology transfer, 23
Temasek Life Sciences Laboratories
  (TLL), 180
Thai Rice Mills Association, 142
Thai Royal Army, 136
Thailand
  COVID-19 in, 20, 135–36, 142, 149,
    151–53, 155–56
  Department of Agricultural
    Extension (DOAE), 141, 144,
    148, 150–51, 153
  gross domestic product (GDP), 16,
    19
  rice exporter, 6, 25
  rice sector, 137–42
  subsidies, 143, 146, 148, 156

Thaksin Shinawatra, 7, 138, 140
"tiger" economy, 16
Tradewinds, 14
TRT (Thai Rak Thai), 7, 20, 136, 140,
  157
tsunami, 36

U
Ukraine, and Russian invasion, 13,
  28, 117
undernourishment, 182–83
undistorted price, 139–40
  see also distorted price
unemployment, 13, 37, 61, 106, 115,
  156
UNICEF, 61
United Malays National Organization
  (UMNO), 14, 35
United States Agency for
  International Development, 85
"Upgrading the Mega Farm with
  Modern Agriculture and
  Connecting the Market" project,
  141–42
urban food cluster, 166
urban poverty, 11

V
vaccination programme, 37
venture capital, 166
Vietnam, and rice exports, 25, 58, 98,
  168, 171, 181, 184

W
wage subsidy, 62, 167
Walker, Andrew, 7
Water Management Policy, 144
weedicide, 40
wheat, 9, 13, 28, 36, 51, 58, 106, 116,
  122, 161, 163

white rice, 71, 142–43, 158
Wilmar Group, 120
World Health Organization, 161
world rice stock-to-use ratio, 58
World Trade Organization (WTO), 87–89, 101
World War I, 7
World War II, 7–8

Y
Yellow Shirt Movement, 140
Yield Lab, 166
Yingluck Shinawatra, 7, 20, 25, 138, 140, 142, 153

Z
Zoning by Agri-Map, 143–44

www.ingramcontent.com/pod-product-compliance
Lightning Source LLC
Chambersburg PA
CBHW072236290426
44111CB00012B/2115